METALCRAFTING
ENCYCLOPEDIA

COMPILED AND EDITED
By STEVEN MORGENSTERN

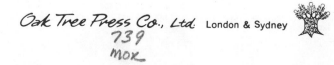

STERLING PUBLISHING CO., INC. NEW YORK

Oak Tree Press Co., Ltd. London & Sydney

739
MOR

OTHER BOOKS OF INTEREST

Practical Encyclopedia of Crafts
Family Book of Crafts
Giant Book of Crafts

Contents

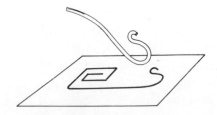

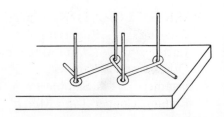

Acknowledgments

The materials contained in this volume were adapted and condensed from the following sources:

"Aluminum & Copper Tooling" by Chester Jay Alkema, © 1974 by Sterling Publishing Co., Inc., N.Y.

"Creating Silver Jewelry with Beads" by Marianne Seitz, © 1972 by Sterling Publishing Co., Inc., N.Y.

"Creative Enamelling and Jewelry-Making" by Katharina Zechlin, © 1965 by Sterling Publishing Co., Inc., N.Y.

"The Embossing of Metal—Repoussage" by Yves Meriel-Bussy, © 1970 by Sterling Publishing Co., Inc., N.Y.

"Etching and other Intaglio Techniques" by Manly Banister, © 1969 by Sterling Publishing Co., Inc., N.Y.

"Horseshoe-Nail Crafting" by Hans Carlbom, © 1973, 1972 by Hans Carlbom and ICA-Förlaget AB, Västerås, Sweden; published by Sterling Publishing Co., Inc., N.Y.

"Junk Sculpture" by Gregg LeFevre, © 1973 by Sterling Publishing Co., Inc., N.Y.

"Make Your Own Elegant Jewelry" by R. Boulay, © 1972 by Sterling Publishing Co., Inc., N.Y.

"Make Your Own Rings & Other Things: Working with Silver" by Elsie B. Ginnett, © 1974 by Sterling Publishing Co., Inc., N.Y.

"Metal & Wire Sculpture" by Elmar Gruber, © 1969 by Sterling Publishing Co., Inc., N.Y.

"Nail Sculpture" by Elmar Gruber, © 1971 by Sterling Publishing Co., Inc., N.Y.

"Pin Pictures with Wire and Thread" by Marie-Claude Riviere, © 1975 by Sterling Publishing Co., Inc., N.Y.

"Practical Encyclopedia of Crafts" by Maria and Louis Di Valentin and others, © 1970 by Sterling Publishing Co., Inc., N.Y.

"Tin-Can Crafting" by Sylvia W. Howard, © 1964, 1959 by Sterling Publishing Co., Inc., N.Y.

Introduction

You have in your hands the key to many hours of enjoyment and achievement, challenge and learning, creativity and exploration. Thumb through this book and you'll soon realize that there is literally something for every metal-minded person here. If you have more imagination than money, you can turn tin cans or aluminum pie plates into dozens of decorative and useful objects. You can transform a handful of nails into an eye-catching candleholder, an abstract sculpture or a stunning pendant. Inexpensive sheet metal can be cut, bent, soldered, embossed, antiqued and cleverly worked into hundreds of exciting projects, some perfect for children with "nothing to do," others challenging enough for the dedicated craftsman. And your investment of time and money in the art of the silversmith will be repaid with stunning, professional-looking jewelry at a fraction of store-bought prices.

There are three basic processes which change the original metal material into a finished work

Chasing gives this belt buckle a medieval look. Complete instructions for the chasing technique are on page 40.

of art—shaping, joining and decorating—and this is where you begin in this volume. If you have an idea for a project, but need to know how to go about it, you'll be able to quickly find the best methods available, requiring the

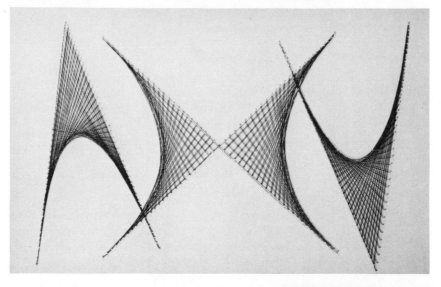

Pictures with pins and wire make fascinating wall decorations. This pin picture utilizes the butterfly design on page 134 and the arc technique.

least number of expensive, specialized tools and materials. Just looking through the descriptions of what can be done with metal will probably start you thinking about a jewelry design you've seen in a store that you know you could improve on, if you only knew how to construct it. Or maybe you've seen an abstract sculpture which gave you the urge to try it yourself. That is the goal of this book, to give you the basic skills and the inspiration to bring your own creative abilities to the pursuit of metalcrafting.

And there's no question that you have the abilities, either. If you can scribble an interesting design, we have instructions for turning your scribble into a beautiful aluminum wall hanging. If you can thread beads onto wire, your jewelry box can be full of exciting and attractive new pendants, belts, armbands and more. Simply hammer some pins into a board, twist wire around the pins and you'll have a shiny "pin picture" perfect to brighten a corner of your home.

There are dozens of projects described fully in each area of metalcrafting, which you can create by simply following the clear, carefully illustrated directions. Be sure to take full advantage of the illustrations as you proceed.

There are hundreds of photographs and line drawings here, many presented in step-by-step sequence to guide you through your first project. In this way, even a relatively complicated craft, like making silver rings, is made available to the eager beginner. Once you have mastered the basic techniques of each craft, there are photos and diagrams of completed projects to provide ideas for the development of your new-found skill.

The editors have attempted to provide everything to make your first attempts at metalcrafting a success. If you find a particular set of instructions confusing, use the index to find another project using the same process. If you find it difficult to locate any of the materials listed, try contacting the companies listed in the Suppliers List in the back of the book. If you want to pursue any of these crafts further, there is more valuable information available in the source books for these articles, listed in the Acknowledgments on page 6.

Now it is up to you. Instead of letting another wasted evening slip by, go to your worktable, pull out your tools, and get started on a fascinating and rewarding craft.

Approximate Equivalents of U.S., British, and Metric Weights and Measures

Volume

1 American fluid ounce	= 1 British fluid ounce	= 30 millilitres (ml.)
1 American teaspoon	= $\frac{1}{6}$ fluid ounce	= 5 millilitres
1 British teaspoon	= $\frac{1}{6}$ fluid ounce	= 5 millilitres
1 American tablespoon	= $\frac{1}{2}$ fluid ounce	= 15 millilitres
1 British tablespoon	= $\frac{3}{5}$ fluid ounce	= 18 millilitres
1 American cup	= 8 fluid ounces	= 240 millilitres
1 British cup	= 10 fluid ounces	= 300 millilitres

Weight

1 ounce	= 28 grams (g.)	9 ounces	= 250 grams
1 lb. (16 oz.)	= 454 grams	11 ounces	= 300 grams
$3\frac{1}{2}$ ounces	= 100 grams	12 ounces	= 350 grams
7 ounces	= 200 grams	14 ounces	= 400 grams

Linear Measures

$\frac{1}{8}$ inch =	3.18 millimetres
$\frac{1}{4}$ inch =	6.35 millimetres
$\frac{3}{8}$ inch =	9.53 millimetres
$\frac{1}{2}$ inch =	12.70 millimetres
$\frac{5}{8}$ inch =	15.88 millimetres
$\frac{3}{4}$ inch =	19.05 millimetres
$\frac{7}{8}$ inch =	22.23 millimetres
1 inch =	25.40 millimetres
$1\frac{1}{2}$ inch =	38.10 millimetres
2 inches =	50.80 millimetres
1 foot =	30.48 centimetres
1 yard =	0.9144 metre

Metals Used in Metalcrafting

The ten metals used since ancient times, namely gold, silver, copper, pewter, brass, bronze, nickel (German) silver, aluminum, and wrought and cast iron, are still used in metalwork today. Gold and silver, due to their cost, are principally used for jewelry work and for fashioning small objects.

Your choice of metal depends upon the object you want to make, the color and finish you like, and your personal taste in design.

Most metals for craft work can be obtained from arts and crafts supply houses and hobby shops, and are sold by weight or in sheets. Mill supply houses are a source for brass, bronze, aluminum and steel. Since, sometimes, a mill supply requires a minimum order which may be far more material than you require, your local hardware merchant may be able to obtain a small quantity for you.

Metals are available in the shapes shown in Illus. 2. When ordering, specify the kind of metal, the shape, the dimensions and the quantity. Thickness of sheet stock is expressed in terms of the Brown and Sharpe gauge system. The lower the gauge number, the heavier the metal.

Illus. 1. For centuries skilled craftsmen have worked with the same metals we use today. This gold pectoral, or breastplate, was made and worn by the Calima Indians of Colombia before the Spanish conquest in the 16th century.

Wires and rods are available either round or square, in a variety of thicknesses which are also expressed in terms of the Brown and Sharpe

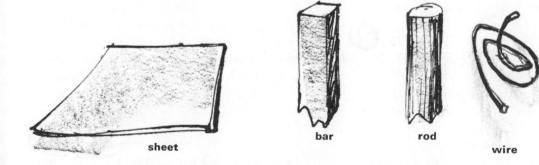

sheet   bar   rod   wire   strip

Illus. 2. You can order metal in any of these forms, in a variety of sizes.

gauge system. The higher the gauge number, the lighter, or thinner, the wire. Any wire that is 12 gauge or heavier is considered a rod.

The following chart shows the gauge size that corresponds to a given metal thickness for some of the more common thicknesses.

Brown and Sharpe Wire Gauge
(Shown Actual Thickness)

B & S Gauge	Metal Thickness	Sheet & Wire (diameter)	
12	0.0808 inches	12	
14	0.0641 "	14	
16	0.0508 "	16	
18	0.0403 "	18	
20	0.0320 "	20	
22	0.0253 "	22	
24	0.0201 "	24	
26	0.0159 "	26	

Metal Characteristics

Malleability and Ductility. When a metal is malleable it can be hammered without cracking; it can be elongated and shaped by pressure. The thicker the piece of metal, the less malleable it will be. When a metal is ductile it can be stretched or hammered until thin without tearing. These two characteristics are required for making formed objects, such as cups, bowls, and dishes.

Most metals "work harden," that is, lose their malleability and ductility after being shaped. By annealing the worked metal it becomes workable again. The process of annealing, described in full on page 26, involves heating the metal to a high temperature, remaining below the melting point.

Density. This is the relationship of weight to size. Copper is about eight times as dense as wood. Our comparisons of the metals will be made with reference to copper.

Nobility. A metal that resists attack from air and chemicals is called noble. Of the metals you will be working with, gold is the only completely noble metal. It does not tarnish or discolor.

Solderability. The ability of a metal to be joined to another metal or to itself, by means of a soft solder or brazing alloy, is known as its "solderability." (Soldering and brazing are explained on page 31.)

Metal Descriptions

Copper is a beautiful reddish metal. When freshly polished, it has a bright lustre, but it will tarnish in air to a black-red color. While its natural color is highly attractive, many different effects can be achieved by heating it. In metalcrafting it is used in the pure state, since, after working, it is tough enough to resist abrasion. When ordering, request cold-rolled and annealed copper. This will give you a smooth, soft material ready for working. If worked extensively, however, copper requires annealing. It is readily solderable with soft solders or brazing alloys.

Brass and *bronze*, usually used like copper in metalworking, have a yellow-red color. Brass, an alloy of copper and zinc, is slightly less malleable than copper. Bronze, an alloy of copper and tin, is less ductile and more brown in tone than brass and is used mostly for casting. It can also be used for small decorative effects on other metals.

Both alloys require annealing, and both tarnish to a dull golden color. Their density is the same as copper.

Aluminum is a malleable and ductile metal that is extremely versatile and easy to handle. It is quite inexpensive when purchased at craft or hobby shops, and is readily available to the home craftsman in the form of everyday aluminum pie plates, which can be hand tooled very effectively.

Whitish and slightly less bright and silvery than silver, aluminum does not tarnish in the same way that other metals do. When attacked by air, a coating forms on the aluminum which is transparent and adheres to the surface very tenaciously. As a result, the coating forms a protection against further attack by air and allows aluminum to retain its color. Aluminum sheets are also available in a variety of colors—gold, copper, red, blue or green on one side, with silver on the other, as well as the standard silver on both sides.

Aluminum requires annealing. Lightest of all craft metals (about one third the density of copper), aluminum can only be soldered with difficulty and requires special fluxes. You would be wise to plan to use riveting methods for joining.

Pewter, an alloy of tin, is very soft and white-silvery when new. It will tarnish with time to a grey-brown metal, losing some of its lustre. The softest of the craft metals, about $1\frac{1}{4}$ times as dense as copper, it does not need to be annealed unless severely worked. It lends itself well to simple metalwork, but has the disadvantage of being more costly than aluminum or copper. Soldering requires a special low melting solder with glycerin as a flux.

Wrought Iron (or mild steel) has a grey appearance with a dull lustre. It has a low malleability and a fair amount of ductility, and is used mainly in wire and strip work. Frequent anneals are required. Iron corrodes easily, producing a reddish scale. As a result, objects made of iron must be painted, varnished or plated to protect the surface. Iron can be soldered or brazed, if the proper flux and solder are used. The density of iron is slightly less than that of copper.

Cast Iron has no ductility or malleability, and is therefore used to make cast or machined objects only. It must be treated with a protective coating after a project is completed.

Nickel Silver, also known as German silver, is a white metal resembling silver in appearance, but is actually an alloy of copper and zinc. It has a malleability similar to brass. Often used in place of silver in jewelry work, as well as for hammered products, it does not tarnish as badly as brass. It requires annealing when worked, and solders readily with soft solders.

Silver in the 100% pure state is seldom used. Instead, an alloy of 92% silver and 8% copper, known as sterling silver, is the metal used for silver work. Sterling is a bright metal, with good malleability and ductility, about $1\frac{1}{4}$ times as dense as copper. Annealing is required when heavy work is done. Silver tarnishes due to the sulphur gases in air, making its surface appear grey and lacklustre. Silver brazing alloys should be used for joining.

Gold is an extremely dense metal, bright yellow in color with a high degree of malleability and ductility. It can be worked to very thin sections without annealing. 100%, or 24-carat, gold is too soft to use for jewelry; 22-carat (92%), 18-carat (75%) and 14-carat (60%) gold are alloys of gold, silver and copper which are used in jewelry. These alloys give longer wearing properties without appreciably affecting nobility or ductility. Gold is $2\frac{1}{2}$ times as dense as copper. To preserve the nobility of work in gold, use only silver brazing or gold solder alloys for joining.

Tools

The illustrations in this section show the basic tools used for most of the metalworking operations you will encounter. Some branches of metalworking require more specialized tools, which will be described at the beginning of these sections. Do not feel that you need to go out and buy all the tools immediately. Pick them up as you plan each project. In a short time you will have an impressive kit.

Cutting Tools

When working with thin sheet metal you will need a variety of scissors-type cutting tools,

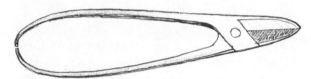

Illus. 3. Cutting shears.

varying in size and design with the weight of the metal you are working with and the cutting requirements for your design. For the lightest gauges of sheet metal and metal foil, a good sharp pair of household scissors will work well.

For heavier metal, varying sizes of cutting shears (Illus. 3) are available. You may also want to try out the specific tools designed for individual problem jobs. For carefully cutting out curves and detailed patterns, jeweler's

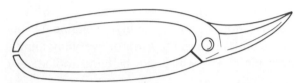

Illus. 5. Circle-cutting shears.

scissors (Illus. 4) may prove handy. For cutting curved lines, you will obtain good results with the circle-cutting shears shown in Illus. 5.

Many metalworkers like the clean flat edge they get by cutting with the "Werindus" sheet-metal shears, which separates the sheet metal by cutting out an approximately $\frac{1}{8}$-inch-wide strip. A double-cut snip, which cuts a $\frac{1}{16}$-inch strip in the metal, will serve about as well, and both are available in specialized crafts shops.

Cutting wire is a simple matter with a diagonal cutting pliers, also called diagonal wire cutters (Illus. 6). With a cutting jaw at an

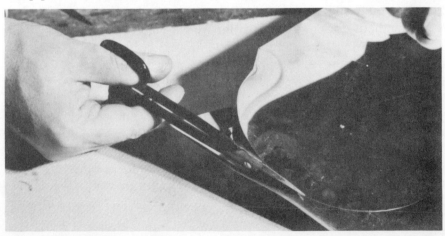

Illus. 4. Jeweler's scissors have short sharp blades, making it easy to cut out intricate designs.

angle up to the point, they are used for cutting both round and flat wire.

Illus. 6. Diagonal wire cutters.

For cutting heavy sheet metal or rods, you will need a saw. Illus. 8 shows a hacksaw, used for straight cutting of all dense metals with a variety of blades, and a jeweler's saw (Illus. 9) for cutting curves and intricate patterns, and also cutting holes within the body of a metal sheet (see page 20). Despite its fragile appearance, the jeweler's saw is a sturdy and powerful tool, capable of cutting the hardest of metals when handled properly.

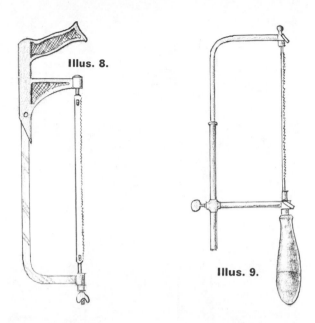

Illus. 8.

Illus. 9.

Files

Illus. 7 shows the various shapes of files you should have. A smooth-cut file 6 inches long is a good size to begin with. Using the five shapes on the top, and the two small "needle" files at the bottom, you will be able to handle all of your filing work. You will also need a file brush and a universal handle to place on the files as you use them.

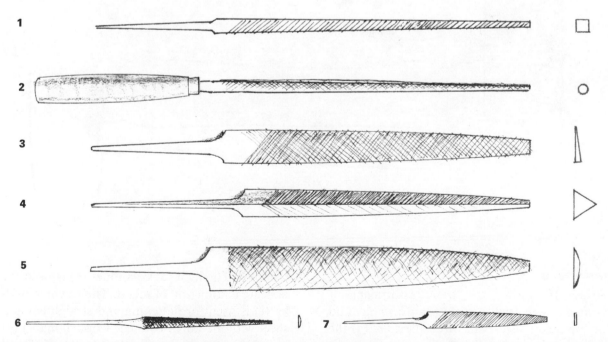

Illus. 7. The shape of the point determines the use of the file. Use a universal handle (shown on #2) for all but the small needle files.

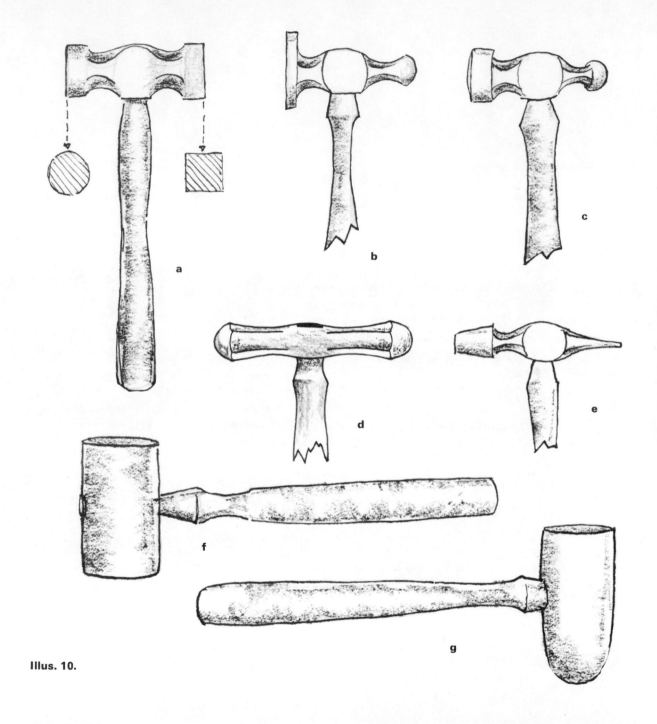

Illus. 10.

Hammers

Illus. 10 shows the basic assortment of hammers you will need for forming and shaping metal sheet and wire. These are (a) the planishing hammer, (b) the chasing hammer, (c) the ball-peen hammer, and (d) the forming hammer. The light tack hammer (e) is used for delicate hammering of metal. The rawhide mallet (f) is used for flattening and straightening a sheet without marring it. The wooden mallet (g) is used for raising metal when a smooth-finish surface is desired.

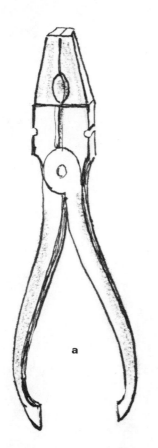

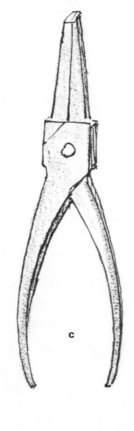

Pliers

Shown in Illus. 11 are (a) multi-purpose pliers with wire cutter, (b) flat-nose pliers, and (c) a thin-nose pliers for work in close places. These three will serve adequately as a starting set. You probably already have an adjustable-grip pliers, which you will find useful for holding and bending in many projects (Illus. 12).

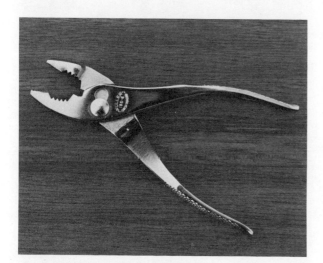

Illus. 12. Adjustable-grip pliers.

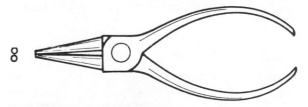

Illus. 13. Round-nose pliers.

For bending cut metal into the shapes you desire, you will need both the flat-nose pliers mentioned above and round-nose pliers, which have two round jaws that taper to points (Illus. 13).

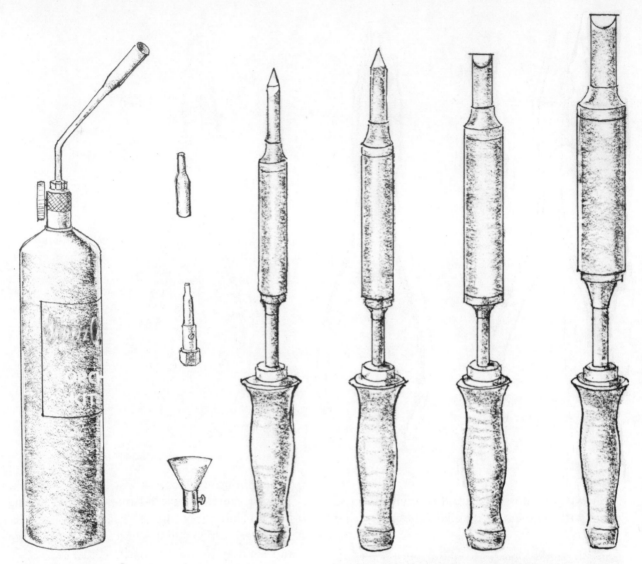

Illus. 14. On the left are a propane torch and several tips used to direct the flame. The torch is used for both soldering and brazing. On the right are several shapes and sizes of soldering irons, used exclusively for soft soldering.

Soldering Torch and Soldering Iron

In many of the projects which follow, metal pieces are joined by soldering or brazing. Soldering requires an electric soldering iron (100–150 watts) and, if possible, a butane torch. The soldering iron can be more precisely directed, and is therefore preferable to the torch when working on delicate constructions. The soldering torch (which may burn butane or propane) creates a higher heat and is faster to work with on sizeable projects. While the tips shown in

Illus. 14 assist in directing the flame of the torch, they cannot duplicate the pinpoint heating accuracy possible with a soldering iron.

If you are interested in brazing, a process similar to soldering which is used primarily in jewelry and precious metalwork, you will need the higher temperatures of the soldering torch. Both techniques are described fully in the section beginning on page 31.

The soldering torch in the illustration has a disposable cylinder, is economical, and is available in hardware departments or from mail-order suppliers. It has a clean flame and the temperature is easily controlled.

You can also use a gas-air torch which utilizes a combination of gas and compressed air. The gas can be either manufactured illuminating gas, natural gas or propane. Air pressure is supplied by a foot bellows or by a motor-driven compressor.

Acetylene torches are portable, and although they are initially expensive to buy, the refill tanks are low in cost and readily available.

Another recommended torch unit uses a tank of oxygen and the natural gas that is normally supplied in homes. Many artists today are using this set-up.

You will also need a heat-resistant base for soldering and brazing work. Start with a fire-brick or even an ordinary brick as a base. This will be adequate for small soldering jobs, but for complete protection, place an asbestos mat about $\frac{3}{8}$ inch thick over the brick or bricks, depending on the size of your project.

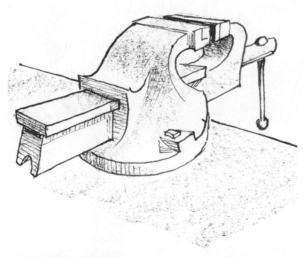

Illus. 15. Bench vice.

Worktable

A sturdy bench with a hardwood top fitted with a vice (Illus. 15) mounted about 12 inches from the left-hand side of the bench is all you will need to start. You will also find that a number

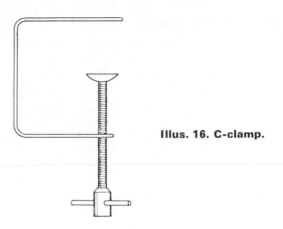

Illus. 16. C-clamp.

of C-clamps (sometimes called G-clamps, Illus. 16) come in handy when you need to hold a piece of work steady against your worktable or to clamp pieces of a structure together for glueing.

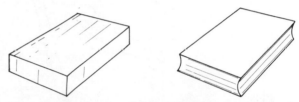

Illus. 17. Wooden bench block (left) and steel bench anvil (right).

For shaping sheet metal and wire with hammers you will need a wooden bench block and a steel bench anvil (Illus. 17). Another welcome addition to your worktable, if you plan to saw very thin pieces of metal, is a bench pin. This can be made simply at home by cutting a V-shaped notch in a sheet of masonite or thin plywood, as shown in Illus. 18. By holding your work in the point of the V, you support it and keep it from bending while you saw.

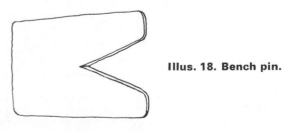

Illus. 18. Bench pin.

Miscellaneous Tools

Drill. For much of your work with thick sheet metal, an electric drill will speed up your work and lead to neat, clean results. However, the hand drill pictured in Illus. 19 should still be a part of your basic tool kit if you plan to do delicate work, when the slower action of the hand drill will aid you in working accurately. You should obtain drill bits up to $\frac{1}{4}$ inch in diameter.

Accessories. Illus. 20 shows (a) two types of punches, (b) a set square, (c) a 6-inch steel ruler, (d) a scribe, (e) a 6-inch compass and (f) dividers, and (g) an awl, all of which will come in handy

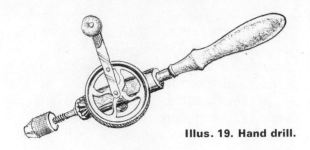

Illus. 19. Hand drill.

as you progress. You should also remember to buy a pair of work gloves, either cloth or leather, thick enough to protect your fingers when working with the sharp edges of cut sheet metal.

Illus. 20. Miscellaneous tools.

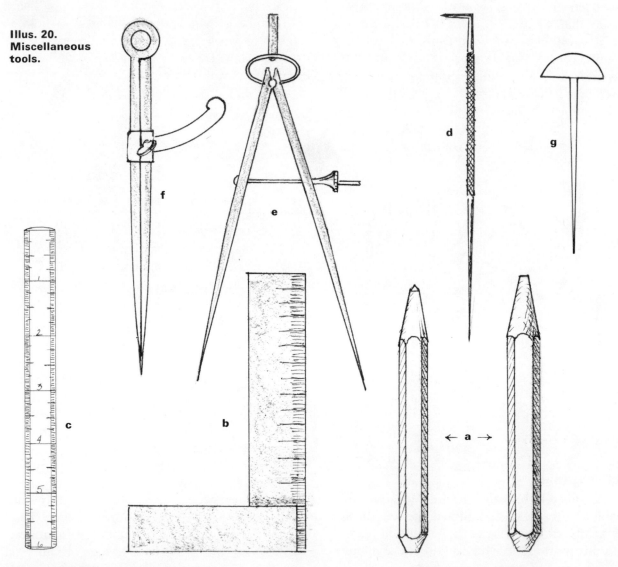

Basic Shaping Techniques

Cutting

The basic cutting tools are saws for thicker sheets or rods, wire cutters for clipping off wires or nails, and ordinary scissors or shears for thin sheet or foil. The shears are faster than the saw, but they tend to deform the metal and require a certain amount of physical strength. Straight shears are used for cutting straight lines. The circle-cutting shears are used for cutting curved lines. Compound-leverage shears, which require less effort in cutting, are also available, but at a higher price.

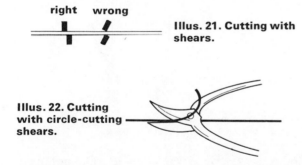

Illus. 21. Cutting with shears.

Illus. 22. Cutting with circle-cutting shears.

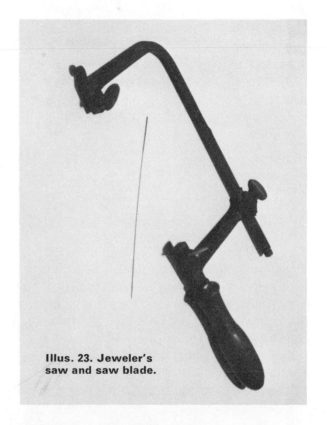

Illus. 23. Jeweler's saw and saw blade.

You must hold the blades of the shears parallel to the flat surface of the sheet of metal and perpendicular to the edge. Otherwise, the thin plate will slip between the blades, crushing it and damaging the tool (Illus. 21). The point of the circle-cutting shears should always be turned upward (Illus. 22).

For a straight, rough cut through a thick sheet of metal, you can use a hacksaw, selecting the blade which is recommended for the material you are sawing. For intricate work, however, the seemingly fragile jeweler's saw will cut through any of the metals you will be using. You can even cut a hole out from the middle of a sheet of metal using the jeweler's saw.

Cutting with the Jeweler's Saw

Unlike other kinds of saws, the teeth of the jeweler's saw point backwards, towards the handle, so that all cutting is done on the downstroke. Therefore, you must always set the blade so the teeth face *out* from the frame, and *down* towards the handle.

Loosen the wing nuts at each end of the jeweler's saw frame. Fasten the blade in the top holder first. Place the tip of the frame against the edge of the table, while holding it by the handle with your left hand. Push firmly against the table until the frame bends slightly and fasten the blade in the bottom holder. Fastened properly, the blade should make a musical ping when you strum it with your thumb.

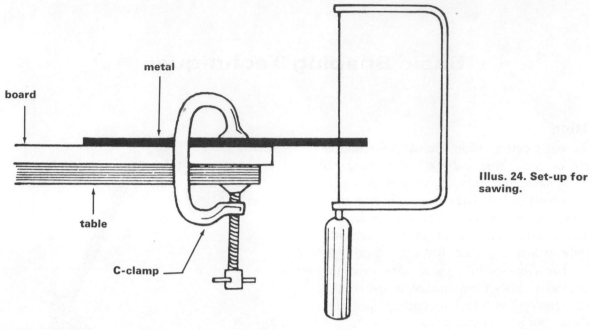

metal

board

table

C-clamp

Illus. 24. Set-up for sawing.

You will have to take into account the type of metal you will be sawing when you set up your worktable. If the sheet is heavy and rigid enough not to bend under the pressure of the saw, then your set-up should look like Illus. 24. You should always clamp the work horizontally, so that the saw will move downwards in cutting and not side-to-side.

Illus. 25. Use a bench pin when you saw thin sheet metal.

If you are sawing a thin sheet you should replace the board between the table and the metal with a bench pin, which you can make at

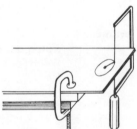

Illus. 26. You can make an internal cut with a pre-drilled hole and your jeweler's saw.

home as described on page 17. Do not lean heavily on the saw. Let the teeth bite lightly into the metal (Illus. 25).

Don't just jiggle the saw up and down—you might break the blade. Cut a downward stroke; draw the blade back a trifle so that it is not touching the metal and lift it; then make another downward stroke, and so on. If you rasp the teeth backward over the metal, you will quickly dull them.

If you want to cut out the middle of a piece, begin by drilling a hole just large enough to pass the blade through, *teeth pointing downward*, and clamp it again in the saw frame (Illus. 26).

If a piece of metal is pulled out of shape by cutting, you must flatten it out (see page 23).

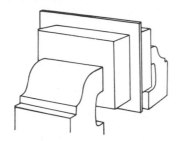

Illus. 27. Jaw covers will protect the workpiece in the vice.

Illus. 28. Hold your file at a right angle to the work surface.

Filing

The purpose of filing is to finish the work of the saw or the shears, removing the burr from the edges of the metal and correcting the imperfections of the cut. You will need not only semi-fine flat, half-round, or round files, but, in addition, very fine needle files, which will permit you to file out the smallest indentation. Needle files, which come in sets containing all useful shapes for the jeweler's purpose, will be used to make distinctive textured effects when making silver jewelry.

Grip the workpiece in the vice, placing between the metal and each jaw of the vice a piece of wood or lead to protect it (Illus. 27). Jaw covers can be made from fairly thin sheet lead and left permanently in place. This is better than trying to juggle three separate pieces between the vice-jaws without dropping them. If the pieces to be filed have a simple shape, you will do just as well by holding the workpiece in one hand and filing with the other.

The edge to be filed should not project more than $\frac{1}{8}$ inch or $\frac{1}{4}$ inch above the vice-jaws. If it sticks up too high, the metal will vibrate and be distorted. If you place it too low, you run the risk of filing the vice.

Place the flat side of the file perpendicular to the flat surface of the metal you are about to attack, as shown in Illus. 28. Holding your file at a 45° angle to the edge of the work, file with the full length of the toothed blade. Alternate filing from left to right and from right to left. Apply enough pressure to the file to cause the

teeth to bite into the metal, but keep the pressure steady at all times to avoid filing irregularities into the edge.

Finish the job by smoothing the file marks from the edges with emery cloth. Cut this into small pieces, about 2 inches square for easy handling or, for larger areas, roll into a tube as shown in Illus. 29.

Try to work only the edge of the metal and avoid scratching the surface. Following filing, the edge should feel perfectly smooth when you run a finger along it.

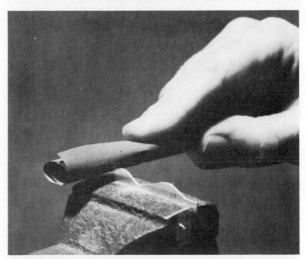

Illus. 29. Emery cloth rolled into a tube will smooth away marks left after filing.

Hammering Wire and Rod

You will need:
steel bench anvil
2 C-clamps (optional)
dapping punch
ball-peen hammer
planishing hammer
gas torch (for annealing)

Hammering the End

Place the end of the wire on a bench anvil or a $\frac{3}{4}$-inch-thick plate of cold-rolled steel. Holding it with one hand, strike the piece with the flat face of the planishing hammer, inclining the hammer head at such an angle that the blow tends to push the metal towards the end of the wire, and not the other way, that is, towards the body of the wire (Illus. 30).

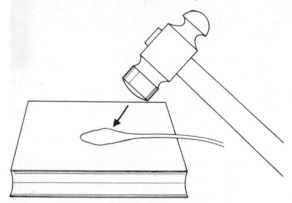

Illus. 30. Hammering the end of a wire.

Continue hammering with light, successive strokes. Try to keep the surface as smooth as possible, avoiding rough "ledges" marking each separate stroke.

This technique is used to keep a bead from slipping off the end of a wire (the hammered part is smoothed down to make it invisible). It is also used for clasps, as you will see. It provides a better hold when you are soldering wire to a flat surface. Decorative effects can be obtained when the flattened end is then shaped with a file.

Hammering Flats in Wire

A flat is a small, flat spot within the length of a wire, hammered in for decorative purposes or

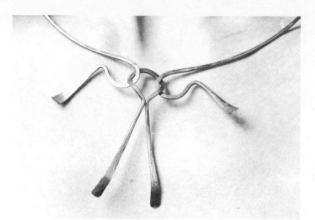

Illus. 31. A simple necklace made of 18-gauge nickel-silver wire which has been hammered, flattened on the ends, and shaped.

to provide a place for drilling through the wire.

You can clamp the wire to the bench anvil with a pair of C-clamps if you have them, or simply hold it by hand. Place the ball end of a dapping punch (Illus. 32) on the wire where you want the flat, and strike it with a precisely

Illus. 32. Dapping punch.

vertical blow of the hammer to avoid skidding. If you do not have a dapping punch, a good substitute is the ball side of a ball-peen hammer. Strike the wire directly with it (if you're very

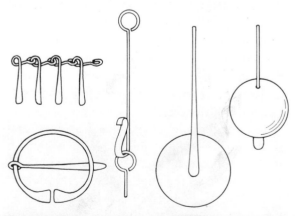

Illus. 33. Some applications of hammered ends in jewelry-making.

Illus. 34.

adept at hammering), or hold it with the ball against the wire and hit the flat face with another hammer. Avoid thinning the metal too much, as this makes it fragile.

This technique is used particularly to isolate a bead on a wire or, as mentioned before, to provide a space for piercing the wire (Illus. 34).

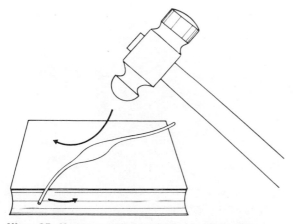

Illus. 35. Hammer wire equally on each side.

Over-all Hammering

You may want to hammer the full length of a wire to make a wire ribbon, or to flatten a piece that has already been shaped. Use the flat face of the hammer, holding the work firmly in place on the anvil. To straighten the metal in the course of hammering, always, after striking one side of the wire for a while, turn it

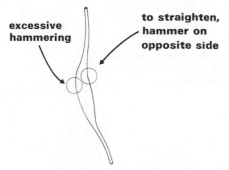

Illus. 36. Aim your hammer blows carefully to maintain an even width.

over and strike the other side in exactly the same place with exactly the same force (Illus. 36).

If the metal becomes too hard after a few hammer blows, you will have to anneal it (see page 26).

When you want to flatten a piece that has already been shaped, be particularly careful working the bent parts, where you will have to adjust the force of your blows to the condition of the wire.

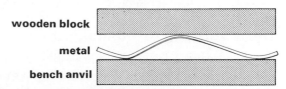

Illus. 37. Set-up for flattening.

Flattening

You will need:
wooden bench block
steel bench anvil
flat-faced hammer

Flattening is necessary when a piece of metal has been deformed by cutting, or during any other process. You will also find that, when you curve a wire for a design, you are actually twisting it in three dimensions. You will often want to flatten the shape of the wire after twisting, using the following technique.

Place the sheet or wire to be flattened on the steel anvil and cover it with a block of wood. If one surface has been hammered or chiselled for texture, that face should be in contact with the wood.

Hammer on top of this sandwiched assembly until the piece held between the two plane surfaces is straightened or flattened out. Where very small pieces are involved, you can bring them back into shape by tapping directly on them with a flat-faced hammer. In this case, you must strike with the face perfectly flat.

You are far better off using a rawhide mallet when the hammer will directly contact the work, since the rawhide will not mark the workpiece, as is likely with a steel hammer face.

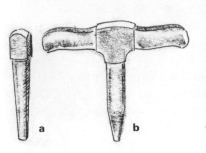
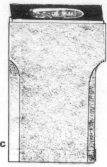
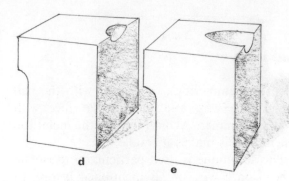

Illus. 38. For deep forming you will need (a) a stake, (b) planishing hammer, (c), (d) and (e) molds.

Deep Forming or Bumping Up

Deep forming is the operation that makes a metal plate concave on one side and convex on the other. Both happen simultaneously, of course. It involves two operations: Beating in and beating out. The following instructions for making a small cup will illustrate the basics of this technique.

You will need:
forming hammer
planishing hammer, or, ball-peen hammer
metal block or bench anvil
soldering torch
wood block
dividers
circle-cutting shears
semi-fine file
copper sheet

First, trace a circle with dividers of the desired diameter and cut it out of 22- or 20-gauge copper with the circle-cutting shears. Smooth down the circumference with a semi-fine file.

Beating In: Place the copper circle on the steel bench anvil. Strike four or five blows in the middle of it with the ball side of the ball-peen hammer. Starting from the edge of this central hammering, hammer the copper along a spiral line that "unrolls" all the way to the edge (Illus. 39).

Since hammering hardens the metal considerably, next heat it red-hot with the torch; then cool it in a bucket of water. This is the process called annealing. Then, you will be able to hollow out your little cup deeply by beating out.

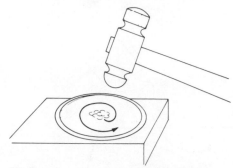

Illus. 39. Beating in using spiral pattern.

Beating Out: First, you must hollow out a depression in a thick piece of wood which will serve as a mold. The depression should be bowl-shaped, about 5 inches across and $\frac{3}{8}$ inch to $\frac{3}{4}$ inch deep. You can also use commercially available molds, as shown in Illus. 38.

Center the beaten-in and annealed piece in the depression. Then, with the ball end of the ball-peen, start striking the metal, starting at the middle (Illus. 40). As soon as a wrinkle shows up in the metal, wipe it out by hammering from the base of the fold, working towards the edge.

Illus. 40. Start beating out from the center, working toward the edge.

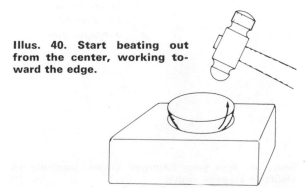

Illus. 41 (left). Start the raising process by hammering four impressions to align the plate in the mold.

Illus. 42 (below). Shape the plate with a wooden mallet, as shown. The surface can be smoothed and straightened later with a rawhide mallet.

If the cup is not deep enough and the metal becomes too hard for working, start the whole procedure over again—beating in, annealing, and beating out.

When the cup is finally hollowed out enough to suit you, get rid of the irregularities in shape and the little bumps left from hammering by working with a planishing hammer on a wooden bench block, taking care that each blow of the hammer strikes with the face *flat* against the metal.

Now, you can re-cut the edge of the cup to straighten it out, if necessary, or file it until it is flat and smooth.

Raising

Essentially similar to the deep-forming technique, raising refers to the process of hammering sheet metal against a mold or block in order to raise part of it in relation to the starting material. In the following example, raising is used to form the lip of a metal disc for a plate or tray.

You will need:
12-inch-diameter sheet-copper disc, 18 gauge
12-inch mold with a 10-inch hollow
wooden mallet
rawhide mallet

After dressing down the edge of the disc, place it over the mold so that the edge of the disc and the edge of the mold correspond exactly. Hit the copper with the round end of the wooden mallet at the four points of the compass and at the outer edge of the mold. This aligns the disc in the mold. Illus. 41 shows the plate in the mold with the four impressions in the copper. Note also the angle at which the mallet strikes the metal.

Continue to hammer the copper with light blows, but now move it continuously in one direction. Each blow should slightly overlap the previous blow. Go round a number of times with light blows rather than trying to raise the edge in one go-round. The middle of the plate does not require hammering. Working the edge will give you the depth you want.

In working, the plate may tend to buckle. If it does, turn it upside down, place it on a flat surface and straighten the edges with the rawhide mallet. The proper way to strike with this tool is to hit so that the mallet comes down *flat* at the bottom of the stroke.

After the completion of the hollowing, pits and scratches can also be smoothed out with the rawhide mallet, by placing the spot over a hardwood block held in a vice and hammering.

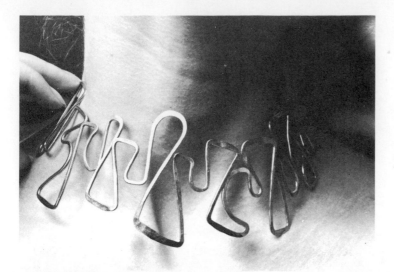

Illus. 43. A necklace made of 20-gauge nickel silver which was first annealed, and then shaped and hammered.

Bending Curves and Angles

Annealing

This is the process of heating a metal to a high temperature, but below the melting point, in order to soften it for further work. Most metals "work harden" after being hammered, formed, or shaped. They become hard, lose their malleability and ductility, and become difficult to shape or form further. Annealing puts the metal back into a workable condition. You will need a torch or kiln to anneal.

A wire that has been bent and straightened too many times becomes hard and brittle. It must be annealed by heating it red-hot with the gas torch, and then dipping the piece into water to cool it. (Use copper tongs for this purpose.) You must always anneal brass wire before working it.

Rods (wire over 12 gauge) cannot be bent as easily as the lighter-weight wire. You will have to anneal them several times to make them malleable enough to work with.

Measuring

You cannot measure accurately while handling a whole roll of wire, nor can you judge the length of sheet metal needed for an intricately bent design. When cutting off a piece of wire or sheet metal by eye, you can make a mistake and cut the piece too short for your project, or cut it too long and waste your material.

The best thing is to lay, right on your design, a length of thin, pliable copper wire or a piece of string which will unroll and roll up easily, allowing you to measure the length of each piece with precision.

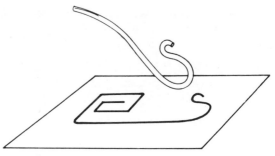

Illus. 44. Check your work against the design drawing frequently.

Cut the measured length with an inch or more to spare (for safety's sake), using the appropriate cutting tool. Then file the sharp ends smooth with a semi-fine file.

From time to time, refer to the drawing (Illus. 44). If you are working on several identical pieces at the same time, compare them not only with the original design, but also with each other.

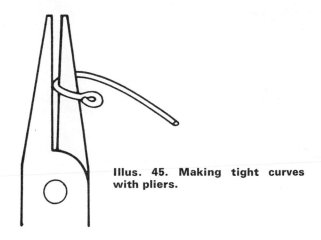

Illus. 45. Making tight curves with pliers.

Working with Pliers

Tight curves are made with the point of the round-nose pliers, and large curves are made with the base of the jaws of the same pliers

Illus. 46. Make large curves and bends in wire with your hands.

(Illus. 45). Long, graceful curves are best made with your fingers (Illus. 46).

You can bend a wire or thin strip of sheet metal at a right angle between the jaws of the flat-nose pliers by bending it down while pulling it over either the thin end or the thicker base of the jaws (Illus. 47).

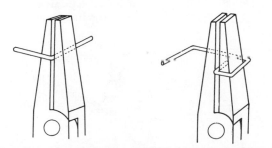

Illus. 47. Forming right angles with square-jawed pliers.

Shaping a Simple Wire Loop

Begin by bending the end of the wire back upon itself with the round-nose pliers. You must bend it into a circle, not an oval (Illus. 48).

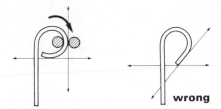

Illus. 48. Forming a circular loop.

Proceed with a succession of small twists with the pliers, then bring back into the axis of the the wire loop which was first formed off to one side (Illus. 49).

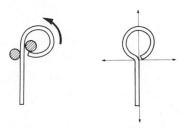

Illus. 49. Form the loop to the side, then center it.

Little eyelets such as these are very important in making pieces composed of links or clasps, and in many jewelry and wire sculpture designs.

Bending Simple Clasps

Simple clasps for pendants, necklaces and bracelets are easy to make. Bend the two open ends of your wire figure with round-nose pliers to form the appropriate clasp. Snip off any excess wire with your diagonal wire cutters. If the edges are rough or pointy, file them down.

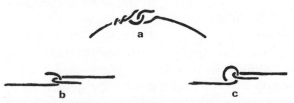

Illus. 50. Simple wire clasps for (a) necklace and (b)(c) bracelets.

Shaping a Series of Wire Loops

With a simple bending device made from a strong board or thick piece of plywood and some 8d or 10d nails with the heads cut off, you can form a series of loops which fits well with many different styles of jewelry. Lay out the pattern for the bending device in pencil on a piece of wood in accordance with the measurements of your design. Drive headless nails into the board as shown in Illus. 51, spacing them as on the design. Twist the wire back and forth round the nails in the pattern as shown.

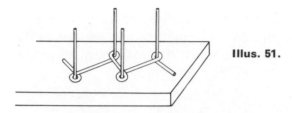

Illus. 51.

To avoid having the same lines always on top or underneath, which would make a piece of jewelry too thick, *alternate the crossing* of the wires, over and under, as shown in Illus. 52.

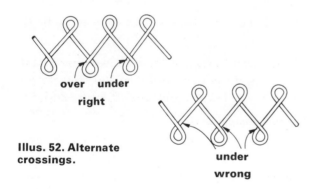

over   under

right

under

wrong

Illus. 52. Alternate crossings.

Shaping Repeated Forms in Wire

For many works you will need a large number of wire pieces bent into the same shape. You obtain these construction elements by bending the wire over a form. Hammer wire nails into a piece of wood in a pre-designed pattern. Then bend the wire around the nails so that it takes the desired form. (Illus. 54). The nails have to be strong and hammered deeply into the wood in order to withstand the pressure created by

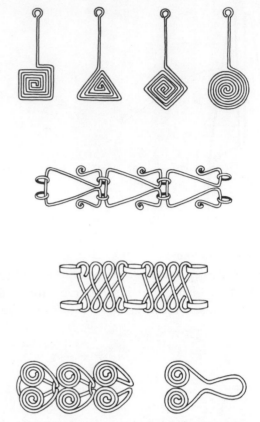

Illus. 53. Sections of earrings, bracelets and necklaces made from shaped, looped and spiralled wire.

bending the wire. Pinch the nailheads off with wire cutters so that the finished piece of wire can be lifted off easily. When the end of the wire reaches the starting point, you cut it. The two ends that touch are soldered together. In this way you can duplicate a form as many times as you wish.

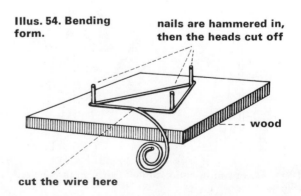

Illus. 54. Bending form.

nails are hammered in, then the heads cut off

wood

cut the wire here

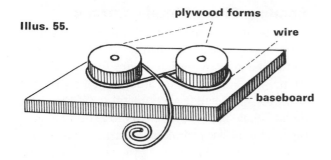

Illus. 55.

plywood forms

wire

baseboard

After removing the finished spiral, cut off the inside end, which will be sticking up.

Spiralling can also be done very simply with your flat- and round-nose pliers. Take a narrow string and make a spiralled form of the desired length. Unravel and measure.

Now, cut a piece of round wire about 1 inch longer than the length of the string. Then, with

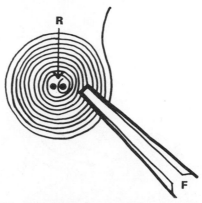

Illus. 57. Use both the round-nose (R) and the flat-nose (F) pliers for spiralling.

In dealing with more complicated forms, it is advisable to use plywood shapes instead of nails. Take pieces of plywood sawed out according to the desired figure and fix them onto a baseboard (use all-purpose glue and small nails). Then bend the wire around the plywood contours (Illus. 55). Proceed with cutting and soldering each wire shape as you did when forming the element around nails.

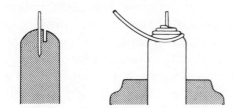

Illus. 56. Shaping a spiral.

Spiralling

In addition to the basic tools for wire bending, you will need a wooden tool handle with rounded end (or a large dowel), a nail with the head cut off, a hand drill, a hammer and a bench vice in order to make decorative wire spirals.

Drive a headless nail into the middle of the rounded end of a wooden tool handle. Use a 3d or 4d nail, leaving about $\frac{1}{4}$ inch sticking out at the top (Illus. 56).

Right next to the nail, drill a hole, having the same diameter as the wire, to a $\frac{3}{8}$-inch depth. Grip the handle in a vice, with the rounded end up. Slip the end of the wire into the hole and wrap it tightly round the nail, then round each turn of wire as it is laid down.

your round-nose pliers, grip one end, and with the aid of the flat-nose pliers, wrap a spiral around it.

Wire rings of uniform size can be made by winding the wire around a piece of round wood dowel. The wire spiral is then slipped off the wooden core and cut open longitudinally with wire cutters (Illus. 58). Then the two ends of each wire ring thus obtained are soldered together. Wire may also be wound around a bar of wood in the same fashion, resulting in squares or rectangles. This is similar to the method used for making "jump rings" (page 38).

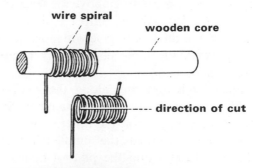

wire spiral

wooden core

direction of cut

Illus. 58. Winding wire rings.

Bending Sheet Metal—Right Angles

In order to form a crisp, clean right angle in a piece of sheet metal, you will need angle irons to fit between the jaws of the vice. By bending your sheet metal tightly against the pre-formed shape of the angle iron, your right angles come out perfectly uniform each time.

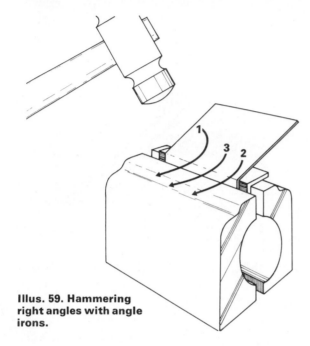

Illus. 59. Hammering right angles with angle irons.

With marking pen and ruler, mark the line along which the plate is to be bent. Place the angle iron between the jaws of the vice (for bending light-gauge metals, aluminum angles will work just as well and, as the inside corners are square instead of rounded, they will fit the vice-jaws more closely). Adjust the metal plate between the angles in such a manner that the bending line appears just above the level of the angle (Illus. 59). Always grip the shorter side of the bend in the vice to give you more bending leverage with the long side. Gently bend the plate over by hand.

Finish by hammering along the bend with the flat face of the planishing hammer. Strike first at one end, then at the other, working the hammer blows towards the middle (Illus. 59).

To avoid damaging the plate with hammer marks, protect it with a thick rag.

Bending Sheet Metal—Curves

Many of the same principles which were used for bending wire are applicable for bending sheet metal. To repeatedly bend wire in a particular shape, you coil it around a dowel. This will also work for light-gauge sheet metal, or if the sheet metal is heavier, it can be curved around a steel pipe. This is the technique used to bend horse-shoe nails (p. 66); clamping the steel pipe in the bench vice, holding the nail against the pipe with adjustable pliers and bending the nail by hand to the desired angle. If the sheet is too heavy, you may have to begin the curve with a few taps of the hammer.

The techniques outlined in the section on deep forming and raising (page 24) allow you to form the perfectly curved forms needed for bowls. However, for most of the sheet-metal projects outlined in this book, you will be able to bend the metal to the desired shape with your hands and, if the curve then needs smoothing, press it or gently hammer with a rawhide mallet against a steel pipe, metal bowl or other round, hard object of the proper shape.

Remember, whenever you handle sheet metal with sharp edges, it is extremely important to wear heavy work gloves to protect your fingers.

Illus. 60. A piece of sheet brass bent into a bracelet was adorned with strips of soldered-on wire to make this design.

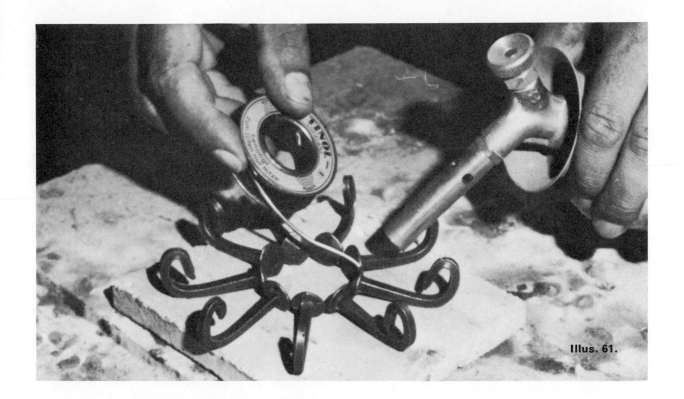

Basic Joining Techniques

Soldering and Brazing

Soldering and brazing are processes which join two pieces of metal by the fusion of another metal with a lower melting point. Soft soldering uses lead-tin solder, melting in the range of 400° F. The parts to be joined are heated with a soldering iron for smaller parts, or a torch for larger pieces. Brazing, a process similar to soldering, uses an alloy of silver and copper for joining, and a torch for heating. Brazing is used most for jewelry and precious metalwork.

As a rule, tin, lead or pewter are joined with soft solder, while brass, copper, iron and steel may either be soft soldered or hard soldered, depending on the strength of the joint required. Another factor to consider when choosing between the two methods is that discoloration is likely to occur when metals are heated to the substantially higher temperatures required for brazing. For nearly all of the projects in this book, soft soldering will provide a sufficient bond.

Soft Soldering

Cleaning

It is essential that all surfaces to be soldered are completely clean. Dirt, oxides or even the oil from fingerprints will prevent the solder from adhering properly. Dirt or oil can be removed with some cotton or a cloth dipped in alcohol. For even better results, use steel wool, sandpaper or emery cloth to clean down to the bright metal. After cleaning, do not touch the metal with your bare hands—use gloves or tweezers.

Illus. 62. You must tin a new soldering iron before using it.

Flux

You can use a compound called flux which cleans the metal surface of oxide and thus promotes fusion. Acid-core solders are also available which perform the same function as flux. You will want to either use self-fluxing solder or be sure to flux the individual pieces before you solder them. Sometimes the core of the self-fluxing solder is not strong enough to adequately clean the particular material you are using, and you will have to use flux in addition. Whether it is brushed on separately or is inside the hollow-core solder, be sure to use only acid flux with zinc, lead and iron, only resin flux with copper or tin.

Depending on the project you are assembling, you will apply the solder in different ways. If two pieces come to a joint, you can apply solder directly to the work. When one piece needs to be soldered on top of another, you must tin them. Tinning consists of first covering the surfaces to be joined with a thin film of solder. Then place the tinned pieces together and, by heating the pieces themselves, melt the solder to form a bond.

Soldering without Tinning

For joints which occur between the edges of pieces of metal, apply solder directly to the work. When the pieces to be soldered have been cleaned thoroughly and fluxed if necessary, apply heat. If you are using a soldering iron, apply solder by melting it with the tip of the iron until it flows into the joint. For best results, the hot iron and the solder should touch the joint at the same time.

Before you can use a new soldering iron, the copper tip has to be "tinned." Bring the temperature of the iron up to "hot" (6–8 minutes). Place some rosin on a flat piece of copper and rub the tip of the iron into the rosin while you hold the solder next to the tip. The solder will melt onto the tip, making it shiny (Illus. 62).

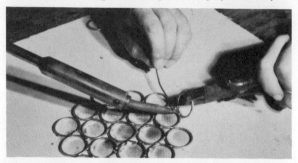

Illus. 63. To apply heat for soldering upright constructions you need a soldering iron.

The oxide that accumulates at the tip of the soldering iron during use has to be removed frequently. File it off and "re-tin" the tip by dipping it in rosin and then coating it with solder.

Illus. 64. Use a soldering torch to quickly join pieces of flat constructions.

If you are using a soldering torch, simply hold the end of the solder at the joint and heat the area with the torch, being sure to adjust the flame so that it heats only the area to be soldered.

The soldering torch has one advantage over the soldering iron: it heats the junction to be soldered much faster and over a wider area and thus spreads the flux and solder to form a very good fusion. However, you must take care not to burn the metal, since overheating produces a change in color.

Illus. 65. Clean the metal.

Illus. 66. Apply soldering paste.

Illus. 67. Laquering.

Tinning

Spread a layer of soldering paste over the surfaces to be joined, apply a coat of clear brushing lacquer, and let dry. This will be burned up in the course of tinning the piece, but it will, at the same time, keep the solder from flowing where it is not wanted. The pieces are now ready for tinning.

Flux the pieces to be joined, if necessary, and place the prepared pieces on your asbestos pad or on a firebrick. If you are soldering pieces longer than 2½ inches, you must avoid the waste of heat caused by conduction. To do this, place a little support, no more than ⅛ inch high, between the asbestos pad and the metal. It must present the smallest surface possible to the workpiece (Illus. 69).

If the pieces are of good size, heat them with the propane torch. Smaller pieces, such as wire jump rings, can be heated with a soldering iron.

Before a piece gets red-hot, remove the flame or soldering iron and touch the end of the wire solder to the hot piece. If the temperature of the metal is high enough, the solder will melt on contact and flow out over the surface. If it was not heated enough, the solder may still melt, but it will form a granular cake. In this case, turn the flame back on the piece, or touch it again with the soldering iron, until the solder spreads out in a shiny layer. Remove the source of heat at once in order not to damage the strength of the solder by excessive heat.

Take note! A thin film of solder is enough. Too thick a layer will only jeopardize the soldering job. If you get too much solder on, reheat until the solder flows well; then at once quickly wipe the surface with a rag. This will pick up the surplus solder.

When the tinned pieces have cooled, examine them to make sure that they are ready for the actual soldering, or joining.

The solder should look glossy and brilliant. This is an opportune time to renew the lacquer which was burned by the flame.

Illus. 68. Place the piece to be soldered, using pliers.

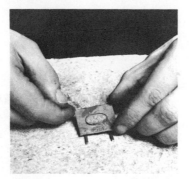

Illus. 69. Place piece on support.

Illus. 70. Apply soft solder.

Soldering Tinned Pieces

Now you must place in close contact the surfaces you are going to solder together. In soldering flat work, you do not need a holding device for the parts to be joined. Where you do need such a device, however, you can use a vice, or jam the parts between bricks. The important thing is to avoid large losses of heat caused by contact with a large, heat-conducting surface.

When the different pieces are ready, heat them all at once, either with the torch or with the soldering iron, concentrating the source of heat towards the thickest and largest piece. Remember, the parts to be joined must reach the melting point of the solder at the same time. The solder melts rapidly and shines brilliantly.

Remove the flame immediately and let the work cool for several minutes, watching to see that the surfaces being soldered together continue to be pressed tightly against each other.

Cleaning after Soldering

Remove all traces of oxidation with emery cloth or a file, as well as the spots of burned lacquer (if you used any) and the excess solder. If flux (as rosin flux or tallow and sal ammoniac) has been used, the greasy residue has to be washed off the completed workpiece with a hot alkaline solution. (Use a brush.) For the preservation of the brightness of non-ferrous metals a coating of cellulose lacquer, obtainable from paint shops, is recommended.

Illus. 71. Heating with soldering iron.

Illus. 72. Heating with propane torch.

Illus. 73. Final soldering.

Brazing or Hard Soldering

This is the process, used mostly for jewelry work, that calls for silver-copper solder and a torch.

The silver solder or brazing compound should flow and penetrate, by capillary action, into the joint between the two pieces being soldered. This means that the metal sheets must be perfectly flat, and the ends of wires very straight. There must be no spaces between the joining surfaces. If there are, eliminate them first by filing.

Cleaning

As for soft soldering, scrape the metal bare with emery cloth or a file, and wipe with a rag,

avoiding any contact with your fingers, as they are always a little greasy.

Next, brush on a layer of flux. This is some-

Illus. 74. Flux the metal.

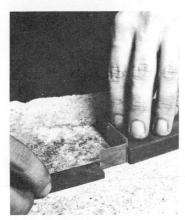

Illus. 75. Position the pieces.

Illus. 76. Heat with torch.

Illus. 77. Apply silver solder.

times available in a liquid form. After fluxing, the pieces are ready to be silver-soldered together.

Soldering

Place all of the pieces to be assembled in position. Make sure the set-up is very stable and arranged so as to avoid large losses of heat by conduction. Light the torch and begin by heating the largest pieces. At the precise moment when the entire assembly is glowing cherry red (a very bright red), carefully touch the rod or wire of silver solder to the soldering point.

If the piece is at the right temperature, the hard solder liquefies immediately and is drawn by capillary action between the two pieces joined together. Take care to remove the silver solder immediately after the touch, to avoid overrunning the piece with solder.

Allow the flame to heat the piece for a few seconds longer; then, take it away. Wait a minute longer, and then cool the piece quickly by plunging it into water. Next, with emery cloth and file, clean away all traces of oxidation and excess solder.

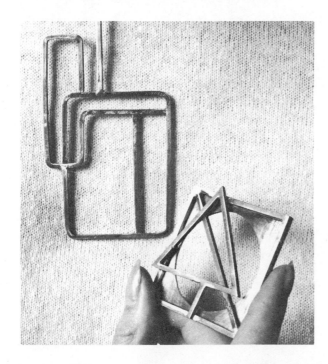

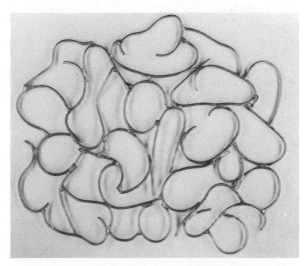

Illus. 78 (left). These lovely modern pendants are composed of simple soldered shapes.

Illus. 79 (above). Free-form shapes were soldered together with a torch to form this attractive abstract decoration.

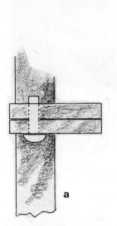

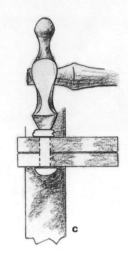

Illus. 80. The basic steps in riveting are (a) placing rivet through the pre-drilled plates, (b) compressing the two parts together with rivet set, (c) "upsetting" the rivet by hammering, (d) rounding rivet with ball-peen hammer, and (e) shaping rivet with riveting-snap.

Riveting

Riveting consists of joining two plates of metal together by means of rivets, a kind of unpointed nail fixed in position by hammering. In many cases you can incorporate the shape and pattern of the rivet heads into your design. Riveting is especially useful when working with aluminum, since this metal is extremely difficult to solder.

You will need:
grease pencil
center punch
hand drill
drill bits of the correct size for the rivets
square-pointed reamer
metal-cutting shears or a jeweler's saw
bench vice
planishing (or ball-peen) hammer
rivets
riveting-snap (a tool having a cup-shaped depression in one end for forming rivet heads)

There are three basic kinds of rivets: Buttonhead (roundhead), panhead (flat), and countersunk head (Illus. 81). Because of their decorative qualities, the buttonheads are most suitable for use in jewelry-making (Illus. 85).

The rivets can be of copper or steel; however, aluminum rivets are also available.

Mark the location for the rivet first with grease pencil, and then with the center punch,

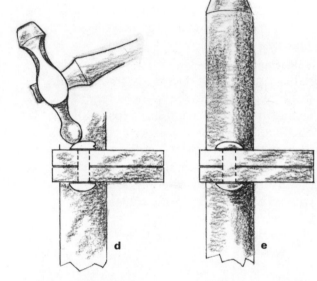

on the metal plate that is to be on top. Then drill a hole. Mark the bottom piece to be attached through the drilled hole. In some cases, both pieces can be clamped together and drilled simultaneously. The holes should be of the same diameter as, or of a diameter slightly smaller than, that of the rivet. Where necessary, the holes can be reamed a trifle with the square-pointed reamer (see "Piercing" on page 39).

Rivets come in various lengths and you should be able to get hold of a length just right for your

Illus. 81. Rivets: (a) buttonhead, (b) panhead, (c) countersunk.

work. The end of the rivet should project above the work no higher than the length of its own diameter. If it does, cut off the excess with the cutting pliers.

In order to hold the rounded head of the rivet and keep it from being deformed as you hammer at the other end, you will need either a riveting-snap or rivet set. A riveting-snap, shown in Illus. 80, is a tool with a cup-shaped indentation, usually used to form the rounded shape of the hammered end of the rivet. However, if you clamp it in your bench vice, it will protect the pre-rounded head of the rivet as you work.

A rivet set is easily prepared by holding the round end of a rivet against a hardwood block and striking the rivet to make an indentation in the block (Illus. 82). Whichever method you use for holding the rivet in place, be sure that the rivet, when placed in the indentation, stands perfectly vertical and that, when the work is placed over the rivet, it remains perfectly horizontal. Otherwise you will not get a firm riveting, and you may mar the work.

With the work in position, strike a vertical blow smartly on the end of the projecting

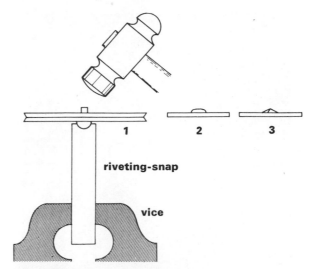

Illus. 83. Shaping the rivet end.

rivet with either a planishing hammer or the flat face of a ball-peen hammer. This will bulge it and hold the pieces firmly together. Do not hammer too hard, but continue hammering from all sides so that the crushed metal expands and begins to round off (Illus. 80). Then, with care, continue hammering until you have shaped the end of the rivet into a pyramid with four sides (Illus. 83). If the hammered side of the rivet will be visible in your design, you may prefer to round it by shaping it with the ball end of the ball-peen hammer and finishing with the riveting-snap (Illus. 80).

The most modern method for riveting in crafts work is a riveting plier, as shown in Illus. 84. Pre-formed rivets, which are available in assorted diameters and lengths for different

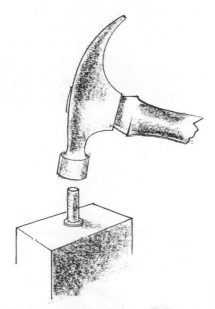

Illus. 82. To prepare a rivet set, make an indentation in a wood block with a hammer and rivet as shown.

Illus. 84. A riveting plier provides a strong riveted connection in very little time.

Illus. 85. Buttonhead rivets were used to create this unique pendant.

jobs, are inserted in a pre-drilled hole. The pointed end of the rivet is placed in the hole at the front of the riveting plier, the handles are squeezed together, and, after a few squeezes, the riveting is complete. If you plan to use rivets frequently in your project, this tool should be a good investment, since it provides a neat riveted join with a fraction of the effort involved in hammering rivets.

Wire Jump Rings

Some projects will require the use of *jump rings*, tiny loops of wire used to connect individual parts of earrings, pendants and necklaces. They can be made simply by winding a length of wire around a knitting needle. Remove the spiral thus created and cut across one side as shown in Illus. 87, using your diagonal wire cutters.

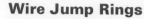

Illus. 87. Cut your wire spiral as indicated.

After cutting, file the ends of the rings off square. They can be soldered together as needed.

If your project requires a substantial number of jump rings of uniform size and shape, you will need these additional materials:

small rod, having same diameter as wire being used
hand drill
bench vice
fine-toothed hacksaw or jeweler's saw

Take a round, square, or oval rod, according to the size and shape of the desired rings. Insert the rod in the chuck of the hand drill along with the end of the wire chosen for the rings. Grip the drill in a bench vice so that the turning handle is on top (Illus. 88). Turn this with one hand while, with the other, guiding the wire as it wraps round the rod.

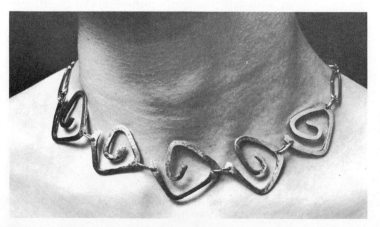

Illus. 86. Wire jump rings connect the various pieces of this 18-gauge nickel-silver wire necklace.

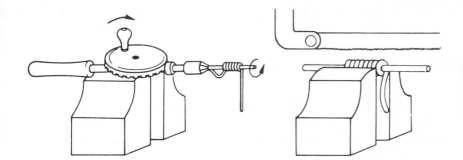

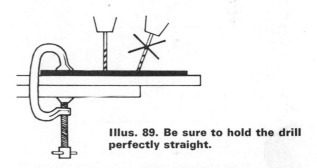

Illus. 88. You can make a great number of wire jump rings quickly by using a hand drill to twist the wire into a spiral, and cutting the spiral into separate loops with a hacksaw.

Remove the rod and the wrapped-around wire from the drill chuck and grip them in the bench vice. Saw the turned wire parallel to the rod with the saw. When released from the vice, the "turns" fall apart, each becoming a ring. Be sure that you hold the saw vertical so that the kerf (cut) will be clean and narrow. If the wire is fine, it is preferable to remove the rings from the rod and cut them apart one at a time with the diagonal cutters, making sure always to cut at the same point in the spiral.

Piercing

You will need:
grease pencil
center punch
ball-peen hammer
C-clamp
wooden board
hand drill
3 drill bits of high-speed steel, numbers 60, 55, and 52 (these come in a set)
square-pointed reamer
round needle file

Piercing allows you to make the holes in sheet metal necessary for passing jump rings and rivets through. First, mark the point to be pierced with a grease pencil; then mark it plainly and precisely with the center punch, lightly tapping it with the hammer. Clamp the workpiece to a wooden board with a C-clamp.

Choose a drill bit slightly larger in diameter than that of the wire of which the jump ring is made and smaller than, or equal to, the size of any rivet you might be using. Insert the bit into the hand drill, place the point on the punch

mark, and start drilling. Turn the handle *slowly and put little or no pressure* on the drill. Bits such as these are very tiny and break easily. It is highly important that you always hold the drill perfectly perpendicular to the metal plate (Illus. 89).

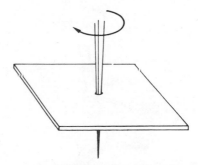

Illus. 89. Be sure to hold the drill perfectly straight.

Do not let the piece be held by a "helping hand." If the bit should break, you could not prevent the drill from jumping aside and causing injury with the remainder of the broken bit. Once the hole is drilled, you can enlarge it with the reamer if necessary (Illus. 90); then remove the burr with a round needle file.

Illus. 90. Use a reamer to enlarge a hole after drilling.

Basic Decorating Techniques

Chasing

You will need:
chasing or other flat-faced hammer
punches, dapping punches and chasing tools
flat block of lead or soft wood

Chasing is a process in which a pattern is repeated by tapping a shaped tool with light strokes of a chasing hammer. The tool is moved along the work and the result is a design made by the repeated pattern.

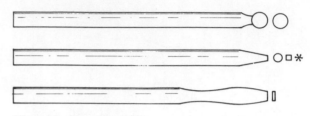

Illus. 92. Chasing tools.

Chasing is a rather delicate operation and requires a good deal of care. You can buy ready-made punches, or you can make them yourself from large nails or spikes, filed or ground to the desired shape. You can buy small chisels and ball-headed dapping punches at a jeweler's supply house.

To hold the workpiece, drive three nails into the block of wood or lead, as shown in Illus. 91. Make the impressions in the metal by tapping the punches, chisels or dapping punches with a hammer. Hold the punch nearly perpendicular to the metal plate and strike it with a sharp blow of the hammer (Illus. 93).

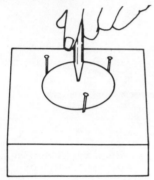

Illus. 91. Hold the workpiece securely in place with three nails.

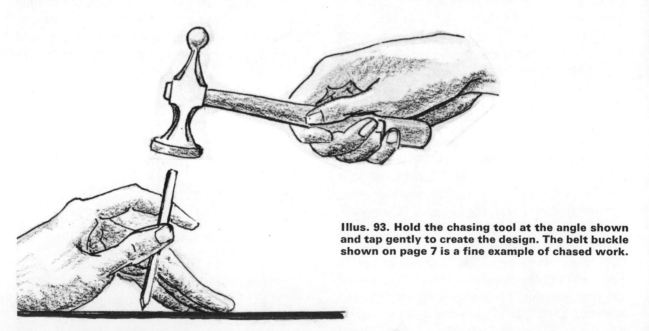

Illus. 93. Hold the chasing tool at the angle shown and tap gently to create the design. The belt buckle shown on page 7 is a fine example of chased work.

Engraving

Decorations made by the engraving method allow you to give vent to your artistic inclinations. The design is carved into the metal with tools such as those shown in Illus. 96. Illus 94 shows a bowl with engraved decoration.

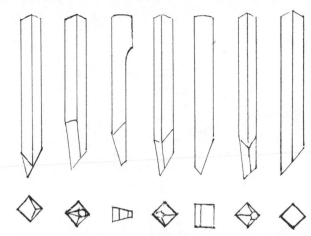

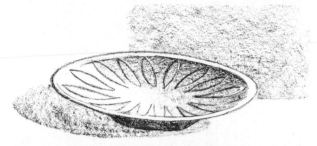

Illus. 94. Engraving a simple design adds interest to a basic deep dish.

Illus. 96. There is a great variety of tools available for incising lines into metal.

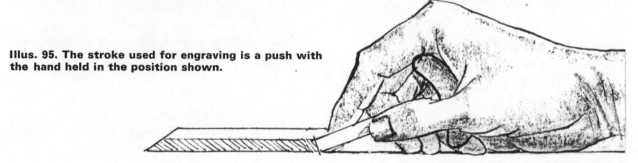

Illus. 95. The stroke used for engraving is a push with the hand held in the position shown.

Stamping

Stamping consists of making impressions from a hard object serving as a "master": a coin, bolt, key, spool, etc. The màster may be repeated by itself or combined with other objects to form a varied pattern. You can also combine it with repoussage and embossing techniques, discussed in the section on page 136. Repetition permits innumerable variations—you can apply the master in a number of positions, or use different parts of it as shown in Illus. 97.

Place a sheet of copper or tin on a hard rubber or thick felt mat. Hold the master in one hand (the key in Illus. 97) and rest it in the desired position on the metal. Strike it with a light hammer blow. (Be sure to make several tests on a piece of scrap metal so you will acquire the proper striking force without

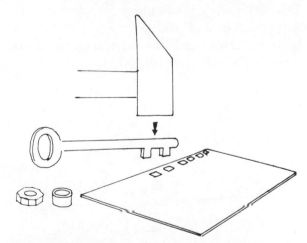

Illus. 97. Use your imagination to come up with new and different objects for stamping "masters."

breaking the metal.) By repeating this process, you will achieve a sharp imprint of the master as many times as you wish in the metal sheet.

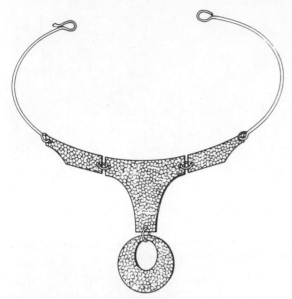

Illus. 98. A hammered necklace.

Hammering for Texture

You will need:
forming hammer
ball-peen hammer
steel bench anvil
dapping punch

Hammering consists of covering the surface of the plate with tiny facets, or hammer marks. This technique gives an attractive, antique look to the metal, and also gives you a chance to hide scratches and the accidental hammer marks that may mar the work.

Illus. 99. A forming hammer is good for creating hammered textures.

Hold the metal on the steel bench anvil with one hand and strike it with the ball of the hammer with the other. If you want to get the smallest possible facets, use a dapping punch and a hammer. Do not let the facets overlap. You must also regulate the force of the hammer blows—heavy enough to produce the effect desired, and even enough to make all the facets the same. However, be sure also to hammer the edges of the piece more lightly to avoid deforming them.

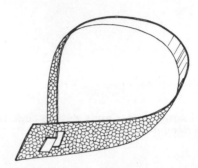

Illus. 100. This elegant bracelet is a simple bent sheet, made interesting by hammering. It is shown in color in Illus. F1.

After having hammered in the decoration, which will be in the form of depressions, polish the surface with fine emery paper or steel wool. This will affect only the uppermost surface, and the hammered impressions will remain unpolished and contrast pleasingly with the brilliance of the surface.

Polishing and Lacquering

You may feel that your metalwork will be more beautiful with a bright, shiny surface. To achieve this finish, first take out the deep scratches and marks with coarse steel wool. Follow this with fine steel wool. To obtain a high lustre, rub with jeweler's rouge or fine pumice on a soft rag.

If your work does not have any deep flaws to begin with, you can start polishing by using ordinary kitchen cleanser on a slightly damp rag. However, it is preferable to use the kind of polishing paste used by automotive body builders. Emery cloth should *not* be used at this stage because it will scratch the metal. You can also use whiting, which is powdered chalk, on a damp rag, but be sure to wash off the residue thoroughly.

Polishing is then done with a metal polish which you can buy at your hardware dealer's. Apply with a soft cloth, let dry, and polish well with a dry cloth. This will not produce the sort of high lustre possible with jeweler's rouge, but it is an easy method which will be applicable to many larger pieces of work. For a full explanation of the fine polishing techniques used in making silver rings and similar work see page 191.

Pieces made of metal sheet and wire will tarnish quickly unless properly protected from moisture and harmful gases in the air. To protect the metal from tarnishing and to maintain its brightness, you must coat it with clear brushing lacquer. Jewelry pieces are especially subject to tarnishing, since they come in contact with the corrosive oils found on the skin surface. They are also particularly difficult to lacquer, since the lacquer tends to clog the delicate holes and bends in the work.

To protect such pieces, mix clear brushing lacquer with an equal quantity of lacquer thinner in a glass jar. Fasten the jewelry piece to a short length of wire, dip it in the lacquer, and hold it above the surface to drain. Then, hang it up by hooking the upper end of the

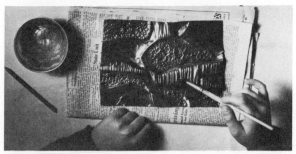

Illus. 101. Use diluted liver of sulphur to antique copper.

dipping wire over a drying line on the edge of a table.

The thin, fluid lacquer will continue to run down the piece and collect in a drop hanging from the lowermost edge. Touch this drop from beneath with a toothpick, and the lacquer will instantly flow down the toothpick. Wipe it off on a rag, and continue touching the spot until the lacquer ceases to form a drop. Continue with all the pieces ready to be finished.

In 15 or 20 minutes, you can apply a second coat in the same way to the first piece. Three or four coats are enough.

Antiquing Copper and Brass

A long time ago some craftsman found that he could help nature along in the tarnishing process, and he produced results that outdid in beauty the natural ageing process. This so-called

Illus. 102. When the liver of sulphur has completely dried, the copper will be black. Use steel wool to bring out the highlights.

Illus. 103. This striking varie-gated effect is the result of a rapid exposure of the metal to the flame.

antiquing, particularly effective on etched work, is a process in which copper is treated with a solution of liver of sulphur (potassium sulphide). Because of the irregularities of the surface, the copper is affected unequally by the solution. When subsequent polishing is done, the effect is that of a beautifully aged piece of metalware.

The process is simple. Dissolve a pea-size lump of liver of sulphur (obtained from your craft dealer or drugstore) in $\frac{1}{2}$ cup of hot water. Rub this onto the copper surface with a soft rag. Allow it to dry. Polish with fine steel wool, pumice or rouge. Experiment for effects. The process can be repeated as often as desired until you obtain the effect you want.

Artificial Patinas

True patina is a gift age bestows on metals. It is caused by the natural oxidation of the metal, which becomes coated with a colored layer—it is this layer of oxidation that is called the patina. For our purposes, we can scarcely wait for natural oxidation to occur, since it takes a very long time. So, in order to simulate natural patina, you can use commercial patinas if you wish, or you can use the following formulas. You will soon discover that the best "recipes" are often the result of trial and error. No doubt your own experiments with artificial patinas will lengthen the list of existing formulas.

Heating Copper

Heating copper will not only make it more malleable—according to the intensity of the heat and the duration of exposure, the metal undergoes a change in appearance. It passes progressively from fiery red to deeper hues, with a whole succession of intermediate tints. A rapid passage through the flame, or through repeated firings, results in magnificent natural patinas. To preserve the effect, rub the surface with oil as soon as the colors show up. You could also spread soap over the surface; then polish it with a piece of newsprint (newspaper that has not been printed on).

Illus. 104. Use pliers to pass the copper over the flame. The intensity of the heat and the length of exposure determine the final effect.

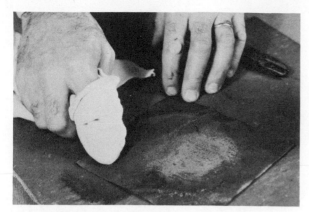

Illus. 105. When the burning is very intense, the red-hot copper oxidizes. After cooling, wipe the metal thoroughly with a rag.

If you have either a butane gas burner or a Bunsen gas burner at your disposal, either is suitable for the purpose. Be sure, however, to use a heat-resistant base such as an asbestos mat during the heating process.

Other Copper Patinas

A blue-green patina on copper:
Dissolve together:
4 teaspoonfuls of distilled water
3 teaspoonfuls of ammonium carbonate
1 teaspoonful of sal ammoniac
Apply with a brush. The patina will appear within a few hours.

A clear, grey patina on copper:
Brush perchloride of iron on the piece. When the desired tone is reached, stop the reaction by washing in running water.

Patinas on Other Metals

A bronzelike patina:
Rub the piece with a little *used* crankcase oil. Heat, then polish. The bronze particles in the oil (from the auto bearings) stick to the piece. You can get the same effect by using any kind of oil into which a little bronzing powder has been stirred. Bronzing powder is available at paint shops in different shades.

A tin patina:
Flow a little soft solder (or pure tin) on the piece and rub it off with a rag while still hot, so as to leave only traces of tin on the surface.

Greyish-black patina in the hollows:
If your design has either etched or embossed work in it, you can obtain a handsome greyish-black patina in the hollow spaces by rubbing dry, powdered soap into the depressions. Turn the gas flame on it until the soap melts; then polish with newsprint.

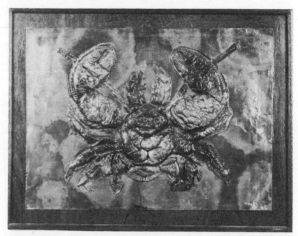

Illus. 106. This embossed crab is mounted on a sheet of copper which has a varicolored appearance resulting from a partial burning.

Aluminum. To apply a patina to aluminum, you have two possibilities: you can brush a black varnish on the metal, which you wipe off lightly with a rag while damp; or, apply a mixture of India ink and fixative with an atomizer. If you use an atomizer, always clean it with alcohol immediately afterward, or the dried fluids will clog it hopelessly.

Pewter. This metal, which has a shiny appearance to begin with, will assume in time a lovely and lasting natural patina. However, if you want to tone down its brilliance, you can use a mixture of lamp black and kerosene.

Illus. 107. Iridescent patina on etched design.

Enamelling

Enamelling is an advanced decorating technique in which glass colored with metallic oxides is fused onto a metal surface. It involves certain potentially dangerous chemicals, and *should not* be attempted by children.

Metals suitable for enamelling are copper (the least expensive and most widely employed), silver, gold, aluminum, pinchbeck, brass and stainless steel.

You will need:

small kiln
kiln cones
tongs
firing stand
stilts
asbestos slab or stone
asbestos gloves
cleaning solution
fine steel wool or emery paper
enamel powder
gum tragacanth or ready-to-use adhesive solution
200-mesh strainer
80-mesh strainer
brush
enamelling fork
carborundum rubbing stone

The cardinal rule of enamelling is cleanliness. *Enamel powder* will not adhere to any surface that is not absolutely clean and grease-free, so

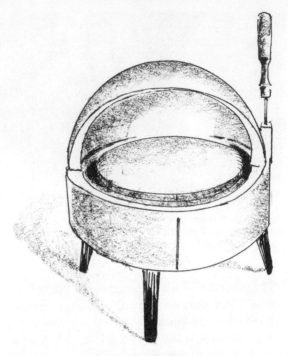

Illus. 110. A typical domed kiln.

the first step is to clean meticulously the surface to be enamelled. A new, inexpensive and *safe acid compound* is now available as a substitute for the traditional nitric acid cleaning solution. It is a dry acid compound for pickling, sold under various trade names. Add one tablespoon of it to each cup of water in a large glass container (*always* add acid to water, according to package directions).

Heat the copper shape for 10 seconds or so in a *kiln*. (You can get a small domed kiln as illustrated here.) This will loosen scale and burn away grease. Let it cool (*never* add a hot metal object to the acid solution or you may be seriously burned and the metal will surely warp). Immerse the metal in the pickling solution, and leave it there until the surface is pink, clean and shiny. Remove it with *tongs* (you

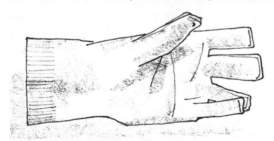

Illus. 108. Asbestos glove.

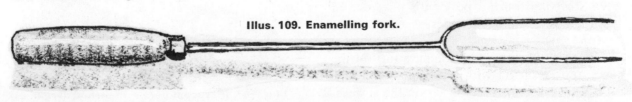

Illus. 109. Enamelling fork.

must not touch the clean surface with your fingers, which will deposit grease on the surface) and rinse it under cold running water.

If the metal surface is not completely clean, or if you want it to show through transparent enamels, you may polish it further by rubbing with fine steel wool or emery paper. Wipe again with a soft cloth, and then with vinegar or household ammonia to make the surface alkaline.

If you are working with children, a solution of 1 cup of vinegar mixed with 1½ tablespoons of salt is an effective substitute for the acid solution, though acid will do a more thorough job of cleaning.

In case the new dry acid compound is unavailable, here is the traditional acid mixture: Add 1 part of *nitric acid* to 5 parts of water in a large, heat-resistant glass container. Heat and cool the metal as before, and immerse it in the solution. Swish it around with your tongs until it is clean. Rinse and polish as before. You may store the acid solution, tightly covered, until it turns brown with dissolved metal.

Characteristics of Enamels

There are three different kinds of enamel: the opaque, the transparent, and the opalescent. Most often used are the opaque enamels. Because they completely cover the color of the metal over which they are fired, they are especially suitable for enamelling on copper. Since transparent enamels allow the surface

underneath to show through, they are used over more precious metals, such as gold and silver, as well as over opaque enamels. Opalescent enamels are seldom used because they are quite scarce. They have an iridescent glow rather than the clear, glassy quality of the transparent enamels.

Ready-to-use enamels are available in various forms, but the best way to buy them is in powder ground to 80-mesh (the powder will pass

Illus. 112. Tongs.

through a strainer with 80 square openings to the square inch). Enamel powder ground to 80-mesh is used for nearly every enamelling technique, with the exception of the "painting," or Limoges technique, which requires enamel ground to 200- or 250-mesh. Although unwashed powders are less expensive, no saving really results in the end as up to 50% of the powder is lost in the washing process.

Enamels also have three firing characteristics: soft-firing enamels mature at 1400 degrees F., medium-firing enamels at 1450–1500 degrees F., and hard-firing enamels mature at 1600 degrees F. You will need *kiln cones* to tell you how hot your kiln is. Although some colors (black, white and beige especially) are available in all three categories, most colors are *either* soft-, medium- or hard-firing. Soft-firing enamels

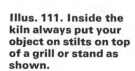

Illus. 111. Inside the kiln always put your object on stilts on top of a grill or stand as shown.

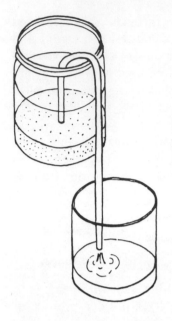

Illus. 113. Using the set-up shown you can eliminate impurities from enamel powders. It is much easier to keep the powders clean to begin with.

burn away sooner than do the more durable hard-firing enamels (which are generally used for counter-enamelling), while the medium-firing enamels are suitable for most purposes. The only way to determine the firing characteristics of each color you buy is to fire a small test sample on a scrap of clean copper and note the results on the label of the jar in which the enamel is to be stored.

The test sample is also an invaluable guide to the exact color of the enamel powder. This is very important because one of enamelling's cardinal rules is that you cannot mix colors as you can oils or watercolors. Yellow and blue enamel will *not* make green, but will remain separate and distinct from one another after firing. Hundreds of color gradations are available, however, so you will not find this a disadvantage if you have made a test sample which you can use to pick out an exact shade at a glance from your stock. For each enamel color, you should also add the manufacturer's number to the label giving the firing characteristics so that when you re-order you will be sure to get the same color. Manufacturers frequently change the descriptive name of the colors, but they always retain the original number for each one.

Cleanliness cannot be overemphasized. Keep your enamel powders tightly capped at all times, for the tiniest speck of dust or grease will loom large on the surface of a finished project. Should transparent colors appear muddy after firing, you will have to clean the powder. Place it in a glass jar. Fill this with ordinary tap water, and siphon off or carefully pour out the water into another jar. Repeat the process until all the impurities have been removed and the water runs clear. Dry the powder on blotting paper thoroughly before rebottling. You can save yourself this tedious chore by keeping each color separate and away from breezes and stray dust at all times.

A Sample Project

Before commencing a complicated project, make a small sample first. This will save you hours of indecision later on, and the grief of spoiling a project because this simple precaution was not taken. These samples need not be discarded, for with the addition of a jump ring and a chain they make handsome pendants or key-chain fobs for gifts.

Illus. 114. The best way to obtain an even coating is to tap the powder out of a slightly inclined shaker bottle, with an 80-mesh strainer at the mouth.

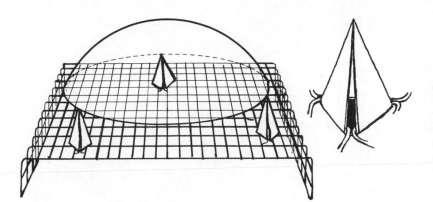

If you do not have a commercial stilt (Illus. 116, below) to support your work during firing, you can improvise a firing stand by bending three pieces of tin into little pyramids and wiring them to a steel mesh stand. The bowl is then inverted over the pyramids. (Illus. 115, left).

Adhering and Firing

After cleaning the metal to be enamelled, coat the surface with an adhesive solution so that the enamel powder will adhere evenly. A *gum tragacanth* solution is usually employed. To prepare this, soak the lumps or flakes of gum tragacanth overnight in water.

On the following day, cook the solution (be sure there is enough water so it will not burn) over low heat until it becomes more fluid and the gum dissolves completely. When cool, dilute the mixture with tap water until it is quite thin and strain it through a 200-mesh sieve (a strainer with 200 square openings to the square inch).

When you apply the adhesive solution to the metal surface it should be as clear and fluid as water. Ready-to-use adhesive is available commercially, and you may find that the higher cost is balanced by its time-saving qualities.

Using a soft, clean brush, paint the adhesive over the surface to be enamelled. Sift the enamel powder over the tacky surface through an 80-mesh strainer, covering the surface evenly but not too thickly. Two thin coats are always better than one thick coat in enamelling, and even the simplest one-color objects must be sprinkled and fired several times. Build up the layer of enamel powder slightly at the edges, however, as this is where it tends to burn away more.

Before you can fire this base coat, you must let the object dry completely, until every trace of water has evaporated, or it will bubble and

crack the enamel coating while it is in the kiln. Either hold the object on your enamelling fork just in front of the open door of the hot kiln (always wear *asbestos* gloves when using the kiln) or dry the piece in a low oven for 25 to 30 minutes. When working with children always use the latter method.

If you dry it just outside the kiln, almost immediately you will see a little cloud of steam rising round the object. This is the water evaporating. Pull the object away instantly or it will overheat.

To fire, put the object inside the kiln on a firing stand on stilts, using an enamelling fork and gloves. If your kiln has a glass door, you will see the powdery surface begin to change color and liquefy.

When it becomes smooth and brilliant, and the metal is heated to a light red (this should take no less than 2 and never more than 4 minutes, depending on whether you have used a soft-, medium-, or hard-firing enamel), the firing process is complete.

Remove the object with your fork, and leave it on an asbestos slab or stone to cool in a draught-free area. The surface will continue to change colors until it is cool enough to be touched with bare hands. Then it will show the color it will always retain. This is one of the most interesting aspects of enamelling, for the gradual color changes are quite beautiful.

If the surface has dents or holes, you can assume that you sprinkled too little powder on the surface the first time. If the surface appears granular, you under-fired.

It is always better to under-fire than to over-fire, for the under-firing is easily corrected, but there is no solution for over-firing. Continue to sprinkle and fire until the surface is smooth and even, and you are satisfied with its appearance. Do not build up so many layers, however, that the enamel is overly thick and puts an unbearable strain on the metal. File the oxidized edges of the metal with a metal file and polish the enamel surface with a carborundum rubbing stone under running water to complete the project.

Since metal expands and contracts at a different rate than the enamel coating, it is always wise and often essential to coat both sides of the metal with enamel, to seal and reinforce it. This is called counter-enamelling. When in doubt as to whether or not to counter-enamel, do so. Always choose a hard-firing enamel for the underside coating, since it will have to withstand as many firings as will be necessary for the top coat.

Illus. 117. The leaf design on this bowl was made with a stencil design. Darker enamel was sprinkled around the edges of the leaf to give it emphasis.

Illus. 118. This deep bowl was counter-enamelled with opaque cherry red enamel. The tiny holes in the middle resulted from slight over-firing.

To counter-enamel, after you have finished sprinkling the top of the object, turn it over on a firing stand very carefully, touching the clean surface as little as possible. (Be sure your stand has little metal stilts or points on which to balance the very edges of the object.) Remove any finger marks with vinegar or ammonia before painting the surface with adhesive solution and applying the enamel, and do not forget to allow the enamel to dry completely before firing. Place the object upside down on its stand into the kiln and fire as usual. If you should hear a cracking sound while an object is being fired, simply leave it in the kiln until the surface heals. The cracking is a result of the metal contracting.

There are many decorative techniques in enamelling. Try them when you have become familiar with the medium and have some experience with simple techniques such as applying colors through stencils, using sgraffito (scratching a design through unfired enamel on top of a contrasting fired enamel surface), and using commercial chunks and threads of enamel barely fused to the surface. Never attempt to be precise, for the colors are simply not easy to control. The 200-mesh powders mixed with adhesive solution can be painted or pushed into shapes and delicate patterns on the surface but this is a demanding and difficult process suitable only for experts. Explore the many relatively simple possibilities first.

Illus. 119. Be sure to label all of your etching solutions carefully, and keep them safely away from everyday household chemicals.

Etching

Etching must be regarded as an advanced metalworking technique, one which should only be attempted by an adult and, even then, with caution. The materials used in this process are potentially extremely dangerous. However, for the careful worker, etching can provide some of the most exciting and beautiful effects in metalcrafting.

The etching process consists of transferring a design to a sheet of zinc or copper-type metal, coating the areas not to be etched with a substance which is impervious to acid, and then immersing the metal in an acid bath which dissolves the exposed design and leaves the remainder untouched. Metal sheet is usually etched before it is shaped.

You will need:
emery cloth
black asphaltum varnish
acid resist or 4-lb. cut shellac
stove polish (available at hardware dealer)
soft brush
graphite
scraper
hydrochloric acid for zinc
mineral spirits (paint thinner)
plastic or glass bowls or trays

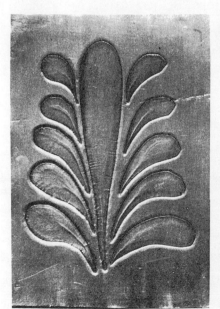

Illus. 120. These designs are etched into copper, zinc and brass. Once the metal has been cleaned and polished, the designs will come to life.

metal polish
70 per cent nitric acid for copper-type metals
single-edged razor blades
utility knives
needlepoint scribers
wooden clothespins
tongs

Before you begin remember to observe these precautions:

You must *always add acid to water*, slowly, and never vice versa. Keep this in mind at all times. If you must add more water to a solution, pour the additional water into an empty glass container. Then *add the solution to it.*

Be sure to work near an open window and keep fumes out of your eyes. If acid or fumes get in your eyes, flush immediately with water, and call a doctor.

Keep a tray of clear water near the etching tray for rinsing your fingers. If acid touches your skin, hold the affected spot under running water for at least 15 minutes. The best thing is to wear finger sheaths for protection. These are better than rubber gloves because gloves are awkward and sometimes slippery and you might drop the acid.

Always use separate solutions for each metal, and store acids or dilute baths in glass bottles having glass or plastic tops. Be sure to *label* each bottle.

POUR ACID INTO WATER!

Illus. 121. Always keep this simple rule in mind.

Etching Zinc

Take the piece you wish to etch and de-grease the surface by a thorough scrubbing with a detergent. Follow this with a gentle abrasive such as fine, powdered pumice.

With a camel's hair brush, coat the back side of the piece and the edges with the resisting medium. If you use shellac, apply two or three coats.

Paint the surface to be etched all over with stove polish and allow to dry. Apply two or three coats, letting each dry before applying the next. The surface should have a flat, black matt finish. When completely dry, trace your design on the surface by loading the back of the drawing to be traced with graphite. The graphite will be set off on the black surface as light lines.

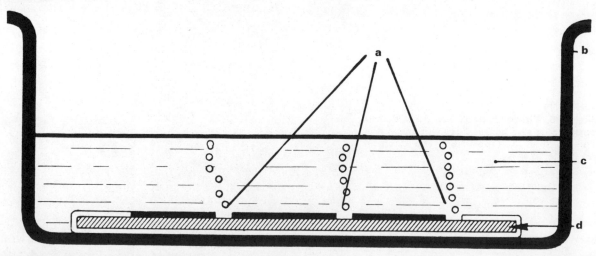

Illus. 122. Etching process: (a) design being etched, (b) glass or plastic container, (c) acid, (d) metal piece.

Then, using needlepoint scribers for thin lines and utility knives or razor blades for large areas, scrape the design out carefully, following the graphite outline.

In preparing the acid bath, begin with a weak solution, say, 1 part acid to 5 parts water. *Put the water in the container first*. Then add the acid. Never fill the container to the top so as to avoid splashing or overflowing. You can easily tell if you have put in too much acid because the bubbles on the plate that will arise because of the chemical reaction will be big and part of the resist will be removed. When you have become

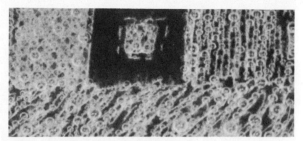

Illus. 124. Bubbles accumulate on the etched lines during the acid bath.

Etching Copper-Type Metals

Before proceeding to etch copper-type metals, familiarize yourself with the method of etching zinc.

After you have cleaned the copper piece thoroughly, paint the back side of the metal with black asphaltum varnish or 4-lb. cut shellac and let dry. Trace the design on the metal using carbon paper. Then scratch the outlines into the metal with a scriber. Clean by washing thoroughly with a detergent, and rinse in running water. Allow to dry completely.

With a small, red sable brush, carefully paint the piece around the outlines of the design with asphaltum varnish or two coats of the shellac, leaving open the areas to be etched. If the paint tends to flow too freely, thicken it with lamp-black (available at your hardware dealer). In any case, lampblack powder in the shellac will darken it and make it easier to see on the metal surface.

Illus. 123. Whether you are etching copper or zinc, you must first clean the surface thoroughly.

more expert, you can use a stronger acid solution than at first, since, as you will discover, the weaker the solution, the longer the etching process. *However, the water content must always be greater than the acid.*

To check how well the etching is going, touch the edge of an etched area with the needlepoint scriber. Keep on until the design is bitten in as deeply as you want it. Remember the acid will bite sideways as well as downwards, so expect that the lines of your design will be somewhat wider than your original tracing.

When the piece is etched to your satisfaction, remove it from the acid with *tongs*. Hold it under running water to wash off the chemical. Then clean it with paint thinner to remove the stove polish. Polish the unetched surface with a good metal polish.

Again, in preparing your acid bath (in this case, nitric acid) begin with a weak solution. Nitric acid is more powerful than hydrochloric acid, but the copper is harder, so try the same 5 parts water to 1 part acid until you are familiar with the effects. In any case, *never use more than 3 parts acid to 5 of water.*

Place the water in the container first. Slowly add the acid. Lay the metal in the bath. Check the action by using the point of a scriber to lift the piece carefully. (Be careful not to splash when lowering back into the acid.) When you are satisfied with the etching, remove with tongs, and rinse in running water. Clean with paint thinner or turpentine, and then polish.

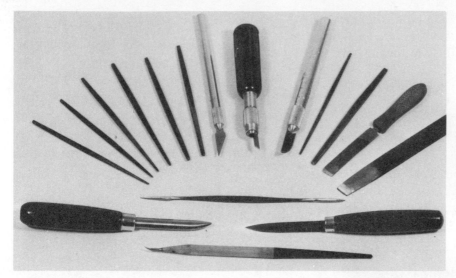

Illus. 125. Pictured are some suggestions for implements to be used as scrapers. The last two scrapers on the far right were made from files by grinding the tip to a cutting edge.

An Etched Copper Tray

You will need (in addition to the basic etching materials):

6-inch compass
tracing paper
a 12-inch-diameter sheet-copper disc, 18-gauge
6-inch file
center punch
dividers
a small jar of white tempera paint
cellophane tape
#2 pencil and carbon paper
soft rags
old newspaper
newsprint pad at least 14 by 14 inches
2 artist's brushes, #2 (fine) and #5 (heavy)

Method

Draw a 5-inch circle with your compass, in the middle of a 12-inch square piece of tracing paper. If you do not wish to use the design shown here, pick any design that will fit into the 5-inch circle and leave ¾-inch to 1-inch space on each side of it inside the circle.

Now trace the design in the middle of this circle on the tracing paper.

Clean the copper thoroughly with detergent and follow with a gentle abrasive such as powdered pumice. Now find the middle of the copper disc by laying the tracing paper on the disc so that they fit exactly and tapping the middle point of the circle with a center punch.

Using the center point, scratch a 5-inch circle on the copper with your dividers. Paint the inside of this circle with white tempera paint. When the tempera is dry, place a sheet of carbon paper face down, over the painted circle. Place the tracing paper, with the design face up, on top of the carbon paper on the copper disc, so that the outside edges match exactly, and tape the paper to the disc.

Now transfer the design to the painted copper by drawing, with a #2 pencil, over the design on the tracing paper. Use firm pressure but do not gouge. Remove the tracing and carbon papers. A clear copy of your design will show on the painted copper. Using the scriber, scratch the whole design into the copper. After you have scribed the design into the copper, wash the copper with water and wipe dry with a soft rag.

Now, place the copper, with the design facing down, on newsprint. With the #5 brush, paint the entire back side of the disc with the black asphaltum varnish. Touch up void spots (they will show up as red spots) with more varnish. Place two sheets of newsprint paper over the fresh varnish. These will stick to the copper.

Wait 5 to 10 minutes until the varnish has partly set and turn the disc over so that the design is now on top. Proceed to paint the top surface and the design. Remember, all the parts of the copper that are covered with the varnish will be protected from the etch. Illus. 126 shows the appearance of the asphaltum-painted copper. Note that the portions of the

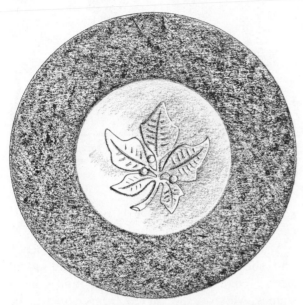

Illus. 126. Copper tray covered with asphaltum after the design has been scribed. The asphaltum protects the metal it covers from the acid bath.

design that appear dark will be unetched. Also note that the outer edge of the disc has about ¼-inch asphaltum running over onto the newsprint. This helps protect the edges from the etching solution. Use the #2 brush for fine work and the #5 brush for the remainder. Allow the asphaltum to dry overnight. Trim away any excess newsprint when dry.

Carefully prepare the copper-etching solution as previously described, remembering to protect your hands with finger sheaths or rubber gloves. Mix thoroughly with a wooden clothespin. Place the cover back on the nitric acid bottle and store it in a safe place.

Then, slide the plate carefully into the etching tray that contains the nitric acid solution. Cover the tray with a piece of cardboard or an inverted cardboard box. Etching will be complete within 1½ to 5 hours. After 1½ hours, remove the plate from the solution, by lifting it to the edge of the tray with clothespins and then picking it up in your protected fingers. Rinse it in the sink very thoroughly. Remove one glove and check the depth of etch with your scriber. Be careful not to disturb the protective varnish during this test. A good etch will be ⅓ to ½ the thickness of the copper. Put back and continue to etch until the depth you want is reached.

When you have the depth of etch you want, rinse the plate thoroughly again and dry it. Pour the acid solution into a half-gallon glass or plastic container, and store it for future use. Remove the asphaltum varnish by placing the dried plate in a tray containing turpentine or paint thinner. Allow it to remain in the turpentine until the varnish and the newsprint on the bottom come off easily. Work with rubber gloves to protect your hands, and use soft rags. If turpentine or paint thinner does not remove all the varnish, use steel wool to clean the last bits away. The plate is now ready for shaping.

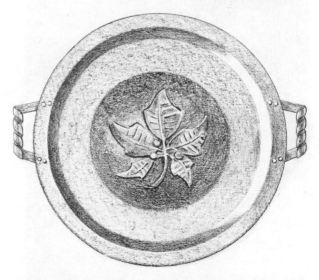

Illus. 127. The finished etched plate. After the etching was completed, the edges of the plate were raised (see page 25) and handles were riveted in place (see page 36).

Nail Sculpture

Nails are available in a surprising variety of sizes and forms, ranging from common builder's nails to specialty products intended for shoeing horses. You can use them as they are, or bend them into new shapes to create all sorts of interesting, decorative and useful objects.

For fastening nails together, you will need a soldering iron (100–150 watts) and, for larger projects, a soldering torch. Follow the general instructions on soldering, and be sure to use soft (acid-core) solder, which forms a strong join between pieces of iron. Your work will be easier if you use rosin flux to cut through the oxides which adhere to nails. As with all

Illus. 129. The straight nail on the left was bent to the shape shown on the right to construct the candleholder on page 63.

soldering, you should work over a brick, a cement patio block or an asbestos mat.

With a vice attached to a sturdy work bench you should have little difficulty bending all sizes of nails into attractive bent and curved shapes. Most of the curved forms you will be using can be made by securing the nail in the vice and twisting it around the jaws of the pliers. Clearly you will want large pliers for larger curves, round- or flat-nose pliers for tight curves. If the nails you are using are too thick to bend easily, you can curve them around a steel pipe with the aid of a hammer. For some especially difficult nails, you may have to apply heat with the soldering torch before carefully bending with pliers. Experimentation will show you the degree of flexibility you have with different types of nails.

For flat designs no special preparation or equipment is necessary to join the nails. Carefully place the nails on the base support in any shape or design you choose, heat the joints with a soldering torch, and let the solder flow. In designing such works, the solder itself is an important element in the over-all appearance.

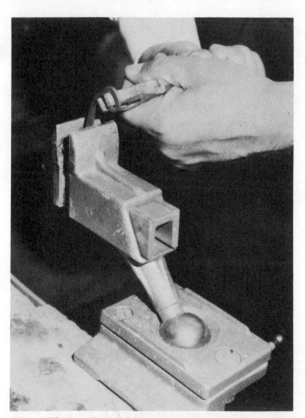

Illus. 128. A nail should bend easily with pliers when it is clamped in a sturdy vice.

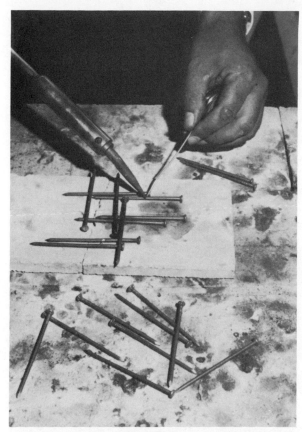

Illus. 130. Flat works are easily soldered with either a soldering iron or torch.

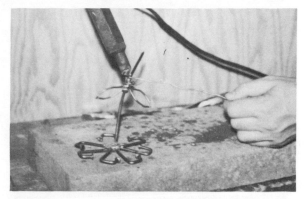

Illus. 131. If you do not have a helper you may have to bind the pieces to be soldered with wire.

Use it generously, keeping in mind the final result.

For upright structures, work your way up directly from the base by adding nail to soldered nail. When you start on such a project you will soon realize that your own two hands are not enough. Have an assistant hold the nail in place with pliers while you fuse it to another nail with a soldering iron and soft solder. A soldering torch is not well suited for these free-standing structural projects, because it heats up too large an area, consequently dissolving those spots that have already been soldered.

If no helper is available, you can keep a piece of your project in upright working position by hammering a nail point into the base, forcing it between pieces of brickwork, or binding the parts together with wire which is removed later.

After the pieces are finished they have to be cleaned of greasy solder residuals. Use a soft brush and a hot alkaline solution or detergent soap. If you do not wash the work thoroughly after soldering, deposits of rust will soon form on the iron (due to the acid in the flux). In order to guard the completed project still further against rust, apply an anti-rust preparation or a coating of colorless varnish, or both. You can use a liquid lacquer, but an aerosol spray covers hard-to-reach areas better. (*Caution:* If you varnish designs that have been soldered, make sure that the solder is cold and the soldering iron or torch is in another room. Lacquer is extremely flammable.)

Illus. 132. After soldering, the wire binding is removed and the finished flower stands upright.

Flat-Surface Projects
with Straight Nails

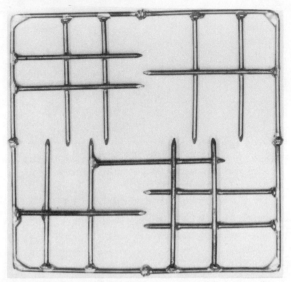

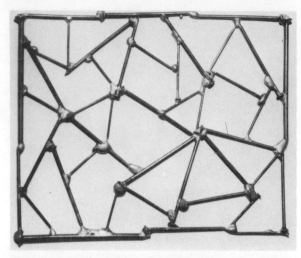

Illus. 134. Nails soldered at varying angles form a wide range of shapes within this frame.

Illus. 133. A rectangular frame adds strength to your construction in addition to enclosing the design. In this example, straight nails were soldered at right angles to each other within the frame of nails.

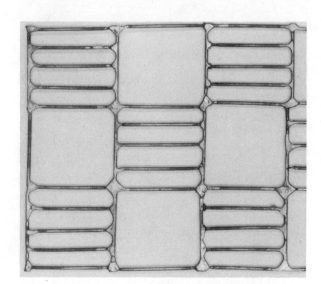

Illus. 135 (right). In this rectangular construction, solder was used to hide the heads and points of the nails, leaving smooth, clean lines.

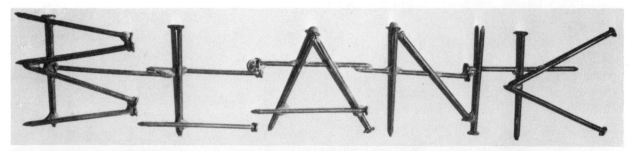

Illus. 136. You can make any letter of the alphabet using just straight, common nails. Connect the letters with a row of supporting nails across the back. If you let some of the points of the vertical nails extend below the rest of the letters, you can fasten them into a strip of wood to make a nameplate for your desk.

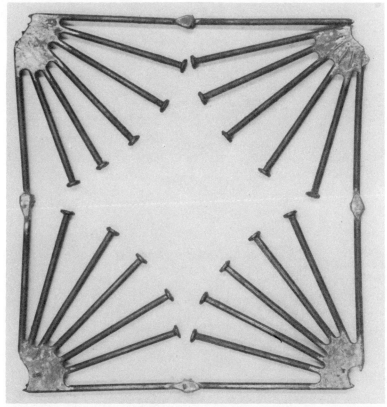

Illus. 137. The liberal use of solder, incorporated into the design, enhances many projects.

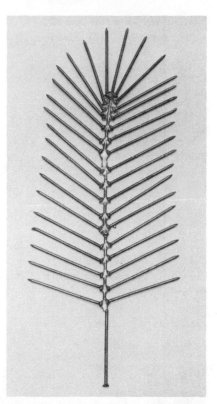

Illus. 139. A straight row of nails provides the base for this leaf-like form. Solder the other nails to the base with their points facing outward.

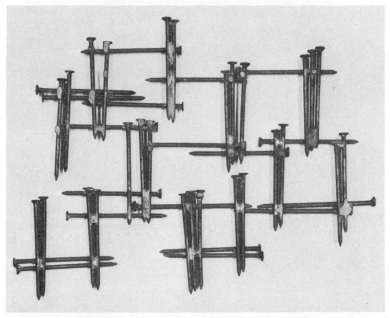

Illus. 138. Flat constructions do not have to be contained within a frame. Note once again the use of solder in the design.

Illus. 140 (below). A different effect is achieved when you solder nails together with the heads pointing outward, as in this circular design.

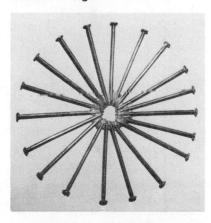

Flat-Surface Projects
with Bent Nails

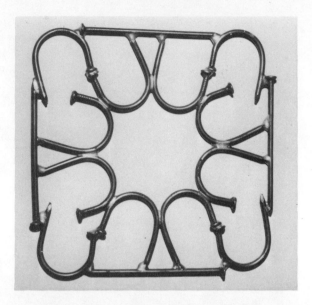

Illus. 141 (above) and Illus. 142 (right) are designs which combine bent nails with straight ones.

Illus. 143. This pattern is made up of uniformly bent nails and a great deal of solder.

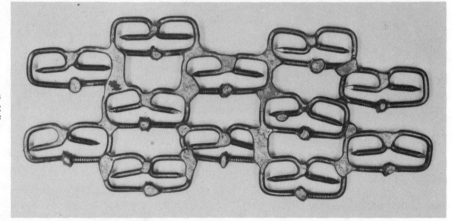

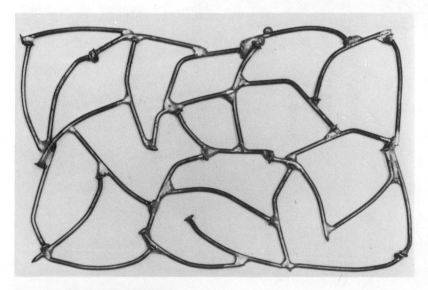

Illus. 144. This interesting abstract form uses an assortment of differently shaped nails.

Three-Dimensional Constructions

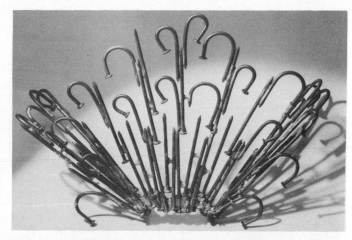

Illus. 147. This sconce consists of three flat-surface designs. You can use a soldering torch for the basic elements, then join the wedge-shaped parts at each side to the middle piece with an iron.

Illus. 145. This lantern was made as four flat pieces, then soldered together in a hollow rectangular shape.

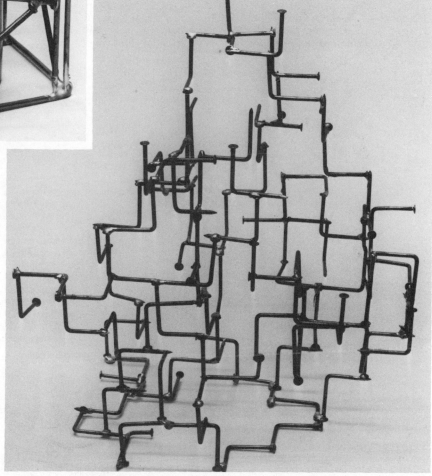

Illus. 146. The basic element of design used here is made up of rectangularly bent nails which form an appealing abstract structure when soldered together with an iron.

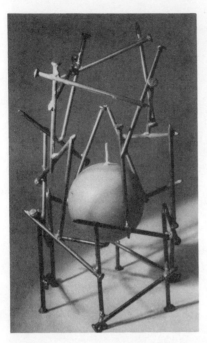

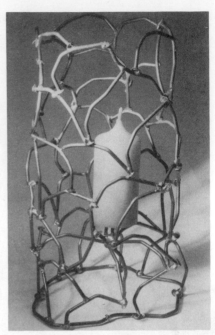

Each of these lanterns has a candle supported by a single nail, bent up directly above its tip at a right angle and soldered with its head to the lantern construction. Illus. 148 (left) consists of straight nails. The nails in Illus. 149 (center) were uniformly bent, and those in Illus. 150 (right) were bent in similar but subtly different shapes.

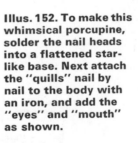

Illus. 152. To make this whimsical porcupine, solder the nail heads into a flattened star-like base. Next attach the "quills" nail by nail to the body with an iron, and add the "eyes" and "mouth" as shown.

Illus. 153. Bend the nails forming the feet of this centipede. Then solder them together at the heads with a soldering iron. For this project, you will need a helper to hold the nails in place.

Illus. 151. This primrose sculpture is constructed with nails which are all the same size.

Projects with Wrought-Iron Nails

Heavy wrought-iron nails are especially decorative, adding a Spanish or Mexican spirit to your work. You can use them straight, with a single bend or with a double bend. Heating the nails with a torch makes them bend more easily, but you can shape them without warming by securing the head in a vice and turning them with a flat-nose pliers. A tap with a hammer may be needed to start the nail bending.

Illus. 155. Simple designs with wrought-iron nails are especially effective.

Illus. 154. This sconce is a flat-surface project made of identically curved wrought-iron nails. The candle is impaled on a nail bent up at a right angle while the head of this nail is soldered to the flat wall bracket.

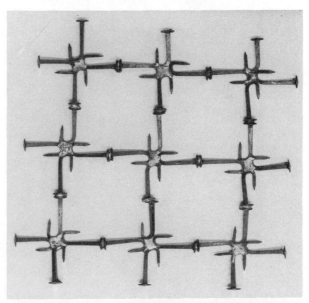

Illus. 156. This flat-surface work makes an excellent wall decoration, particularly in a room with a Spanish or Mexican decorating scheme.

Illus. 157 (right). Bend enough nails to an identical shape so that their heads touching together form a circle of the proper size. Heat the heads with an iron and solder them together.

Begin this construction with a heavy wrought-iron nail for your candleholder. File down the slightly rounded head until it is flat and stands without wobbling. Solder the identically curved nails around this center spike. You can place the candle on a straight center spike (Illus. 159, right) or twist this piece by securing the spike head-down in a vice and heating it until red-hot with the soldering torch, then twisting it into shape (Illus. 158, left).

Illus. 160. To make this wreath-shaped candleholder, draw an outline of the circle on an asbestos mat, sketching in the arrangement of each separate group of nails. After placing the bent nails correctly on the mat, solder them where they touch. Finally, solder four pinched-off nails to the crown for placement of the candles.

Illus. A1. Horseshoe nails are a distinctively different craft material, used here for an eye-catching pendant, ring, and hanging ornament. Find directions for all three in the Nail Sculpture section.

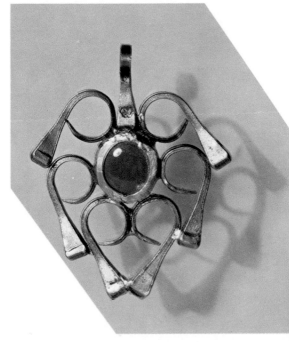

Illus. A2. The nails which went into this horseshoe-nail pendant were bent around a steel pipe, as described on page 66. These nails are made of soft iron, so they bend easily.

Illus. A3. Common nails were used straight out of the box to create the rectangular lantern at left. The circular candleholder at right is made from wrought-iron nails, uniformly bent with pliers and soldered head-to-head.

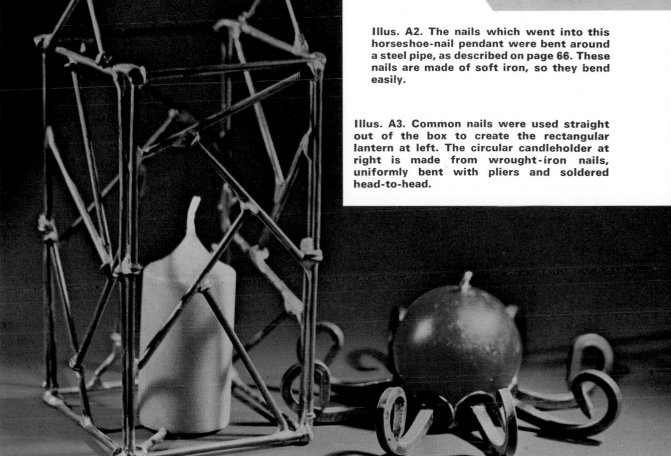

Illus. B2. This one-of-a-kind construction started with the faceplate of a car's headlight, to which a car seat spring, string, magazine cutouts and a pine baseboard were added. A little latex paint completed the decoration.

Illus. B1. This interesting sculpture is a conglomeration of 3 large coffee cans, 5 soda cans, 3 beer cans, 4 vegetable cans, 3 tuna cans, and one small juice can, sprayed with yellow paint and resting on a mahogany block. For more can sculptures you can make, see Constructions from Found Objects, on page 96.

Illus. B3. This can design shines with an aluminum foil coating, applied as described on page 96.

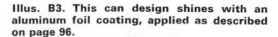

B

Illus. C1. The 12 cans, 7 jar lids and 33 bottle tops which make up this design were first painted, then nailed to the baseboard in an artistic design. Nails with extremely wide heads add to the design.

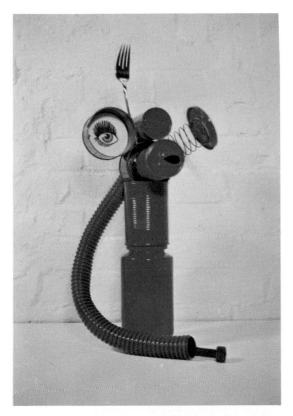

Illus. C2. An ecology-conscious young sculptor improved the environment by recycling a pickle jar, a vegetable can, a tuna can, a juice can, a hair-roller spring, a plastic coffee lid, a metal fork, a vacuum-cleaner hose, a large nut and bolt and a magazine cutout into this fascinating creation.

Illus. C3. You'll find step-by-step instructions for making this "Clown with Hat" sculpture on page 103.

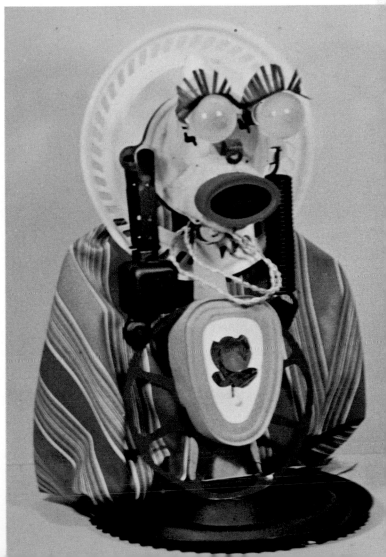

Illus. D1. The richly tooled surface of this aluminum candleholder will add a warm glow to any table. Directions for a similar project are found on page 154.

Illus. D2. Unbelievable as it may seem, this delicately detailed peacock was built entirely from tin cans! By varying the design of the coiled spokes you can come up with hundreds of different designs.

Illus. E1. This dazzling sunburst was made with techniques so simple a child can master them in no time. You will learn to turn a plain sheet of aluminum into designs like this in the section on Working with Metal Foil.

Illus. E2. Complete instructions for this cut-out tooled flower, including the dramatic antique finish, begin on page 141.

Illus. E3. If you'd like to attract birds to your home, try offering them this elegant bird feeder. See page 156 for assembly instructions.

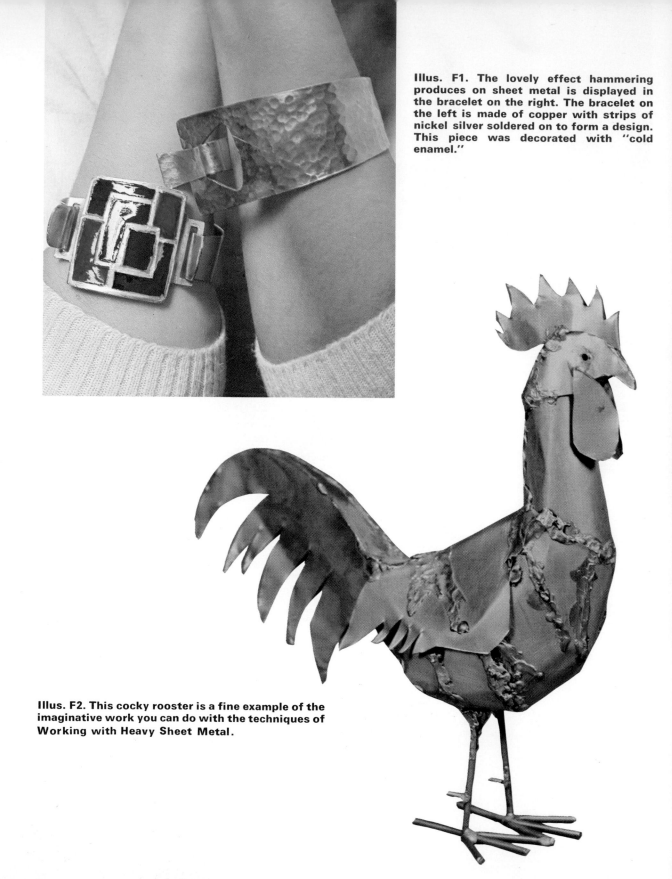

Illus. F1. The lovely effect hammering produces on sheet metal is displayed in the bracelet on the right. The bracelet on the left is made of copper with strips of nickel silver soldered on to form a design. This piece was decorated with "cold enamel."

Illus. F2. This cocky rooster is a fine example of the imaginative work you can do with the techniques of Working with Heavy Sheet Metal.

F

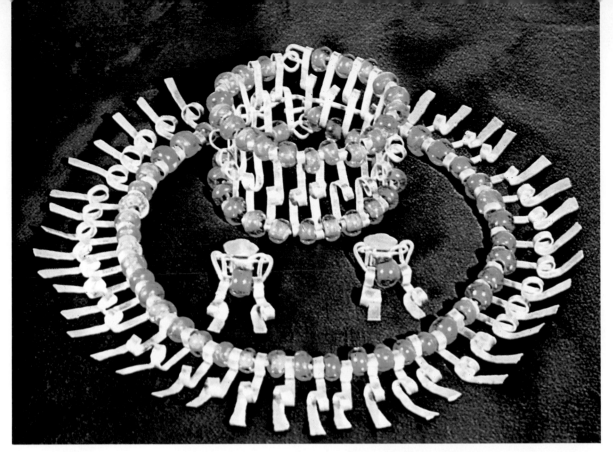

Illus. G1. As ornate as this lovely set looks, it is as easy as your first project in Crafting with Silver Wire and Sheet Silver.

Illus. G2. Silver wire, silver sheet and beads are all that are required to turn out many professional-looking pieces of jewelry. At the upper right, with red handles, is a pair of round-nose pliers and, with black handles, a pair of plate shears.

Illus. H1. Pictures made with pins and wire appear complicated, but if you follow the step-by-step directions for this flower, which begin on page 122, you'll be amazed with your success.

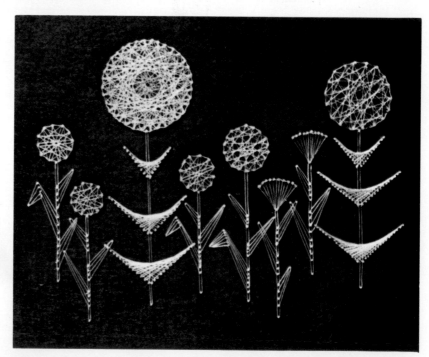

Illus. H2. The basic techniques and designs for making pin pictures can be combined to create an entire wall hanging, like this striking garden design.

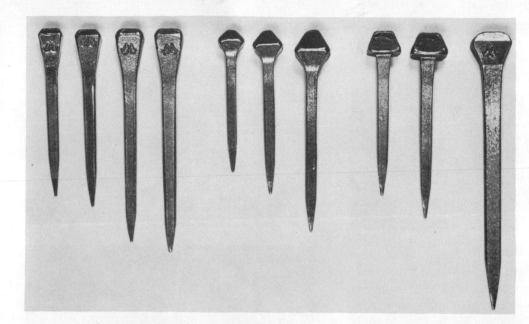

Illus. 161. Types of horseshoe nails.

Projects with Horseshoe Nails

The traditional shape and feel of the horse-shoe nail makes it a particularly interesting material for crafting pendants, rings, home decorations, candlesticks, frames and much more. There are four different types of nails, all suitable for horseshoe-nail crafting. However, one type usually looks better in a given design than another, so don't use them at random. The four types (shown in Illus. 161) are, from left to right: *J* numbers 4, 6, 8, and 10; *T* numbers 3, 5, and 8; *TIH* numbers 4 and 7; and *REG* number 12. Most of the designs in this book are made from *J* number 8 nails.

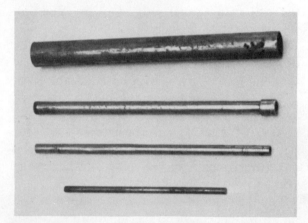

Illus. 162. You will need several steel pipes of assorted sizes to bend horseshoe nails.

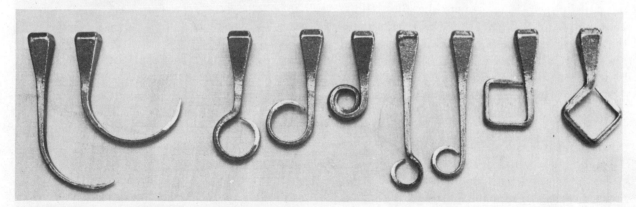

Illus. 163. These are only a few of the varied shapes you can achieve by bending horseshoe nails.

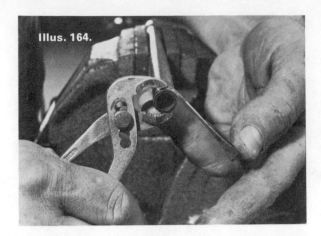
Illus. 164.

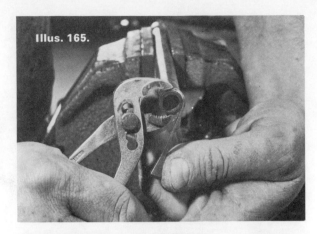
Illus. 165.

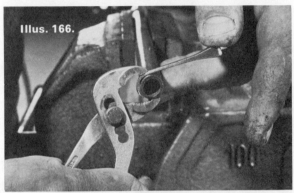
Illus. 166.

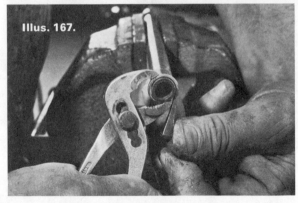
Illus. 167.

Bending Horseshoe Nails

Horseshoe nails are made from soft iron, and you should have no trouble at all bending them. Try it with just a pair of pliers and your hands. If you do encounter difficulties, grip the head of the nail in a second pair of pliers. You will seldom need a hammer.

Bending horseshoe nails to make any of the designs described in this book requires very few tools—a pair of pliers with an adjustable grip, a vice, and several sections of steel pipe of assorted sizes (Illus. 162). Firmly clamp the section of steel pipe (of whatever size your design requires) in the vice. You can clamp it either horizontally or vertically, whichever way you find more convenient.

Lay the point of the nail on the steel pipe and grip it with pliers. Bend the nail down with your thumb (Illus. 164) until it comes in contact with the bottom jaw of the pliers (Illus. 165). Move the nail up, grip it again with the pliers (Illus. 166), and bend it down (Illus. 167). Make sure that the curved part of the nail is flush against the steel pipe. Otherwise the finished shape will be more oval than round.

You can also bend horseshoe nails into square shapes. Hold the pointed end of the nail in the pliers (at a right angle to the pliers) and bend it down. This forms the first side of the square. To make the second side, grip the nail at a point equal to the first length, and bend the nail down again. Do the same for the third side. It's a good idea, before you start bending, to measure the nail, just to make sure that you're not making the sides too big. Otherwise you might not be able to form a square. (See Illus. 163 for two examples of square shapes.)

Experiment with a few nails, just to get an idea of the shapes you can form. There are many possibilities—you can form all sorts of curves, triangles, and uneven shapes, as well as variations on the basic circle and square. Illus. 163 shows a few suggestions.

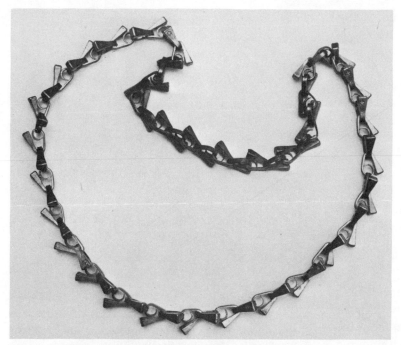

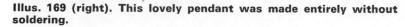

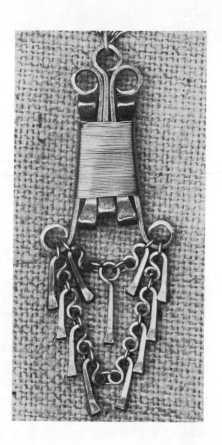

Illus. 168 (above). You can make this unusual necklace by simply hooking small horseshoe nails together.

Illus. 169 (right). This lovely pendant was made entirely without soldering.

Joining without Soldering

Although most of the projects in this section involve soldering, you can make many horseshoe-nail creations with nothing more than the nails and some iron wire.

Hooking-Up

Simply hooking nails together, you can create many bracelets, chains, necklaces, and pendants. Try making the unique necklace shown in Illus. 168. The technique is remarkably easy. Bend the pointed end of the nail into a small circle, but don't close it up. Then bend the nail at its midpoint. Leave a small space, about the width of a nail, between the head of the nail and the small circle. Repeat this process for every nail required by your design. (There are 70 in the necklace in Illus. 168, but this number is arbitrary, and you can increase or decrease this amount.)

After you have bent all the nails, begin joining them. Hook similar sections together. In other words, hook each circle to the circle of the next nail, and each midpoint to the midpoint of the nail following it. Then, with the pliers, press the head and circle of each nail together so that the circle and the space between the head of the nail and the circle are closed up. *Note:* Some types of horseshoe nails have small trademarks on their heads. Your design will look more attractive if the trademarks of all the nails face in the same direction.

Wire Binding

Wire binding is another method you can use to avoid soldering. The only additional material you will need is a quantity of both thin and thick iron wire. Making the decorative pendant shown in Illus. 169 will acquaint you with the techniques involved.

First form the ends of five large (REG #12) nails into small circles. Bend one of the five into the shape of the middle nail in the illustration. Lay the five side by side, in the configuration shown. The trademarks should all be facing away from the center nail. Now, hold the nails firmly together and wrap the thin iron wire round them as tightly as you can. Cut the wire with diagonal wire cutters. The wire and the position of the nails will lock the pendant together.

Next, bend 10 smaller nails into the shape shown in the picture of the finished pendant. Form the end of one additional nail into a slightly larger circle, then bend it into a shape identical to that of the large middle nail above it. Now, using the thicker, less pliable iron wire, form and cut a quantity of small rings. The best way to do this is to wrap 2 or 3 feet of the wire round a small steel pipe and cut off the rings from the resulting coil as you need them.

Finally, hook all the nails together with rings, as shown in Illus. 169, and hang them from the two larger nails. Attach a ring to the large middle nail, run a small chain through it, and your pendant is ready.

These basic methods have endless possibilities. Experiment with them—there are many beautiful designs that you can make without using any solder at all.

Soldering Horseshoe Nails

You will find that soldering horseshoe nails presents few unusual problems. Either a soldering iron or a torch will be adequate. You should use solder which contains a small quantity of silver, which increases the strength of the solder. Be sure to carefully clean any dirt or grease from the heads of the nails before soldering.

Horseshoe-nail designs look best when you keep the amount of visible solder to a minimum. After the solder has cooled and you have scrubbed the remaining flux from the work, you can smooth down any lumps of solder with steel wool or a thin steel-wire brush.

A good beginning project with horseshoe nails is the clothes hook shown in Illus. 170. Be sure to blunt the tip of the nail on which the clothing will hang by turning it down with the

Illus. 170. These clothes hooks are an excellent project to practice your soldering.

pliers. To hang the clothes hook, just hammer either a horseshoe or an ordinary nail through the triangular space formed by the junction of the heads of the three nails.

Illus. 171. Projects with horseshoe nails look best when the solder is used sparingly.

Horseshoe-Nail Jewelry

Illus. 172. To make beautiful horseshoe-nail rings, bend the nails as shown, cut the sheet metal and solder the nails to the sheet. Bend the ring to fit your finger only after soldering. Illus. 173 (right) shows two more ring ideas, along with an easy pendant design.

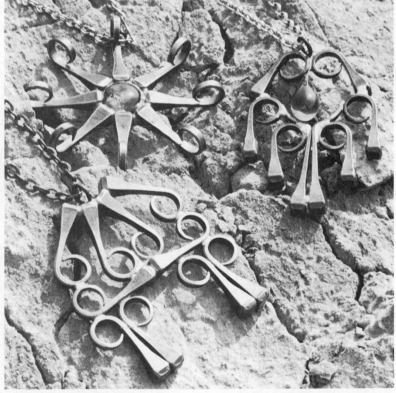

Illus. 174 (left) and Illus. 175 (above). You can make lovely pendants like these with just a little imagination and a handful of horseshoe nails. The glass beads shown are widely available in craft and hobby shops.

Illus. 176.

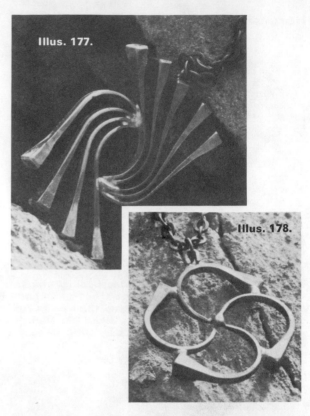

Illus. 177.

Illus. 178.

Using the pendant ideas shown in these photographs, try to come up with ideas of your own. Sketch out your ideas first, keeping the mechanics of construction as simple as possible. When you want to attach a glass bead to your pendant, use a two-part glue—either a synthetic resin glue or epoxy adhesive.

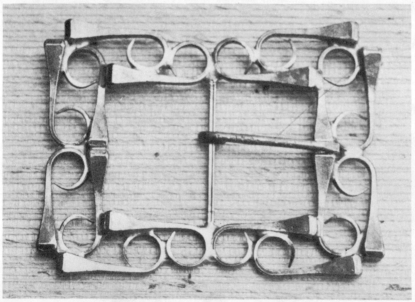

Illus. 179. If you'd like a unique, eye-catching belt buckle, try making one from horseshoe nails. Use small nails and construct the buckle by following the picture. Make the crossbar and the catch from thick, stiff iron wire.

Hanging Designs

Hanging decorations make any room more attractive. Illus. 180 through 182 show some possibilities. Be sure to solder carefully, as lumps of solder will ruin the delicate effect.

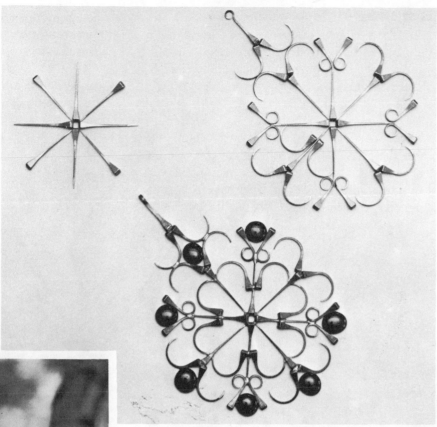

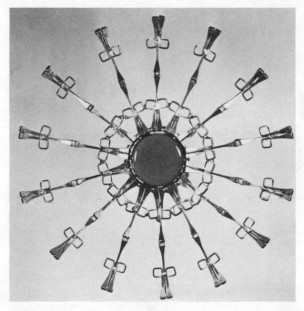

Illus. 180.

Illus. 181.

Illus. 182.

Bell-Shaped Decorations

Illus. 183 shows the procedure for making a bell-shaped hanging decoration. Bend 16 nails over a large steel pipe and then make eight S-shapes from them.

Use a cylindrical piece of wood with a conical hole in one end to hold the nails while you solder them. The wood should have roughly the same diameter as the bell shape you are making.

If you can't find a suitable piece of wood, you can try a tin can. Find one with the right diameter, then tape the S-shapes to the can so that the points all meet in the middle of the can. However, soldering is much trickier with this arrangement, so it's better to use a piece of wood if you possibly can. (Illus. 184 shows the finished decoration.)

By using a simple holding device as shown in Illus. 183 (left) you can create the attractive hanging ornament in Illus. 184 (right). Try using the same method in your own designs.

Creating Your Own Designs

Creating your own designs is not very difficult. There are a few important things you should remember, though. Don't make your design too complicated, for this may give the viewer the feeling that it is cluttered or fussy. Don't mix too many different shapes in the same design—it's better to just repeat one or two curves or patterns. If you are thinking of making a large design, construct it in sections rather than all at once. This makes it easier to visualize and construct accurately.

When you make up any horseshoe-nail design you must deal with certain practical considera-

Illus. 185. Decide on a simple pattern and repeat it to create a handsome wall hanging.

Illus. 186. You can design your own one-of-a-kind horseshoe-nail chess set. In the set shown here the pieces are: pawn (first from left); bishop (second from left); knight (third from left); rook (fifth from left); king (large piece in back row, left) and queen (back row, right).

tions. Make sure that your creation is balanced, and that it won't tilt or tip over. And always remember to distribute the soldering points so that when the design is complete it will stick together. It's easier to make a few revisions in your design than it is to correct it after it has been soldered together.

You can get many good ideas for horseshoe-nail designs from geometric patterns, abstract or even representational paintings and sculpture, flowers, butterflies, and animals—in short, just by looking around you. Above all, use your imagination. Just sit back and relax and see what you can come up with.

Illus. 187 (above). Horseshoe-nail "paintings" look attractive on either inside or outside walls.

Illus. 188 (right). Horseshoe-nail sconces provide a uniquely beautiful opportunity to bring candle-light into your home.

Tin-Can Crafting

Tin-can crafting is an expressive, creative art that is often useful, *always* extremely interesting and decorative. The material required is primarily the "used" tin-can, cylindrical or otherwise. Use seems to give a lasting patina of brilliance or lustre to the metal, whether it is the gold-lacquered lining of a beer can or the soft silver of an empty sardine tin. Much of the fun in tin-can crafting is the salvaging of a useless article, and producing from this no-cost material an interesting and decorative item of lacy beauty.

In the section on "Constructions from Found Objects" on page 96, you will learn how to use whole tin cans to create abstract sculptures. On the following pages you will find an assortment of medallions, sunbursts, plaques, and ornaments which have been cut, twisted, curled, contrived and assembled from cans. They will lead to the point where you can proceed on your own initiative to create many items with increased interest and enthusiasm.

Illus. 190. This delicate sunburst design was made entirely from tin cans.

Tools and Materials

The equipment you need consists mainly of common household items. The few tools you will have to buy are not costly, so don't skimp on the pennies. It is essential to use good tools.

The basic tools are shears for cutting and pliers for bending. Work gloves (leather or cloth) are an important aid to protect your hands against work blisters, cuts and accidents. While your tools and materials are not in themselves dangerous, it is always a good idea to have first-aid materials handy, especially at the start.

You will need three pairs of shears. The #1 shears in Illus. 189 are light metal shears with a strong spring. The #2 shears are ordinary good-quality kitchen shears and the #3 shears are tin shears, also known as tin snips. If you plan on making big pieces from heavy cans you'll need an electrician's tin shears, sometimes called a sheet-metal worker's tin shears. These and the

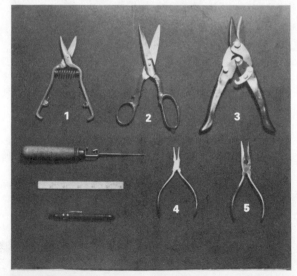

Illus. 189. These are the only tools you will need for most projects with tin cans.

#3 shears shown in Illus. 189 are compound-leverage shears. The compound mechanism allows you to cut the tin without pressing hard by increasing the pressure mechanically. For extra-fine work with small pieces you will need a heavy-duty compound-leverage snips with double serrations. This can be used throughout as a substitute for the tin shears; it is stronger and costs a little more. All shears need sharpening and tightening occasionally.

You may already have a pair of needle-nose pliers, shown in Illus. 189 as #5. The #4 pliers are flat-nose pliers. Both types of pliers are available in a variety of sizes.

Unnumbered in Illus. 189 are an ice pick, small ruler and a grease pencil. A child's crayon may be substituted for the grease pencil. You will also need a tape measure made of cloth or paper, odds and ends of wire, a penny or any coin $\frac{3}{4}$ inch in diameter (and other coins), odds and ends of jewelry (old unmatched earrings, brooches, loose stones, pearls, beads, etc.), a bottle or tube of household cement, bells, buttons, lamp pull chains, other chains, and, of course, lots of cans.

Templates and a Gauge

As part of your equipment you will need a few templates and a gauge for can lids (or bottoms). It will take you just a few minutes to

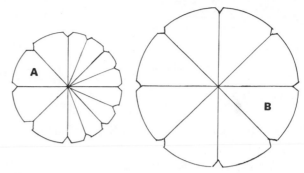

Illus. 191. Templates.

make them out of heavy cardboard. For a template (Illus. 191), cut a circle of cardboard the size of the lid of a No. 2 can (see chart). Draw two diameters at right angles, forming quarters. Now draw two diagonals to form eighths, and then draw sixteenths on half the circle as in Illus. 191. (An easy way to do this is to start with a square and then use a protractor to form the circle after the lines are drawn.) Notch the end of each diagonal sharply.

Make template B (Illus. 191) the same way, but in a No. $2\frac{1}{2}$ can size. These templates will enable you to divide can lids into equal segments simply by putting marks in the desired notches with a grease pencil or crayon and then connecting the opposite marks with pencilled diagonals.

CHART OF CAN SIZES

25-lb. can—used in bakeries, etc. for lard, egg yolks or frozen berries	10″ dia. × $12\frac{1}{4}$″ high
No. 10 can—used in restaurants for vegetables, fruits, flavorings, etc.	$6\frac{3}{16}$″ dia. × 7″ high
46-oz. juice can—used in the home	$4\frac{3}{16}$″ dia. × 7″ high
32-oz. juice can	$3\frac{3}{8}$″ dia. × 7″ high
No. $2\frac{1}{2}$ fruit can	$4\frac{1}{16}$″ dia. × $4\frac{11}{16}$″ high
No. 2 fruit can	$3\frac{7}{16}$″ dia. × $4\frac{9}{16}$″ high
Chili can	3″ dia. × $4\frac{7}{16}$″ high
Frozen juice cans	$2\frac{3}{16}$″ dia. × $3\frac{1}{2}$″ high
12-oz. beer can	$2\frac{11}{16}$″ dia. × $4\frac{13}{16}$″ high
16-oz. beer can	$2\frac{11}{16}$″ dia. × $6\frac{1}{8}$″ high
1-lb. coffee can	$5\frac{3}{16}$″ dia. × $3\frac{7}{16}$″ high
2-lb. coffee can	$5\frac{3}{16}$″ dia. × $6\frac{9}{16}$″ high
Salted peanut can	$3\frac{5}{16}$″ dia. × $3\frac{1}{4}$″ high
1-quart motor oil can	These vary; be guided by the general shape desired
4-lb. lard can	$5\frac{1}{16}$″ dia. × $5\frac{7}{8}$″ high

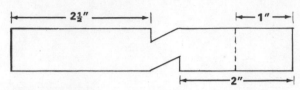

Templates may be used with lids of their own size or larger.

For the gauge, simply take a ¾-inch strip of cardboard and notch it as shown in Illus. 192. It will be useful in measuring even strips.

Basic Techniques

Cutting

If you can cut paper, you can cut cans. It takes a little more effort, but once you become familiar with your tools you will find there is little difference. Use the light metal shears for short cuts and thin strips, the kitchen shears for long cuts with serrated edges, and the compound-leverage tin shears for heavy-duty cutting, like heavy can rims and the starting cut on heavy seams.

You may also find that you want two luxury items, a pair of heavy-duty shears with double serrations for extra-fancy work, and the electrician's or metal-worker's shears for general heavy work. Only a few of the items shown here, however, have been made with these.

To begin cutting, take a can with the lid already cleanly removed (use a wall-type can opener). Use the compound-leverage shears to start the cut through the top rim and then practice removing this upper rim until you can do it in a smooth, even line. Then, firmly holding either light metal or kitchen shears, depending on the height of the can, practice cutting strips as in Illus. 194. Work with all 3 pairs of shears until you get the feel of each.

Curling

Curling is the second basic step in tin-can crafting. Use the flat-nose pliers for curling ordinary-weight cans and needle-nose pliers for large curls.

Take one of the cans in which you have cut strips right down to the base. With the needle-

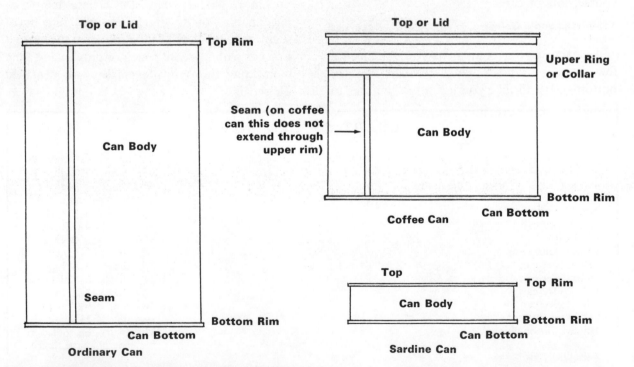

Illus. 193. Construction details of various tin cans.

Illus. 194. Cutting.

nose pliers grasp one strip near the base and turn it at right angles to the others. With the point of the flat-nose pliers grasp the end of the strip and curl once tightly around the point. Continuing to hold the strip firmly, guide it into

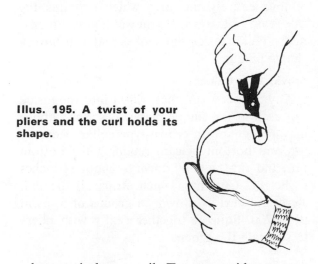

Illus. 195. A twist of your pliers and the curl holds its shape.

a larger circle, or coil. Try to avoid any tendency on the part of the tin strip to form an angle. If an angle occurs, remove your pliers from the loop and apply pressure along the strip gently but firmly with fingers and pliers (here's where thick gloves come in handy) until the arc is smooth.

Making a Collar

A collar is a simple first step in tin-can crafting. You may use it later as a part of a larger project; or you may use it as is for a decoration.

You make a collar from the "body" of a can after removing the top, top rim and bottom of

the can. The bottom rim remains intact. A shallow can (such as a tuna fish can) will be fine for the purpose. Cut the sides into equal tiny strips all around, and then with pliers bend each strip into a petal-like arc as shown in Illus. 196. Now you have a collar. You can use it for a picture frame by glueing on a snapshot cut to the appropriate size, or you can use it as a center decoration in a sunburst.

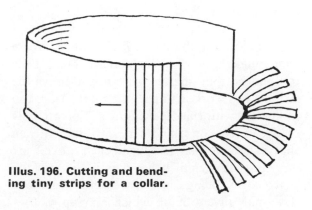

Illus. 196. Cutting and bending tiny strips for a collar.

Arching and Bending

The secret of arching, or curving, is a firm grasp of the spoke, near the can bottom, with your gloved fingers. With a slow gentle pressure, run the spoke between the right thumb and forefinger in the general curve desired.

To give depth to the spokes of certain plaques, you bend the spokes $\frac{1}{2}$ inch from the can bottom before arching. For uniform bends, hold a wooden block about $\frac{1}{2} \times \frac{1}{2} \times 5$ inches tightly against the lower edge of each spoke. (See Illus. 197.)

Be sure to wear a heavy leather glove for arching as the spoke sides are sometimes sharp and often a little jagged.

Illus. 197.

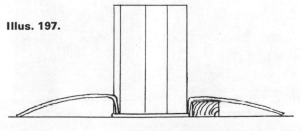

Making Spokes

Take a can of the same size as the one used for making the collar. To divide the can body into spokes of equal size, wrap a tape measure around the can and divide by 8; however if this does not work out evenly or seems to pose a mathematical complication, another way is to wrap a strip of paper around the can. Use a strip slightly narrower than the depth of the can and cut off the excess to get the exact circumference. Now fold the strip in half 3 times until you have 8 equal sections and wrap it around the can edge. With a grease pencil make a mark at each crease, both at the top and bottom, making sure not to move the strip as you work. Connect the marks from top to bottom with ruled pencil lines. You are now ready to cut on the lines with the kitchen shears. Use gloves. Next, bend each spoke back (see Illus. 199) until it lies flat. Watch out for sharp edges, being especially careful to remove any small slivers of tin which may appear.

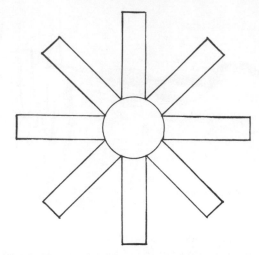

Illus. 199. A can bottom and body cut into equal-sized spokes.

Now take the collar you made previously and remove entirely the strip which contains the side seam of the can. If you want, you can now fit the collar inside the spokes and you have a simple plaque!

Crown-Type Collars

Any diameter can that will fit into the inside can used in the simple plaque described above may be cut into a crown-type collar. Remove top and bottom of can, retaining the bottom rim, and cut the body down to about $1\frac{1}{2}$ inches in height. Cut into $\frac{1}{8}$-inch strips all around. Turn and curl as shown, in groups of 5, as in Illus. 200. Squeeze together gently with pliers to separate the groups.

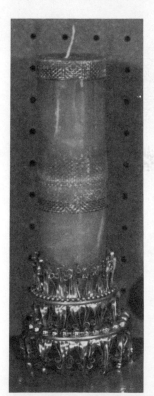
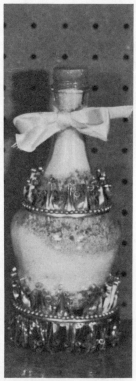

Illus. 198. You can use your crown-type collars to make a fancy candleholder or dress up a bottle.

Illus. 200. Details for crown-type collar.

These collars may also be used upside down and in various combinations to form interesting bottle decorations or candleholders. (See Illus. 198.)

Centerpieces

A basic centerpiece is needed for all medallions, sunbursts, plaques and other wall decorations. These objects all follow the same general construction, so start with a simple centerpiece.

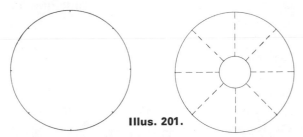

Illus. 201.

Start with a lid from a No. 2 can of pet food, peaches or any can lined with shiny gold color. Use template "A" (Illus. 191). With black grease pencil or crayon divide and mark the lid in 8 sections (Illus. 201) and with the ruler connect the dots.

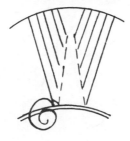

Illus. 203. Cut strips along solid lines. One coiled strip is indicated in final position.

Place a coin ¾ inch in diameter in the center and draw a circle around it. Use the light metal shears to cut the 8 lines, leaving the center circle uncut as in Illus. 201.

Next, use shears to cut a narrow strip down each side of each of the 8 sections. Use the flat-nose pliers to curl both strips to the gold side. Continue around. (See curl in Illus. 203.)

With your light metal shears, make 3 cuts, graduated in length, in both sides of the 8 sections, as shown in Illus. 203. Turn the strips with the flat-nose pliers, one at a time, at right

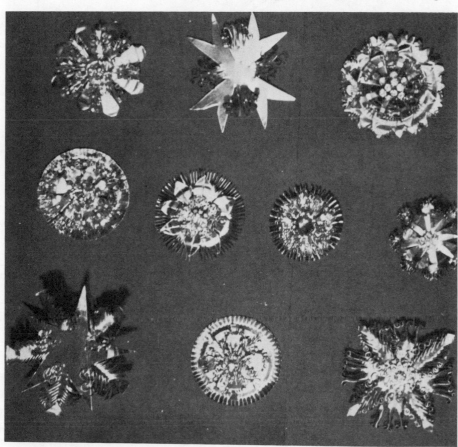

Illus. 202. Make a wide variety of centerpieces and keep them on hand for use in future projects.

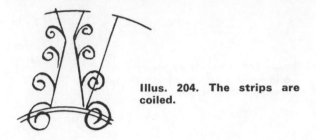

Illus. 204. The strips are coiled.

angles to the center section, and curl outward (to the tin side) as shown in Illus. 204.

Place an odd earring or small brilliant pin (with backing removed) in the center (where the coin was) and tighten the two small curls at the base of each section to hold it in place.

You can vary the design by cutting and curling every second section and trimming the odd sections to a point, or to a gently rounded petal tip. The variations are limitless.

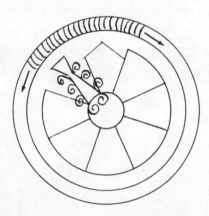

Illus. 205. Detail of centerpiece mounted upon larger fluted circles.

Note that, in Illus. 202, some of the centerpieces are divided into 8 sections and some show alternately curled and shaped petals. For larger lids, or more intricate designs, the lids may be divided into 12 or 16 even sections.

The centerpiece is a complete decoration in itself. You can also go one step further and mount it on another, larger circle. Give the second can lid a fluted look by simply making short cuts all around, of an even width and depth. Turn each small section slightly with the pliers so they face in the same direction, as in Illus. 205.

Patterns

To enlarge the patterns pictured in this section, use the square-off pattern copying system. Rule a grid of equal-sized squares over the design to be copied, making sure that the grid covers all parts of the design. On another sheet of paper rule a larger grid containing the same number of boxes as before, but larger this time. Now, working one square at a time, copy the original design to the enlarged boxes by sketching the contents of each box of the original design in the exact same way. You can reduce a pattern in the same way—simply copy the design onto a smaller grid, each box equally smaller than the original.

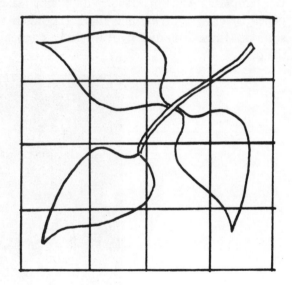

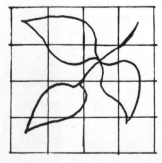

Illus. 206. Use the simple system described here for enlarging the patterns which appear in this section.

Illus. 207. The outermost curls on this plaque show bits of color from the outside of the can.

Coffee-Can Plaques

You will need:

1-lb. coffee can

string of pearls, or other beads, or light pull chain

centerpiece (as shown in Illus. 202)

Your plaque will be silver-colored and have a trim of red, yellow, brown or green around the outside, depending upon the brand of coffee that formerly occupied the can.

First remove the upper ring or collar (see Illus. 193) from the top of the can. Grasp this ring at the top firmly with pliers and jerk it upward. This extra bit of the can is not seamed

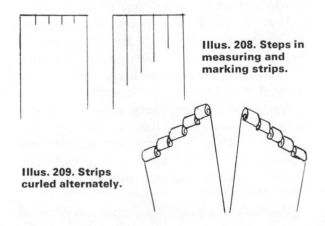

Illus. 208. Steps in measuring and marking strips.

Illus. 209. Strips curled alternately.

or soldered to the can proper, but crimped together and fastened with a staple. You will never use it with the can body, but often separately, as a collar.

With the compound-leverage shears, remove the heavy top rim from the can. Cut down to the bottom on both sides of the can seam and bend this back in a loop for use later as the hanger.

Now, divide the can body into 16 spokes approximately 1 inch wide. Following the directions for making spokes, fold the paper one more time to make 16 spokes.

Note that the plaque in Illus. 207 has its spokes curled right to left, all in the same manner, while the spokes in the plaque in Illus. 210 are curled alternately left and right.

Illus. 210. Cemented plaque with washers of wood or leather to raise the center portions.

Use a $\frac{1}{2}$-inch wooden bar (see Illus. 197) pressed tightly against the lower edge of each spoke to give you a straight, even bend. This results in a uniform depth, essential for this type of plaque.

Next divide each spoke into 5 equal strips (see Illus. 208) and cut the strips down in a graduated sequence going from $\frac{1}{2}$ inch to 1 inch. You can cut right to left or left to right, as in Illus. 209. Use your grease pencil to run a slanting mark from the ½-inch point to the 1-inch point so that the cuts will be uniform on each spoke. The marks will rub off easily after the curls are made. With needle-nose pliers roll each strip toward the front in a tight curl.

The base for the centerpiece can be made from the silver lid of a shortening can. Make ¼-inch cuts all around with shears and turn them with the needle-nose pliers at slight angles to the bottom. This will reflect the light beautifully.

Fill the depressed outer edge of the centerpiece with a silvered light pull (such as is used for an overhead light or for key chains) or a chain of pearls. Complete the decoration with a collar made from the ring which comes off the top of the coffee can just above the heavy rim. Cut this ring into very narrow strips, arch them with needle-nose pliers and fit inside the straight edge which is left by the use of the wooden block. Cement the collar and beads into place.

Small Sunburst

You will need:
46-oz. juice can (gold-lacquered inside)
16-oz. beer can (gold-lacquered inside)
12-oz. beer can (gold-lacquered inside)
jewelled centerpiece
gold enamel spray (optional)

**Illus. 211.
Small sunburst.**

Since this will be a sunburst which is curved, or arched, the rear silver side of some of the finished spokes may be visible from some angles. Therefore, you may want to spray the outsides of the 2 beer cans with a gold enamel before cutting. Stand the cans upside down to prevent spray spots from reaching the inside.

Starting with the juice can, remove the heavy top rim with the compound-leverage shears. Wear a rather heavy glove on the right hand since the juice can is high and the metal quite

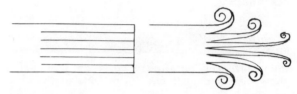

Illus. 212. Two steps in cutting and coiling the spoke ends.

stiff to cut. With the kitchen shears cut down closely on both sides of the seam to the bottom rim. Using the needle-nose pliers gently work the seam back and forth to break it off about 2 inches from the bottom. Then fold it back for a hanger.

Divide the can into spokes approximately ¾ or ⅝ inch wide, marking carefully. Cut down all around and bend spokes outward gently. Do not flatten at rim; leave a curve.

Divide each spoke into 6 equal strips, cutting down with the kitchen shears to a depth of 2 inches from the outer end. Make the 2-inch marks with grease pencil and gauge.

With the needle-nose pliers turn 3 strips to the right and 3 strips to the left. Make sure the gold side is toward the center cut in each case, so that the outside of each curl will be gold colored.

Using the flat-nose pliers, grasp the outside strip firmly and turn to form a tight loop. Then continue turning until the first loop is surrounded by a larger, looser coil or curl. Curl 3 strips to each side in graduated sizes. (See Illus. 212.)

It makes no difference whether you do all of

the cutting at one time or cut each strip and then curl it before going on to the next strip or spoke.

Now, with the compound-leverage shears, remove the top rim and seam from the 16-oz. beer can. Measure and cut into $\frac{1}{2}$-inch spokes (approximately) using kitchen shears.

Divide each spoke into 5 equal strips and cut with light metal shears to a depth of $2\frac{1}{2}$ inches from the end. Curl with flat-nose pliers, making the middle curl of each spoke face the same direction, and the 2 curls on each side face outward.

Cement the finished can into the center of the 46-oz. can with household cement, or fasten it with 2 split-shank paper clips through holes punched with an ice pick.

Next, remove the top rim and seam of the 12-oz. beer can in the same manner as above and cut into $\frac{1}{2}$-inch spokes. Do not pull these out flat. Instead, curl one spoke forward and one slightly backward. Curve both gently to accommodate the overlapping.

Divide each spoke into 6 equal strips and cut down 2 inches.

Curl similarly to the 46-oz. juice can, only a little more loosely, with 3 graduated curls facing outward on each side of the spoke.

Before cementing this can into the 16-oz. beer can, insert the centerpiece and cement it into place.

Now you will observe that this third can is of the same diameter as the second can. Therefore, you will need to cement it to a rather thick wooden washer to hold it away from the second can bottom by approximately $\frac{3}{4}$ inch to 1 inch. A round section sawed from an old broom or shovel handle will come in handy here for a wooden lift.

Now the sunburst is all together, but it needs a little additional work to put it into its final shape. Turn it upside down on several thicknesses of newspaper and gently work the spokes until they all have identical curves and angles, and adjust the spread between spokes so they are all equally spaced.

Illus. 213. A 32-inch sunburst.

Large Sunburst

You will need:

25-lb. lard can, or can that egg yolks are packed in for bakeries—$12\frac{1}{4}$ inches high, 10 inches in diameter and $31\frac{1}{2}$ inches around

No. 10 can—vegetables, flavoring for ice cream and other products for restaurant use come in this size can

46-oz. juice can

1-quart motor oil can

From the 25-lb. can remove the top rim and cut down the seam for a hanger. Divide into spokes approximately $1\frac{1}{4}$ inch wide and cut down. Arch back from bottom ring gently.

Divide each spoke into 10 equal parts, as in Illus. 214. Cut and turn the 10 strips as shown in Illus. 215.

Illus. 214.

4″
2″
1″
2″
4″

Illus. 215.

From the No. 10 can, remove the top rim. Cut down the seam and remove. Divide into 1-inch spokes and cut them down. Divide each spoke into 6 equal parts and cut down 2 inches. Turn and curl as shown in Illus. 216.

From the 46-oz. juice can, remove the top rim and seam. Divide into $\frac{3}{4}$-inch spokes and cut them down. Divide each spoke into 5 equal parts and cut down 2 inches. Curl as shown in Illus. 217.

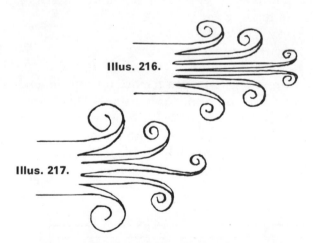

Illus. 216.

Illus. 217.

From the quart motor oil can, remove the top and heavy top rim. Divide into $\frac{1}{2}$-inch spokes and cut them down. Divide each spoke into 5 equal parts and cut down 2 inches and curl as in Illus. 217.

You will find that the spoke ends will tend

to overlap due to the width of the finished curls. To counteract this tendency, pull every other spoke forward slightly.

The centerpiece in Illus. 213 was made from a shiny, rounded can bottom which curves convexly. If you can find this type of can bottom, it makes a good simple center for an ornate sunburst. However, it is only optional. If you prefer a jewelled center, use the conventional flat bottom of the motor oil can.

This 32-inch sunburst, because of its great weight and size, cannot rely on cement to hold it together. Make 2 matching holes in the 2 larger can bottoms with the ice pick and fasten them together with a split-shank paper clip. Then fasten the third can with one clip through the center of all 3. The last can may be cemented on (Illus. 219).

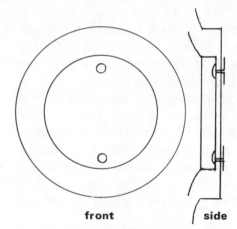

front   side

Illus. 218. Assembly of a two-tiered sunburst.

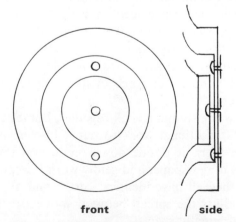

front   side

Illus. 219. Assembly of a three-tiered sunburst.

Tailored Sunburst

You will need:

46-oz. juice can

shorter can with same diameter, or 46-oz. can
    cut down

4-tiered jewelled centerpiece

Either gold- or silver-lacquered cans may be used for these sunbursts. Notice that these large cans have ridges or indentations around the sides. Sometimes labels pasted on the cans hide these ridges and you do not notice them until you remove the labels. In these sunbursts the ridges become part of the design.

Cut the largest can of the set into even-sized spokes about $\frac{3}{4}$ inch wide. Point the end of each spoke. Use the wooden bar to bend the spokes outward, or arch them as desired.

Make the collar from a low can having the same diameter, or nearly the same, as the first can, or from a high can cut down to 3 inches. Remove the bottom, the top and the top rim and cut the body into $\frac{1}{4}$-inch strips all the way down to the bottom rim. These spokes may be pointed, rounded or left straight across the top. Cement the collar into place.

The sunburst in Illus. 220 is finished with a centerpiece whose details are shown in Illus. 221. The first or bottom tier has short cuts all around, turned at a slight angle. Cut the second lid $\frac{3}{4}$ inch deep and shape and curl it as shown. The third is simply round with indentations, and is held in place by curls from the second lid. The fourth lid has 8 petals. Cut the lid into 8 sections as usual, turning the corners under to produce the petals. Leave 2 curls between petals. In the center of the assembled lids make a gold mounting with a sapphire earring.

Designing Sunbursts

Using the techniques and materials outlined in the preceding projects, you can let your imagination run free and create new and unusual sunburst designs. By changing the design of the curled cuttings on the spokes, you will achieve a wide range of different effects.

Illus. 220. Tailored sunburst.

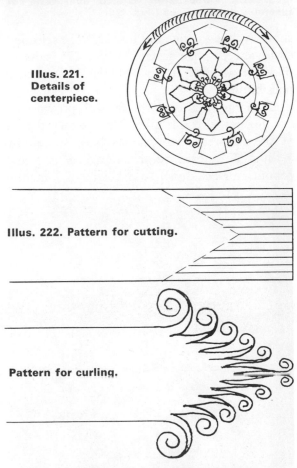

Illus. 221. Details of centerpiece.

Illus. 222. Pattern for cutting.

Pattern for curling.

You can cut the spokes as shown in Illus. 222, and, after curling the strips back, construct a

Illus. 223. Three-tiered 32-inch sunburst. For assembly diagram, see Illus. 219.

sunburst like the one in Illus. 223. The selection of advanced spoke designs in Illus. 225 is meant only to suggest a few of the innumerable possibilities.

Changing the centerpiece will provide an exciting new effect. In Illus. 224, the basic design of the tailored sunburst has been altered by making a 2-tiered centerpiece from a salted peanut can cut down to a height of 2 inches.

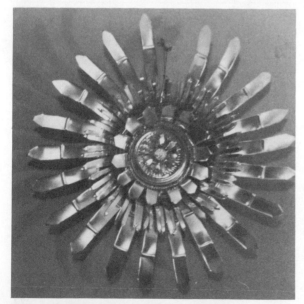

Illus. 224. Variation of tailored sunburst.

Illus. 225.

With the bottom of the can left in, the body was cut into $\frac{5}{8}$-inch spokes. The spokes were pointed, a collar (made from the piece of can just above the rim of a coffee can) was cut into $\frac{1}{8}$-inch strips and cemented in place. You can experiment with a number of centerpieces until you find the one which looks exactly right in a particular sunburst.

Illus. 226. This modern sunburst was made from a 46-oz. juice can cut into 12 pointed spokes, a soup can cut into 16 pointed spokes, and chili and motor oil cans cut as shown at right.

Illus. 227. Details of chili can spokes (top) and motor oil can spokes (below) for modern sunburst.

You may want to change the shape of the spokes entirely. The modern sunburst shown in Illus. 226 was made from four different sizes of cans, each cut into tapered spokes and painted with a different color enamel. In any sunburst design you can use the shiny metallic color of the original can, paint or lacquer the entire project, or alternate painted and unpainted layers for interesting contrasting effects.

Clock Medallions

One of the most interesting and useful objects you can make with tin cans is a clock medallion.

The type of decoration you use will depend on the type of clock or clock works you choose. Your clock, of course, must be round.

For a modern clock medallion you can vary the modernistic sunburst in Illus. 226 for a very unusual effect. Instead of using the face of the clock, use 12 spokes to represent the numerals. Mount the works behind, with just the hands of the clock showing in front of the medallion.

Here's another frame you can make:

Start with a 1-lb. coffee can. Remove the top rim and lid as well as the bottom of the can. Cut down strips ¼ inch wide all around and

bend them out flat. Using the large pliers, turn all of the strips in the same direction. Curl them into fairly large curls in groups of 3, the first one high, the second medium and the third one curled down against the rim. (See Illus. 228.)

Treat the seam simply as one of the strips since it can be coaxed into a large curl such as these.

Illus. 228. Coil the spokes for this clock medallion in groups of three.

Roses

You will need for each rose:
2 can lids, 3¼-inch diameter
1 can lid, 4-inch diameter
1 12-inch stiff wire
green florist's tape

These impressive roses are striking either singly or grouped into floral arrangements.

After enlarging the pattern to proper size, cut the lids to form petals. Choose one of the 3¼-inch lids for the center, and on one petal make the small cut marked "X" on the pattern. With pliers, work this petal into a tight roll (the long way). Then crease the middle of each of the remaining petals (again lengthwise) until each has a cupped shape. Gently bend back the corners of each petal and shape them around the inner roll. You should now have a rosebud.

Make each layer of petals in the same way, but do not draw them up quite so tightly. Nest

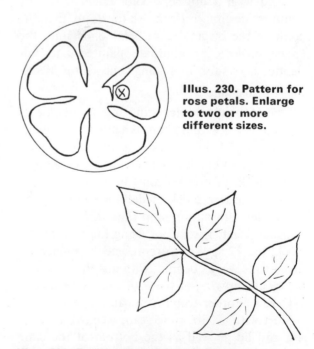

Illus. 230. Pattern for rose petals. Enlarge to two or more different sizes.

Illus. 231. Basic pattern for rose leaves.

the layers together, and add finishing bends and twists to form a well shaped rose.

Wire the layers together, and twist the wire tightly at the base, making sure the rose is firmly held together. Then use the remainder of the wire to form the stem. Wind the green florist's tape around it.

For a realistic touch, add leaves, using the pattern, enlarged, in Illus. 231. To simulate veins, score the undersides of the leaves with an ice pick, and then press down firmly. With a small pliers, crimp the outer edges.

If you want colored roses and leaves, do this *before* you make them. Use shiny tin from used cans and any one of the popular dyes available. Follow the directions given on the package exactly as you would for dyeing any material.

Large Flower

You will need (all matching gold color):
5 can lids, graduated sizes
3 No. 2 cans
6 or 7 46-oz. juice cans
2-inch stove bolt with nut

You make this flower from the center outwards. In the very center use a cuff link held in place by the petals of the smallest can lid. Cut this lid into 8 sections, cutting down to a $\frac{5}{8}$-inch center. Gently round each petal and then, to help you cup the petals into position, remove a small bit of tin from between each 2 petals. Carefully bend up the petals to hold the cuff links in place.

Make 5 layers of can lids into petals in the same manner. With each successive lid leave a slightly larger circle intact in the center. Nest them, in graduated sizes, one inside the other, with the petals cupped upward and tipped outward.

Next use the 3 No. 2 cans. Divide them into spokes approximately 1 inch wide. Now round the ends of each spoke and flatten them out. You can do this best by stepping on the can after you have flattened it as far as possible by hand. Place these 3 cans one on top of the other in such a way as to expose as many spokes as possible.

Illus. 232. This large flower makes a striking, impressive wall hanging in any room.

Take 4 or 5 46-oz. juice cans and cut them down into 1½-inch spokes, gently rounded on the ends and varied slightly as to length from can to can. Each can will have the same length spokes, but some complete cans will be somewhat shorter.

When these cans have been flattened out completely, layer them so that as many spokes as possible are visible.

Use an ice pick to make a hole through each of the layers of the No. 2 cans and the 46-oz. cans. Put a 2-inch stove bolt through the layers and tighten as much as possible to hold these together. Bend the seam on the last, or outside, can to hold a ring by which to hang the piece. Cement the inner petals made from lids into place, making sure that the petals are bent in such a way as to hold all 5 together.

Make the leaves now from 2 flattened 46-oz. juice can bodies with seams removed. Use the patterns given in Illus. 233 and 234. Crimp the leaves with pliers to simulate veins, as shown in the illustrations and then attach them to the flower with cement. A Formica contact-bond cement is good here.

This flower is a heavy, flat, showy decoration which reflects a lot of light from its polished surfaces. Such a flower can be made larger or smaller by using cans of different sizes.

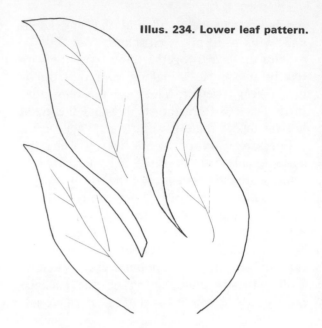

Illus. 234. Lower leaf pattern.

Melodious Bells

You will need:
can lids of various sizes
small sleigh-type bells
Christmas tree beads, or shiny glass beads
lightweight wire
ribbons

Use one can lid to make a fluted bell. First divide the lid into fourths and mark with lines. Then with the needle-nose pliers make a crease from the center outward along each mark. Leave a circular section about ½ inch untouched in the center of the bell. Next make a crease between each of the original creases (Illus. 235). Now go around the lid again deepening each crease. Repeat until the bell has assumed the desired shape.

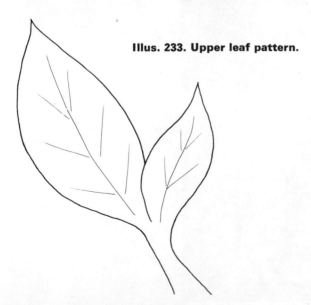

Illus. 233. Upper leaf pattern.

Illus. 235.

Use a bright, shiny lid from a pet food can to make a square bell. Cut out 4 small sections as shown in the pattern (Illus. 239) and bend the sides into shape by hand (Illus. 237).

For the novelty bell (Illus. 238) use a large juice can lid or a No. 2½ can lid. Remove the pie-shaped sections (Illus. 240) completely and bend the bell into shape by hand.

Assembling

All the bells are assembled in the same manner:

Using an ice pick, make a hole in the center of the top of the bell. String a sleigh bell and one bead on a 4-inch length of wire. Place this inside the bell and run the wire through the hole at the top, then through a bead on the top, outside (Illus. 237), ending with a wire loop.

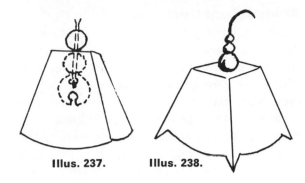

Illus. 237.   **Illus. 238.**

Return the loose end of the loop back into the bell and twist it tightly about itself. String the ribbon through the loop of wire and double it back through the next 2 beads.

Use several bright beads atop each bell if you prefer.

String the bells separately on ribbons, or tie 3 to 5 of them in graduated sizes on one ribbon (Illus. 236). The bells make interesting decorations and tinkle musically when moved. The color of your ribbons and beads should blend with the room decor.

Illus. 236. You can string your tin bells uniformly, as shown here, or mix different bell patterns on each string.

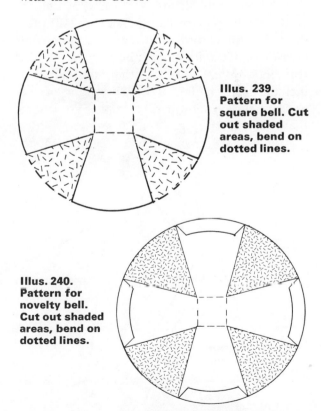

Illus. 239. Pattern for square bell. Cut out shaded areas, bend on dotted lines.

Illus. 240. Pattern for novelty bell. Cut out shaded areas, bend on dotted lines.

Animal Constructions

The patterns reproduced in this section can be used to make charming animal constructions from tin cans. Follow the instructions on page 80 to enlarge these patterns, and then trace them onto flattened tin cans. To prepare the cans, remove the tops, bottoms, rims and seams and flatten them by bending gently with gloved hands. If they will not lie flat, put them between two boards and leave overnight in a vice under pressure.

Rooster

You will need:

4 46-oz. juice cans with gold-lacquered insides (Use the inside gold color for body and outside silver color for wing, tail and feet.)

sequins and jewels

Formica cement (This will hold these birds together more tightly than the usual cement. It comes in pints and is more expensive than household cement.)

Roosters lend themselves well to tin-can crafting. The pattern (Illus. 241 and 242) produces a fancy bird with curls, crimps and creases (made with large pliers) to look like feathers. Note, however, that the patterns include diagramming of the directions of the various curls you will later make, so ignore these curls in tracing.

Attach the 4 tracings, when completed, to the flattened pieces of tin, and you are ready to cut.

Use the compound-leverage shears for cutting. Cut the small strips indicated on the pattern but, before making the curls, crease and crimp the wing and tail pieces here and there with flat-nose pliers. Use the pliers gently to make creases which simulate feathers. The tin will crease readily when held firmly in one hand and grasped with the pliers. Hold the pliers in a position as nearly parallel to the top of the wing as possible and as far inward toward the

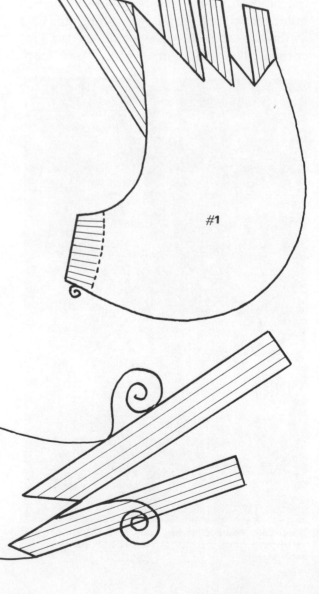

Illus. 241. Pattern for rooster wing, tail and foot.

center of the wing as the pliers will reach. Then "work" the pliers sideways, back and forth as if to stretch the tin. After you repeat this a number of times at different places on the wing you will obtain a slightly concave wing. Always have the creases running as nearly horizontal as possible, since that is the way the feathers lie on a wing. Then make the curls as indicated on the patterns.

Assemble each half of the rooster's body with cement. First attach wing (#1) to the body, using a layer or two of cardboard between the wing and the body. Weight this while it dries. Attach the foot (#3) next in the same way, and the tail (#2) last.

Decorate your rooster halves with sequins and jewels to add glitter. You can also create eyelashes from a small pie-shaped piece of tin by making fine slanting cuts and curling the

Illus. 242. Completed tin-can rooster.

ends. Cement them into place to impart a rakish expression.

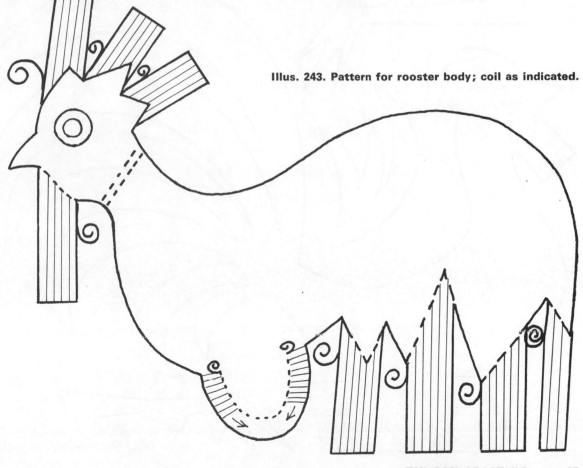

Illus. 243. Pattern for rooster body; coil as indicated.

Game Cock

Follow the pattern in Illus. 245 to make another variety of rooster, a game cock (Illus. 244). You may find him a little more difficult to make than the first rooster, but using a double-serrated tin shears will make your task a little easier.

This rooster may look better when the metal is left flat rather than creased. If you use the gold-lacquered can, cut the wing so that the reverse or silver-colored side of the can body will provide a contrast in color.

Make the eye by cutting a contrasting circle of tin and mounting a jewel stone of whatever color and size is obtainable from your accumulation of "junk jewelry."

Illus. 244. A bold traditional game cock.

Illus. 245. Pattern for game cock.

Horse

This little horse may be cut out from any small piece of tin. When you mount the horse's head on heavy, contrasting construction paper it will make an interesting silhouette.

Illus. 246. This amusing horse's head is easy to make.

Illus. 247. Pattern for horse.

Illus. 248. Sea gull.

Sea Gull

Trace both parts of the pattern in Illus. 249. Trace the wings twice and the body once. Attach the tracings to flattened can bodies. Cut them out. Make the slot in the gull's body by perforating a hole with an ice pick and then working the pick until the hole is large enough to use the light metal shears.

Slip the end of one wing through the slot and the end of the other wing onto the slit at the back of the neck portion. Cement them into place (Illus. 248).

Make an eye from a small piece of contrasting colored metal and cement a rhinestone or colored stone onto it. You can add eyelashes if

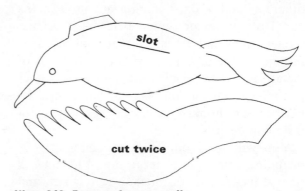

Illus. 249. Pattern for sea gull.

you want. Make the beak of a separate contrasting color, or cut it out of the same tin in one piece with the body.

Constructions from Found Objects

The projects in this section were all created from discarded metal scraps, tin cans, various common fasteners and paint. While specific instructions are given for the design and construction of each sculpture, these are only suggestions, since you will certainly want to alter them and make your own original sculptures. In fact, for many projects you will have no choice, since you will never find exactly the same scrap objects as those in the illustrations.

Several things should be kept in mind when collecting scrap metal for standing sculptures. To begin with, find a solid base for your sculpture. Sections of planks, boards, beams, logs or heavy metal objects, if they rest evenly on a flat surface, make good bases. Hub caps and inverted pots and pans can also be used, if holes for attaching other items can easily be drilled or hammered through them.

When choosing the other objects to include in your sculpture, select pieces which either have holes and brackets already, so you can bolt them together easily, or which are thin enough so that you can make holes. Nine different methods for joining are used in the metal sculptures presented here. You can use screws, nuts and bolts, washers, nails, paper fasteners, glue or solder to join many kinds of metal scraps. Tying pieces together is another possibility, and finally many shapes can be wedged or hooked together without extra fastening devices.

You will need only a few common tools, including a tin-can opener, a saw, a hammer, a screwdriver, a pair of pliers, a wire cutter, and a sharp knife. A soldering iron or torch was used for some projects, but you can usually substitute nuts and bolts. In addition, be sure to have a pair of work gloves handy for handling sharp-edged objects.

Illus. 250. You can paint your modern wall sculpture with flat colors, but why not add excitement with a coating of aluminum foil, applied with rubber cement and carefully smoothed out with the rounded back of a comb. See this construction in color in Illus. B3.

For painting your sculpture, you can choose from a wide variety of products. Spray paints are usually the easiest to use, but must be used before the pieces of a multi-colored construction are assembled. Acrylic paints are expensive

Illus. 251. Arrange the cans, lids, and tops in a design which appeals to you.

and do not cover well with just one coat on many metal surfaces. Latex, on the other hand, scratches easily and, if the metal underneath is rusty, the rust will bleed through. If you are aware of the different problems which come up with each type of paint, you should be able to choose the one best suited for your particular project.

The projects found in this section are unique since, in this area of metalcrafting, there is no standard supply of materials to work with. It is up to you, as an individual craftsman, to find unique and different pieces of scrap metal, either searching for materials to suit your idea or letting the inspiration come from the scrap items at hand. In either case, you will have the special enjoyment of turning junk into sculpture, eyesores into eye-openers.

Modern Wall Sculpture

This is a fairly simple project—it involves only selecting an assortment of tin cans and jar tops and mounting them in a pleasing arrangement on a board. You will also need a hammer, some nails with wide heads, and three or four different colors of acrylic paints.

Once you have collected everything, clean all the cans and lids. Wash them out and peel off the labels. Also remove the plastic and card-

board sealers from the lids and tops. If any dirt or paper is left on the cans when they are painted, the paint probably will not hold.

Remember, too, that the insides of the cans and tops may be sharp. *Wear gloves when you work.*

Next, place your cans and lids on the board and experiment with different arrangements and designs. When you have made a design which you like, carefully move it off of the board, one

Illus. 252. Make a hole in the middle of each can, lid and top.

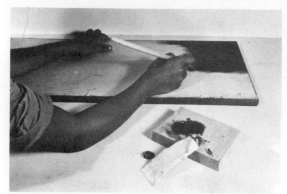

Illus. 253. Paint the edges and the front side of the backboard.

Illus. 254. Paint the cans one at a time.

can at a time, and set it up in the same way on a piece of newspaper off to the side of your work space. This is done so that you won't forget where each can goes as you work on the rest of the project.

Now punch holes in the cans, paint and assemble as shown in Illus. 252–257.

You should give careful consideration to the colors you choose. Too many colors will detract from your design. It is best to paint your cans and lids with two or three colors which go together well, and then paint the background a dark color so the design will stand out.

By using different sized and shaped cans and backboards, all sorts of tin-can wall sculptures are possible. You can also add on other materials, such as wood scraps, spools, bottle caps, string, and wire, to give your tin-can design more variety.

Illus. 255. Nail on the tops, lids and shallow cans with a hammer and nails.

Illus. 256. For the tall cans, use a nail-set to finish pounding the nails in, or screw them in instead.

Illus. 257. Attach a hanging wire to the back of your piece. Screw eyes or bent-over nails can be used to attach the wire.

Tin-Can Tower

You can approximate the original design for the tower in color Illus. B1 by arranging cans on the floor and then viewing them from above. Attach the cans together in one of three different ways: glue them together, using small wooden stir sticks and glue between the vertical cans to be positioned side by side; bolt them together; or solder them together.

To achieve a strong bond in soldering, you must first remove all grease, dirt and oxide from the two metal surfaces to be joined. Flux can be used to clean oxides from the surface. Next, heat both surfaces with a soldering iron or gun, and after they are hot, apply the solder. Use acid-core solder for iron, and multicore solder for non-ferrous metals (copper and brass). There is also a solder especially designed for soldering aluminum.

Regardless of how you attach the cans, it's best to start with a central core of 3 or 4 large, heavy cans, and then attach the other cans one or two at a time. Prop them into position with blocks or wedges, or hold them in place with masking tape, transparent tape or a clamp. Then solder, glue, or nut-and-bolt them.

Metal-Strip Sculpture

While a chrome strip from the side of an automobile was used for the sculpture in Illus. 258, you can use any long metal strip for the same purpose. Aluminum siding, counter siding, or metal framing strips can all be employed in similar sculpture. Or, bolt shorter pieces together to make strip designs.

Begin by applying masking tape in several

Illus. 258. Untitled. 19" x 14" x 35"; 7' x 4" chrome automotive siding strip, 2 tuna fish cans, redwood base.

lines along the entire length of both sides of the metal strip. Spray-paint the strip. Remove the tape and you should have stripes of color alternating with the metal finish.

Next, use a piece of wire the same length as your strip to experiment with different designs. When you have worked out a suitable design, bend the strip into the same configuration.

Then bend over a short portion of the bottom end of your strip, make several nail holes in it, and screw it down to your base block. A redwood 4 × 4 mounted on top of a pine-wood square was used for the base block in Illus. 258.

To add motion to your piece, bolt together two tin cans with the tops and bottoms removed, and suspend them on a string or wire from the strip design.

A piece like "Chrome on Chrome" (Illus. 259) can be constructed from a number of other materials besides those used here. Start by fastening three vertical strips to a base block. The longer strip in Illus. 259 measures 39 × 3 inches, and the two shorter strips 31 × 3 inches. They are all fastened to the base board with L braces and screws.

Next, solder or bolt on the two cross-pieces. Tricycle fenders were soldered in place in the construction shown. Finally, shape a metal strip by bending or twisting it, and then solder it onto the tops of the vertical pieces.

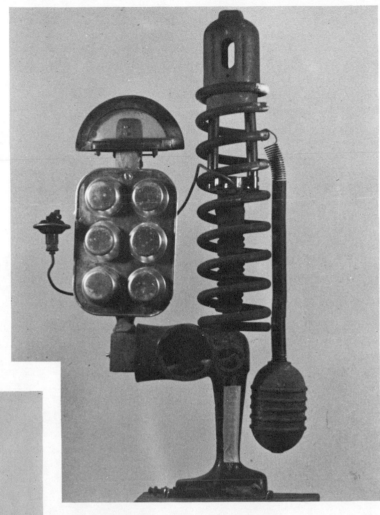

Illus. 260. "Junkman and the Ms." 19" x 9" x 36"; parking meter top, table leg, muffin tin, fuel pump and tubing, sewing-machine body, 17" truck spring, bicycle pump and air hose, oxygen tank cap, 15" spring, toilet-tank float, and a wooden beam base.

Illus. 261 (below). "Boing" by Sandrea Lopez, age 11. 10" x 5" x 12"; mattress spring, 4 pop-tops, windowshade pulley, toy wheel, bumper hook from an auto jack, and an electric outlet box; painted with latex.

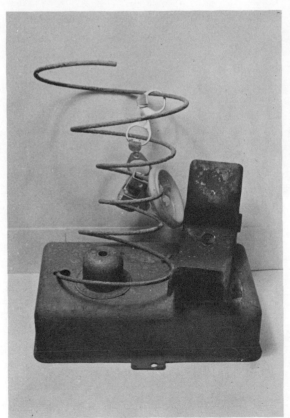

Boing

The construction in Illus. 261 was made by simply threading the pop-top chain, the wheel and the pulley onto the spring, and then twisting it through a hole in the base box. Then the metal bumper hook was bolted down and the different parts were painted with red, green, and blue latex paints.

Junkman and the Ms.

In spite of the size and weight involved, large constructions such as Illus. 260 are not difficult to make. While you will probably not be able to collect the same junk parts to start with, the following instructions will provide some ideas for assembling the junk you do have.

A sewing machine turned on its side is

Illus. 262. "Martian Sunday Hat" by Aixa Ledee, age 11. Plastic washing-machine agitator cap, heavy strainer screen, engine casing, wooden chair leg; painted with purple, red and yellow tempera.

Illus. 263. "Crazy-Horn" by Evelyn Luciano, age 11. 20" x 12" x 17"; hub cap, pipe brace, lamp fitting, party horn, construction paper, and a spring; painted with enamel.

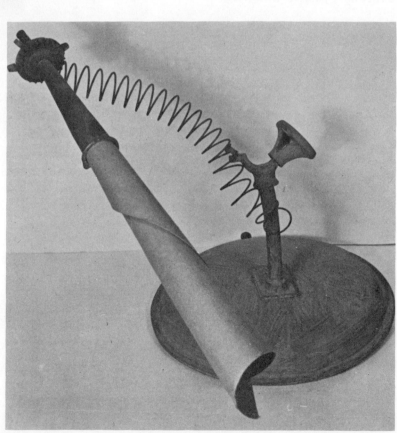

mounted to the base block by driving heavy spikes into the block and then bending them over, around the machine. Next, the table leg is attached to the sewing machine, through a hole, using a nut, bolt, and washer. Then the meter top and the muffin tin are mounted on the vertical table leg with screws.

The bicycle sprocket with the air hose slid around its stem is now hammered into a large hole in the sewing-machine body. The truck spring can then be lowered down around this sprocket, and the oxygen-tank cap forced down onto the sprocket above it, holding the spring in place. Both the long narrow spring and the fuel-pump tube can be hooked onto the coils of the truck spring. Finally the toilet-tank float is threaded onto the free end of the narrow spring.

Martian Sunday Hat

The sculpture in Illus. 262 is also very easy to assemble. Hammer the chair leg into the engine casing hole. Then hammer a nail through the agitator top and the strainer, into a hole on top of the engine casing. Then use any type of paint.

Imaginative figures such as this are so easy to construct, using only a few materials, that you should find no end to ideas. Often the shapes of the junk you find will immediately conjure up images in your mind.

Crazy-Horn

When pushed, the piece in Illus. 263 gives a long-lasting and unique series of motions. To build one like it, bolt a pipe brace onto a hub cap; then twist a long spring onto one side of the brace top, and another junk object on the other side, like the lamp fitting. Next, thread a party horn onto the free end of the spring. By inserting some rolled construction paper into the mouth of the horn you will throw it off balance, and add to the crazy motion of the piece.

Clown with Hat

All the different pieces of junk in Illus. 264 were used in constructing "Clown with Hat" (color Illus. C3). On the following two pages are step-by-step instructions for constructing this whimsical figure.

Illus. 264. The ingredients for the "Clown with Hat" are, from left to right, top to bottom: desk lamp arm base, T-hinge, hub cap, wheel ring surrounding metal spring and carburetor section, anchovy can, pulley, light socket, film reel, heavy spring, and ham can.

Illus. 265. First you must hammer holes in the hub cap in order to bolt in the central support for the sculpture, in this case a large T-hinge. Hold nail with pliers for safety, and keep it from skidding out of place.

Illus. 266. Bolt the square end of the T-hinge onto the hub cap, holding the nut from one side and turning in the bolt on the other side with a screwdriver.

Illus. 267. Bolt the pulley on at the top of the hinge.

Illus. 268. Paint the piece.

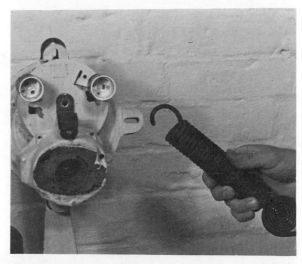

Illus. 269 (left). Solder an oval anchovy can onto the carburetor section. The oval can forms the mouth and the carburetor section forms the cheek, jaws and lower face. Bolt the triple light socket onto the face of the pulley; break off the lower socket and you have the eyes and nose. Bolt the anchovy can-carburetor construction in place. Attach the "earrings" to the clown's face. The desk lamp arm base goes on one side, and the hook on the spring goes on the other (Illus. 270, right).

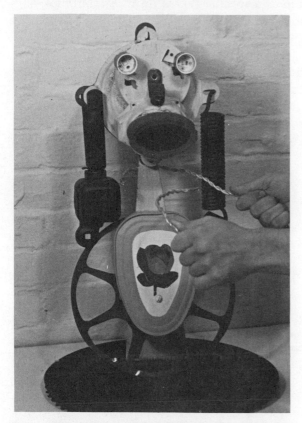

Illus. 271. Drive a hole through the ham can. Insert a bolt through this hole and through the middle hole in the film reel, and attach to the hinge. Add the wire necklace as shown.

Illus. 272. Finishing touches include the cut out flower on the ham can, light bulbs for the sockets and paper eyelashes. See the completed sculpture in color in Illus. C3.

Metal and Wire Sculpture

In this section you will learn how to make original, unusual sculptures, using the standard techniques of cutting, bending and soldering. Your basic materials are pieces of sheet metal and wire, both made of medium-hard copper or brass. The sheet metal should not be thicker than 20 gauge. The wire should be from $\frac{1}{16}$ to $\frac{1}{8}$ inch in diameter.

Illus. 273. All you need for this craft are an electric soldering iron, a soldering torch, pliers, compass, solder, jeweler's scissors, brass or copper sheet, and an asbestos mat.

Cutting

For cutting sheet metal, use shears made for the purpose (the type used by a jeweler). "Werindus" sheet-metal shears, which separates the sheet metal by cutting out an approximately $\frac{1}{8}$-inch-wide strip, is an excellent cutting tool. However, if you do not wish to go to this extra expense, use a double-cut snip, which cuts a $\frac{1}{16}$-inch strip in the metal. Both types of sheet-metal shears may be obtained from specialized shops. In thin sheet metal, even a simple scissors will do. The wires can be cut effortlessly with diagonal wire cutters or multiple-purpose pliers.

Perforating the sheet metal is done with the aid of a nail or other puncturing tool, such as

an iron rod or a chisel, and a hammer. Before doing this, the workpiece is placed on a yielding base (wooden board).

Shaping

The same basic techniques used to shape wire for jewelry (page 26) are applicable to the copper and brass wire you will use in your sculptures. With the aid of your pliers and a vice you should be able to shape the wire into every imaginable design. You can also make a simple bending jig which will allow you to repeat a specific curved form several times, and aids generally in making smooth bends in thicker wire.

The simplest bending aid is a length of dowel, around which you can coil your wire to make rings of a consistent diameter. The fixture around which wire is coiled is known as a mandrel (or core). The size and shape of the coil is determined by the size and shape of the

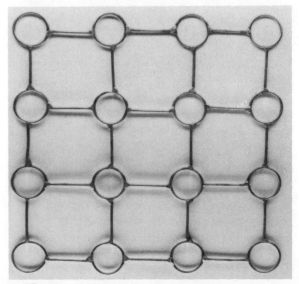

Illus. 274. Uniformly-bent wire rings and equal straight lengths make up this design.

Illus. 275. Copper coil being formed over a wooden dowel.

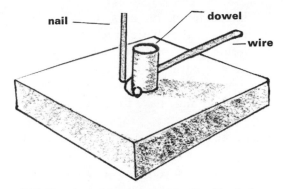

nail ———   dowel

wire

Illus. 277. The dowel is screwed to the block from the bottom to form this bending jig.

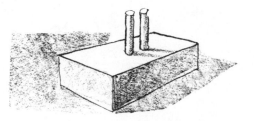

Illus. 276. Simple jig is made by driving two nails into a block of wood and clipping off the heads.

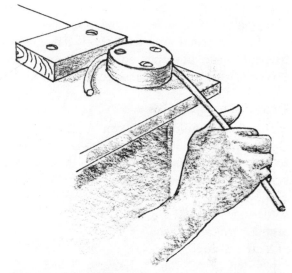

Illus. 278. A similar jig is used to make the candle-holder on page 103.

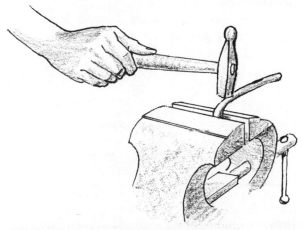

Illus. 279. Make a right-angle bend in a vice like this or on an anvil.

mandrel. Illus. 275 shows a dowel used as a mandrel for making a light copper-wire coil. Illus. 276 shows a jig for making simple bends. Illus. 277 is a simple jig made with a dowel rod and nail in a block of wood. When the wire is inserted between nail and dowel and gradually wound around, each successive bend forms a curve or loop. For making bends with heavy wire and the bar stock, you need a jig similar to Illus. 278. The brass candleholder on page 108 will be made on a modified version of this jig. To make right-angle bends, use a vice (Illus. 279) or an anvil and hammer.

Soldering

Any kind of solder, except acid-core, may be used for the soldering of non-ferrous metals like copper and brass. If ordinary solid-wire solder is used, you must use it together with a flux (either rosin flux or a mixture of tallow and sal ammoniac). Solder containing rosin flux in its' hollow core is convenient to use. The addition of extra flux may be necessary if the chemicals in the core of the self-flux soldering wires are not strong enough to remove the oxide present on the metal.

When you solder you will want to be careful not to burn the metal. If the metal is over-heated it will change color. This may sometimes fit in well with your design, but experiment before you begin, so you will be able to control the final effect.

Flat soldering presents no difficulty if you understand the basic process of soldering. Soldering construction works, however, requires an extra set of hands. In addition to holding the soldering iron or torch and the solder, you must have the piece you are soldering held in the proper three-dimensional position, and it must be held steady for the solder to work. The easiest solution is an assistant with steady hands. If you do not have a ready volunteer, you will have to fashion a holding device by pushing the metal into the asbestos soldering base, by jamming it between pieces of brick, or by using a vice or clamps. You may also be able to solder several pieces of your construction together lying flat on your fireproof base, and then solder them into their position within the construction.

Brass Candleholder

For this candleholder you need to solder together a number of curved brass wire pieces to form a lacy tube. Two jigs will be needed, a bending jig to bend the brass wire to shape, and a soldering fixture to hold the pieces while soldering.

STEP 1. *Making a bending jig.*

You will need:

1 wooden dowel, $\frac{3}{8}$-inch diameter, $\frac{1}{2}$ inch long
1 finishing nail, 6-penny size, $1\frac{1}{2}$ inches long
2 small wire nails, 17-gauge, $1\frac{1}{2}$ inches long
hammer and saw
1 wooden block (2 × 4 cut 4 inches long)

Nail the $\frac{3}{8}$-inch dowel on to the block with the two 17-gauge nails. Hammer the larger nail into the block in the position shown in

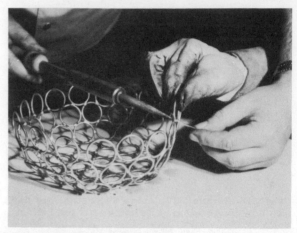

Illus. 280. The easiest way to solder upright constructions is with a helper.

Illus. 281. To determine the spacing between the nail and the dowel, place a short length of 14-gauge wire next to the dowel. Position the nail so that there is a small clearance for the wire between the nail and dowel.

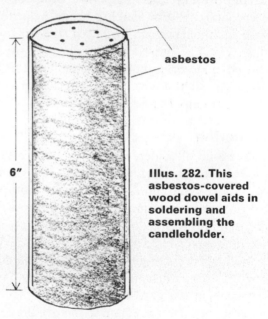

asbestos

6"

Illus. 282. This asbestos-covered wood dowel aids in soldering and assembling the candleholder.

STEP 2. *Making a soldering fixture.*

You will need:

1 wooden dowel rod, 6 inches long, $1\frac{1}{2}$-inch diameter
several sheets of asbestos, 6 inches square, .050 inch thick
1 package brads, 17-gauge, $\frac{3}{8}$ inch long

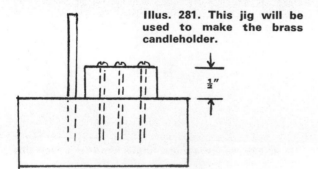

Illus. 281. This jig will be used to make the brass candleholder.

$\frac{1}{2}$"

Illus. 283. Your finished project will look handsome on any table.

Wrap the asbestos around the dowel so that it makes a smooth, tight fit. Start the asbestos by nailing one edge to the dowel. Wrap and nail the second edge flush to the first. Do not overlap.

Cut a circle of asbestos 1½ inches in diameter. Nail this to the top of the dowel rod (Illus. 282).

STEP 3. *Planning and layout.*

You will need (in addition to above):
brass wire, 14-gauge, 15 feet
soft copper wire, 22- to 28-gauge, 2 feet
brass sheet, 18-gauge, 2 × 2 inch square
1 small smooth file
1 propane gas torch

1 medium soldering iron with wedge tip
1 1-lb. spool of 50/50 solder (50% tin–50% lead) of the solid type, .032 inch (20-gauge)
1 small can of soldering flux

Illus. 284 shows the way the individual curved brass pieces are to be laid out and joined. Note that the pattern is one of alternately upright and inverted swan shapes.

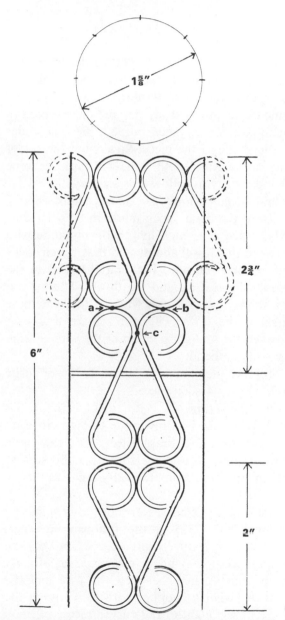

Illus. 284. Follow this pattern for your candleholder. The top view (above) shows the size of the brass plate which fits across the middle.

Illus. 285. Here you have to pull in order to hug the dowel and form an almost closed loop.

The layout will enable you to determine the number of pieces in each row, the number of rows, and the size of the brass circle. To determine the length of straight wire you will need to make one curved piece, curve a piece of solder to the shape of the piece. Straighten the solder and measure its length. This will turn out to be $4\frac{1}{4}$ inches if you follow this size layout.

STEP 4. *Bending the brass curves.* (Illus. 285.)

Using the bending jig made in Step 1 (Illus. 281), place a $4\frac{1}{4}$-inch length of 14-gauge wire between the dowel and nail so that $\frac{1}{4}$ inch sticks out beyond the nail. Holding the wire in the middle, bend it around the dowel. The motion is a slight pulling action while at the same time hugging the dowel. Bend till there is $\frac{1}{8}$ inch between the straight portion of the wire and the start of the bend.

Reverse the wire and repeat at the opposite end. Make 24 such pieces.

STEP 5. *Soldering.*

Make a disc by drawing a $1\frac{5}{8}$-inch circle on the 2-inch-square brass sheet. Cut the circle with a tin snips and file the burrs. Be sure to file in one direction, forward only, not back and forth.

Arrange eight curves around your soldering fixture (Illus. 282) in the following manner. Encircle the fixture with one strand of fine copper wire, leaving a clearance of slightly more than $\frac{1}{16}$ inch between the wire and the fixture. Twist the copper wire to maintain the circle. Insert eight of the curved pieces of brass you have made between the wire and the asbestos, by sliding them in. Lay the fixture down on its length. Tighten the wire, by twisting, so that the pieces can be moved, but will not fall down when the fixture is held upright. Adjust the pieces now so that the tips extend $\frac{3}{4}$ inch above the end of the fixture. Tighten the copper wire to hold them firmly in place. Place the fixture in a vice, so that the bottoms of the curves clear the vice.

Trim the brass disc with a file so that it fits inside the circle of pieces. When a good fit has been obtained, mark with a pencil the points at which the disc and curves touch. Remove the disc and notch these points to a depth of about $\frac{1}{32}$ inch. Place the disc back, adjust the curves to fit into the notches, tighten the copper wire, and proceed to solder.

With a pencil, place a small dab of flux at the junction of the disc and each curved wire. Cut eight pieces of solder, each $\frac{1}{16}$ inch long. Place a piece of solder on each of the fluxed meeting points of the disc and the brass curves. Make sure that the solder touches the wire curves. Light the torch and adjust to a 2-inch flame. "Play" the flame over the disc with a circular motion, starting from about 2 inches from the disc and moving closer. Continue this circular motion while moving closer to the disc until the solder melts and flows. Remove the flame. When the solder has hardened, the disc will be soldered to the eight curves. Allow the part to cool thoroughly, and remove the copper wire used as a clamp. Prepare for the soldering of more brass curves to make the complete holder.

Build up a second row of eight curves on top

of the first row of curves, using the copper wire as a clamp. Tighten the clamp and lay the fixture so that you are looking directly at two curves. Place a small dab of flux at the meeting points of the curves, marked a, b and c, in Illus. 284. Make sure that the curves touch each other. Illus. 286 shows the positioning of the soldering iron when soldering a, b and c. Hold the iron in one hand and a short length of solder in the other. Touch the spot to be soldered with the solder every few seconds. When it becomes hot enough, the solder will melt and flow to make a good joint. When the solder flows, remove the iron IMMEDIATELY. Allow the solder to harden before going to a new joint. Be careful to supply heat to each joint as quickly and for as short a time as possible, so as to prevent softening of the previous joint.

Turn the fixture one eighth turn so a new curve faces you. Adjust the pieces so that they touch, and solder as before. Continue until the row is completed. Allow the parts to cool thoroughly.

Turn the fixture upside down and proceed

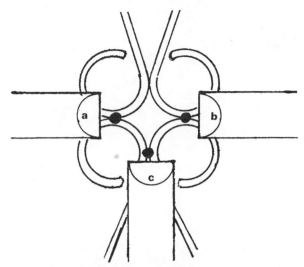

Illus. 286. Place the tip of the iron and spot of solder as shown for the three points.

to add the last row. Use the same soldering procedures as before.

STEP 6. *Cleaning and finishing.*

Remove the flux residue by wiping with a rag dipped in cleaning fluid. Polish. Coat the holder with clear lacquer.

Flat Works in Wire and Sheet

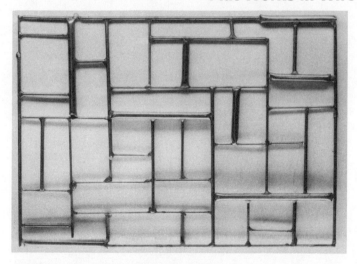

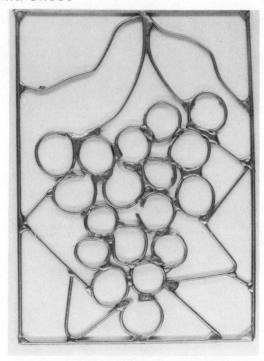

Using the techniques you have learned for bending and soldering, you can make interesting forms like Illus. 287 (above) which incorporates wire of varying widths and brass tubing into rectangular shapes, or Illus. 288 (right), which abstractly represents grapes on a vine.

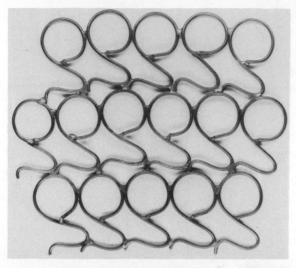

In Illus. 289 (above) and 290 (below), notice the effect of using the same wire form repeatedly. It is easy to create your own design in this way.

Illus. 292. Here is a spider web made of wire spokes and slightly bent wire pieces.

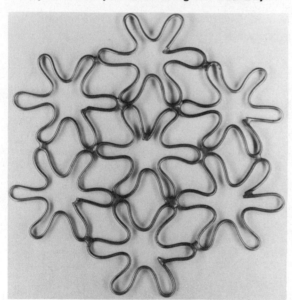

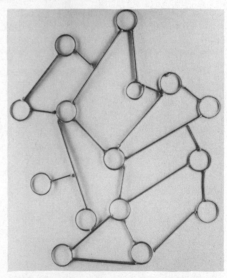

Illus. 293 (above). By varying the wire segments between rings, this design takes on an interesting feeling of motion.

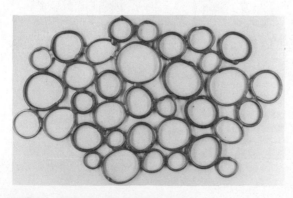

Illus. 291 (left). This design is meant to represent soap bubbles.

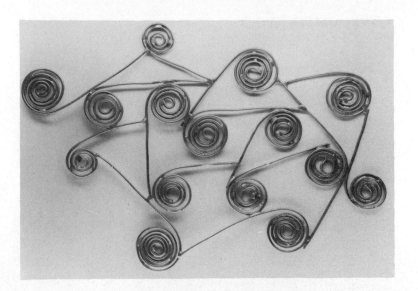

Illus. 294. The elements of this work were bent without a bending jig. Each wire was spiralled with the aid of a pair of pliers.

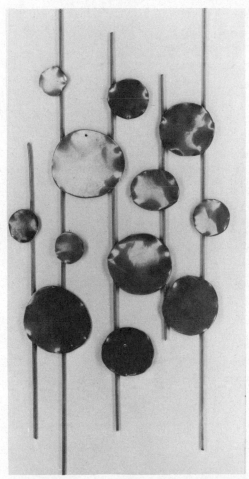

Illus. 295 (left) and Illus. 296 (right) show the effect of combining wire and pieces of sheet metal. The middles of the metal pieces in Illus. 296 were perforated.

Construction Works

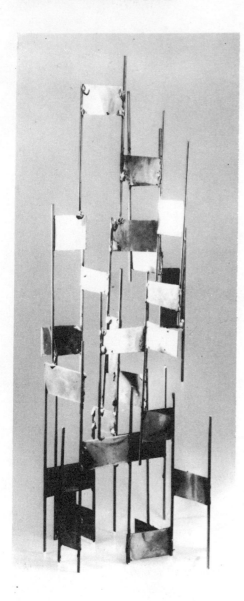

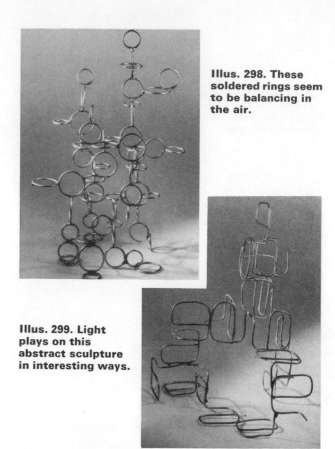

Illus. 298. These soldered rings seem to be balancing in the air.

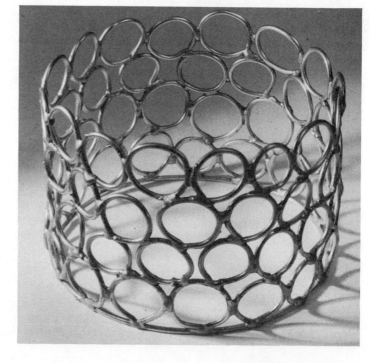

Illus. 299. Light plays on this abstract sculpture in interesting ways.

Illus. 297. Upright abstract forms can be created by combining metal pieces and wire rods. Notice the effect of generous use of solder on the design.

Illus. 300 (right). This upright structure is used as a candle sleeve or holder. It was made with a soldering iron.

Flowers

Simple flower heads are formed by cutting metal discs to the desired form using the radii as guides (see Illus. 302). The flower petals are shaped and bent up according to your own taste. The longitudinal ribs in the petals can be formed with a hammer and a chisel, using a wooden base and hammering just enough to indent the metal, not cut it. The bottom of the blossom can be created by perforating the metal sheet with a nail. Bore a hole for the stem.

Rosette-like flower heads combine three to five bloom-discs of different diameters, each created as described above. Hold the stem in a vice. Put the bloom-discs on the stem one on top of the other so that the smallest disc appears as the core of the flower head (Illus. 303). Solder each disc to the stem immediately after lining them up. Rods of hard brass are most suitable for the stems.

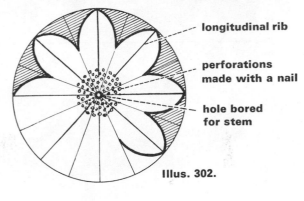

longitudinal rib

perforations made with a nail

hole bored for stem

Illus. 302.

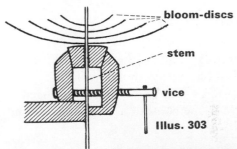

bloom-discs

stem

vice

Illus. 303

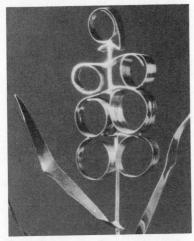

Illus. 305. This rose looks lovely alone or in groupings.

Illus. 304. For this tulip, three pairs of petals were cut, with opposite petals cut symmetrically from one piece of metal.

Illus. 306. Strips of copper foil were cut out with ordinary scissors.

Illus. 307.

A Play with Light

This project utilizes the mirror-effect of unpainted sheet metal. Individual "sails" are soldered as flat works and are then arranged in a semicircle in the holes of a baseboard so that the sheet parts (the sails soldered on to wire rods) are interlocked.

The flame of the candle itself ought to be covered by the sails; only its rays ought to come into play through reflections on the metal. Turning the sails produces different effects.

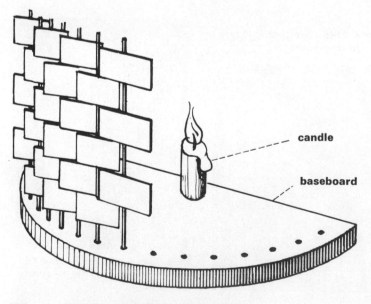

candle

baseboard

Illus. 308. Set-up for your play with light.

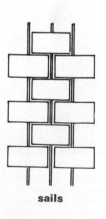

sails

Pictures with Pins and Wire

By stretching wire between pins you can produce geometric figures or stylized forms. This section will show you the effect of using wire in various ways, so that you can plan your own design to produce the result you want.

Since the same design can be executed in wires of different colors, you must consider color harmony in your work as well as the design itself. Although this technique calls for precision and care, anyone can learn it easily and produce really attractive works.

Materials

Pins

You can use all kinds of brads or small nails for pins. They are available with or without heads, long or short, and in a variety of thicknesses. You can also use more decorative types such as escutcheon pins made of brass, fancy upholsterer's tacks, and others. The proper size and thickness to use depends on the thickness of the wire you choose.

Types of Wire

For working with wire, you need something very fine and very malleable—gilt or silvered brass, copper, or very fine steel. The pins you use should also be fairly strong and must be deeply inserted into the background material, since wire calls for firm support.

The Background

For the background of your work, you can use matt or glossy painted surfaces, varnished wood if you wish to keep the natural color and grain, or stained wood (mahogany, oak, walnut, and so on). Use a colored varnish or apply a coat of clear varnish when the stain is dry. You can also cover the mounting base with a fabric such as burlap (hessian), linen, felt, corduroy, or velveteen (some of these come with adhesive backing, making them easier to mount on plywood). The background material and the mounting base play an important rôle in your finished pin picture. Give some thought to how

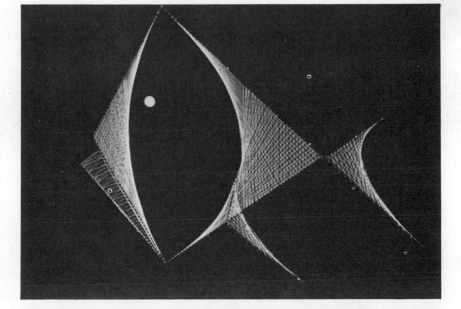

Illus. 309. Once you have mastered the basic techniques of pin pictures, you will be able to follow the diagram on page 132 and make this abstract fish.

and where you intend to display the picture. Consider the color of the wire you plan to use and the lighting conditions in which it will appear.

The Mounting Base

You can mount pins in any flat surface that is sturdy enough to hold them securely—wood, plywood, composition board, or heavy cardboard. You can also drive pins directly into a wall, a door, or even a piece of sheet metal (in which case, you have to bore some holes first).

Preparing the Mounting

Work out your design on paper and cut a piece of plywood to the appropriate size. (You may find it helpful to draw on graph paper.) Smooth the surface of the plywood with very fine sandpaper. Always rub with the grain of the wood to avoid scratches and to achieve a smooth surface.

If you are going to use the wood itself as the background for your work, transfer the design to tracing paper. Flatten the paper out on the board, centering it carefully. Follow the outline exactly, making a dot with the point of a pencil or nail at each spot where a pin is to go. Alternatively, you can drive the pins right through the paper. Next, hammer in all the pins.

The pins must hold firmly and be accurately placed. Try to drive the pins in so they are perfectly perpendicular to the surface of the board. This is a task that requires dexterity and patience. Some pins can be straightened up a bit by bending them, but those made of hardened metal will break off if you try this. The head of each pin must also be the same distance from the surface of the board. Look at Illus. 310. The pins are $\frac{3}{16}$ inch apart and the head is the same distance from the board.

If you are going to paint the pins, wait until they are placed on the mounting base to apply first coat. Some paints require two coats (follow the instructions on the label of the can). If this is the case, sandpaper the surface again, very lightly without pressure, to remove any brush strokes before you apply the second coat. Also

use a damp cloth to remove any traces of dust before applying the final coat.

Even if you choose to cover the mounting board with cloth, sand the surface first to eliminate any roughness, ensuring close contact between the cloth and the board. Next, glue or

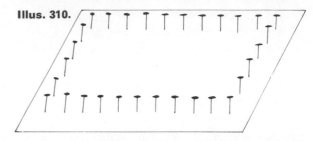

Illus. 310.

staple the cloth to the board. Stretch the cloth evenly and tightly over the surface. Cut out the excess material from the corners and pull the edges of the cloth tightly over the edges of the board, fastening it firmly to the back.

Rather than putting any marks on the cloth, fasten the paper diagram to it with masking tape. Then drive in the pins, right through each dot marked on the diagram. When this is done, simply lift the paper away.

With a cloth background, it is attractive to use gilt or brass pins.

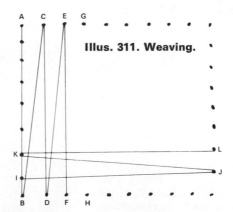

Illus. 311. Weaving.

Techniques

In this craft, all designs spring from four basic methods of connecting the pins—weaving, making pyramids, twisting, and forming arcs.

Weaving

To weave, tie the end of the wire to the first pin, marked A in Illus. 311. Pass the wire around

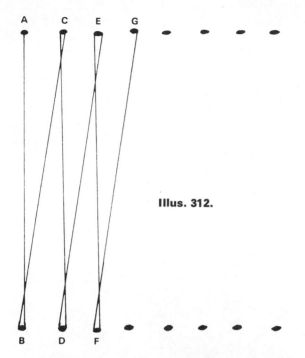

Illus. 312.

Tie the wire securely to pin A, which will be the peak of the pyramid. As you pass the wire around B, twist it completely around the pin and do the same for each of the following pins. For an example of this technique, see Illus. 353.

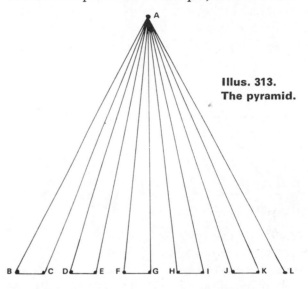

**Illus. 313.
The pyramid.**

pin B, directly opposite A, keeping it taut, but not excessively so. Next, run the wire around C, then opposite to D, continuing in the same manner until you reach the end of the row. Turn the board 90°, and repeat the procedure connecting I to J, J to K, K to L, and so on. Note that if you loop the wire around the tack from right to left, as in Illus. 312, the crosspoint of the wires adds an additional element to the design.

This technique is very simple, but studying it will give you a feel for the materials. It is important that you always begin and end the weaving process by tying secure knots—if the wire gives at either end, you will have to start over again. The knots will be hidden by the wires and will not show in the finished design.

The Pyramid

This design is easy to make: all you do is set up a row of pins facing a single, centrally located pin opposite as in Illus. 313. The design develops by running your wire from A to B, B to C, C to A, A to D, D to E, E to A, and so on, until you tie-off at L. In the case of an even number of pins in the row, you will finish back at A.

Twisting

Tie the wire to pin A and carry it over to pin B diagonally opposite, at the end of the second row. Run it back to the second pin in the first row, marked C in Illus. 314. Proceed in the same manner, passing the wire around all the

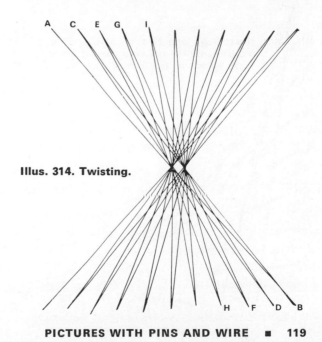

Illus. 314. Twisting.

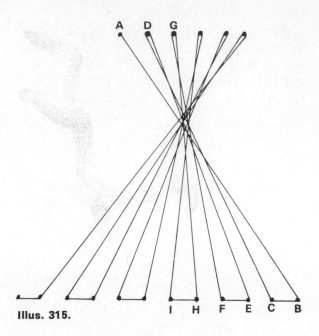

Illus. 315.

You can vary the design by passing the wire around a single pin in the upper row, but 2 successive pins in the lower row. The result, as you can see in Illus. 315, is to move the crosspoint of the wires away from the midpoint and closer to the top row.

Passing the wire around 2 pins at a time in both rows creates another slight variation, shown in Illus. 317.

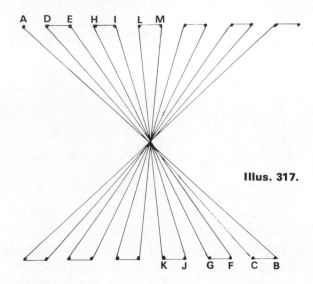

Illus. 317.

pins in both rows. In this example, you must have an equal number of pins in both rows.

Illus. 316. Use this technique of connecting points on two angled lines to form an arc or portion of a circle.

Arcs

The design in Illus. 316 is worked on 2 rows of pins set at a right angle to one another. Do not set a pin at the intersection of the lines. In this example, the 2 rows have the same number of pins. To make an arc, start at pin A at the top of the vertical row, passing the wire around pin B, at the beginning of the horizontal row. Run the wire back up to C, the second pin in the vertical row, then down to D, the second pin in the horizontal row. Continue connecting the pins in the same sequence until you arrive at the last pin in the horizontal row, completing the curve or arc.

Again, you can vary the design by looping the wire around a single pin in the vertical row, but 2 pins in the horizontal row as in Illus. 318. In this case, set an even number of pins in the horizontal row, only half the number plus one

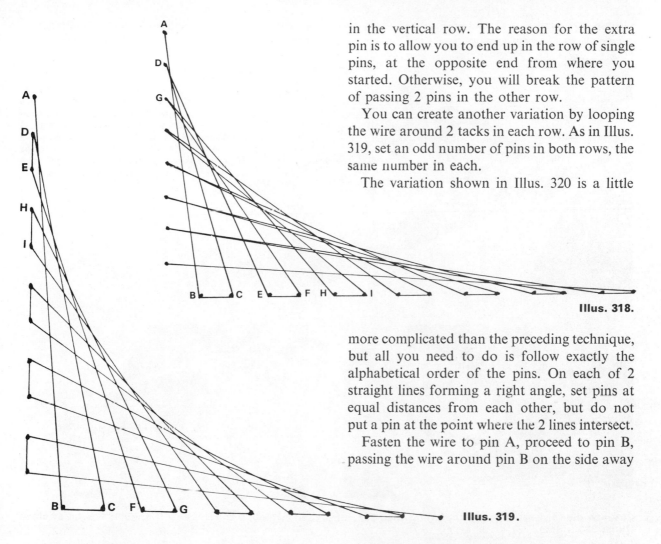

in the vertical row. The reason for the extra pin is to allow you to end up in the row of single pins, at the opposite end from where you started. Otherwise, you will break the pattern of passing 2 pins in the other row.

You can create another variation by looping the wire around 2 tacks in each row. As in Illus. 319, set an odd number of pins in both rows, the same number in each.

The variation shown in Illus. 320 is a little

Illus. 318.

more complicated than the preceding technique, but all you need to do is follow exactly the alphabetical order of the pins. On each of 2 straight lines forming a right angle, set pins at equal distances from each other, but do not put a pin at the point where the 2 lines intersect.

Fasten the wire to pin A, proceed to pin B, passing the wire around pin B on the side away

Illus. 319.

from pin C. Carry the wire around pin C on the side away from B and run it up to pin D. Now, from D, go back around C, passing the wire around the side towards B, the opposite of what you did before. Go on to B, once more passing the wire first around the side away from C. Continue on to E, passing the wire around the side away from A. Can you see how the pattern develops? Go on to F, then G, then H in the same way. Pass the wire around H and go back down again to G, passing the wire around the side facing C. Go back to F once more, passing the wire around the side away from B, going on then to I. Proceed according to this pattern until you have completed the arc.

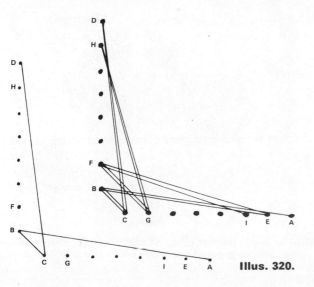

Illus. 320.

In Illus. 321-341 you will find step-by-step instructions for making the flower shown in color Illus. H1.

Illus. 321. The first step in making any pin picture is to prepare a sturdy base. Cut a piece of wood to the exact size of your plan, and a piece of felt or other material so that it extends at least 2 inches beyond each edge of the board. Staple or glue two opposite flaps of the material to the back of the board.

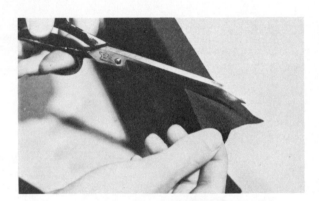

Cut into the top corner of the material (Illus. 322, left), then cut again to remove a triangular wedge of cloth (Illus. 323, right).

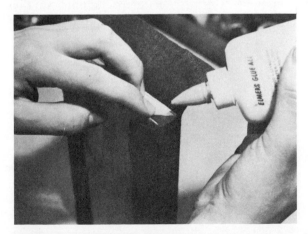

Wrap the remaining material around the corner of the board, using a spot of glue to hold it in place (Illus. 324, left). Fold the remaining flaps of cloth over onto the back of the board and secure them in place (Illus. 325, right).

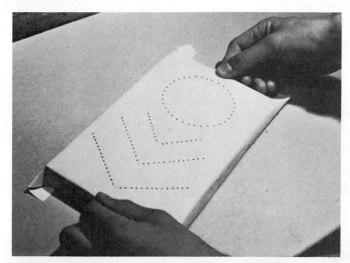

Illus. 326. Fold your paper pattern over the base, adjusting it for the proper margin on all sides. Your pattern should have a dot where each pin is to be placed.

 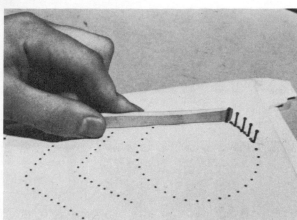

Now hammer the pins into the board (Illus. 327, left). Choose pins that are long enough to go at least $\frac{1}{4}$ inch into the wood and still leave at least $\frac{1}{4}$ inch exposed. Use a stick to check the height of the pins to be sure that they are all the same (Illus. 328, right).

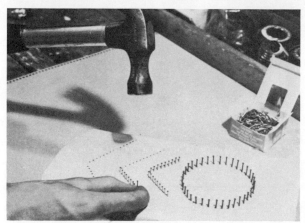 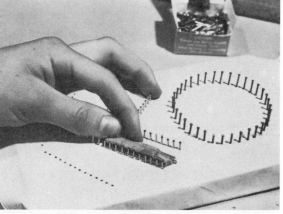

Illus. 329 (left). You will need to use taller pins when you plan to use several layers of wire for a three-dimensional effect. This project calls for 1-inch panel nails for the flower head, $\frac{5}{8}$-inch brads for the leaves. Again, use a piece of wood to check the height of the pins rather than measuring them one at a time (Illus. 330, right).

Illus. 331. When all of the pins are in place, just pull the pattern up over the nails.

Illus. 332. Check to be sure that all of the pins are evenly spaced. Use the blade of a screwdriver to make any necessary adjustments.

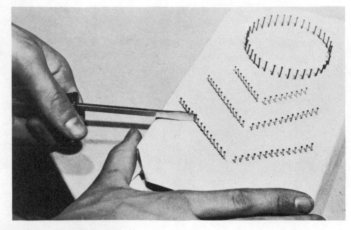

Illus. 333. When all of the pins are in place and properly spaced, you are ready to begin stringing the wire.

Illus. 334. Attach a #26-gauge (or finer) wire securely to one of the pins. The plan for this flower calls for you to connect pins along the circumference of a 36-pin circle. In making your pattern, use a protractor and mark off 10° angles so that the pins will be evenly spaced.

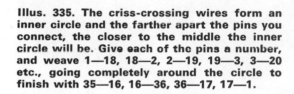

Illus. 335. The criss-crossing wires form an inner circle and the farther apart the pins you connect, the closer to the middle the inner circle will be. Give each of the pins a number, and weave 1—18, 18—2, 2—19, 19—3, 3—20 etc., going completely around the circle to finish with 35—16, 16—36, 36—17, 17—1.

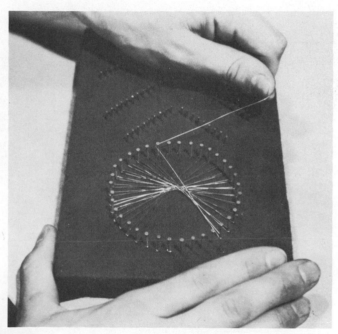

Illus. 336. When the first layer is complete, secure the end of the wire to the pin where you started. For a pleasing contrast, switch to a different-colored wire for the next layer.

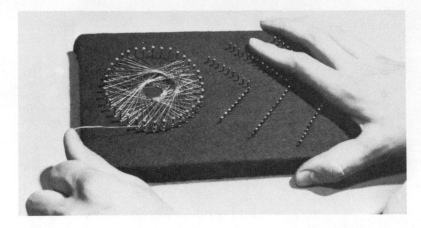

Illus. 337. For the second layer, run your wire 1—14, 14—2, 2—15, 15—3, 3—16, etc.

Illus. 338. The wiring plan for the top layer is 1—10, 10—2, 2—11, 11—3, 3—12, etc. Finish this before starting on the leaves.

Illus. 339. Make the leaves by connecting equal numbers of pins along two lines. The crisscrossing wires form an arc, a portion of a circle.

Illus. 340. For the final touch, add a stem. This can be a thicker wire fastened in place or two pins with thin wire stretched between them.

Illus. 341. Here is the finished flower which you can see in full color in color Illus. H1.

Illus. 342. This abstract design makes an excellent project for beginners. Note the change in effect when the rod is moved up or down, or the work displayed vertically (Illus. 343).

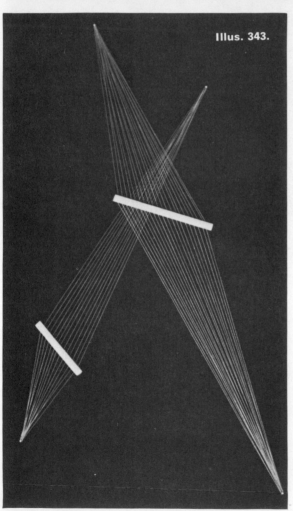

Illus. 343.

Abstract Designs

The abstract form shown in Illus. 342 is easy to do. You need only set 2 pins into a plywood board and pass the wire back and forth between them. To create a decorative composition, place 4 pins at varying distances from one another. Drill 10 or more small holes into 2 little rods of soft wood, which serve to hold the wires apart.

Knot the end of your wire to one of the nails, then pass it through the first hole of one of the rods. Pass the wire around the opposite pins, then back through the second hole in the rod and to the first pin. Continue going back and forth between the pins, passing the wire each time through the next hole in the rod. When the wire has been passed through all the holes, tie it to the next pin.

Proceed in the same manner with the second rod and pair of pins. By sliding the rod up or down, you can change the structure of each group of wires.

Linear Structures

To make the design shown in Illus. 344, place your pins $\frac{3}{16}$ inch apart along the straight lines. The exact form of these depends upon the apertures of the angles marked BHJ and KLM

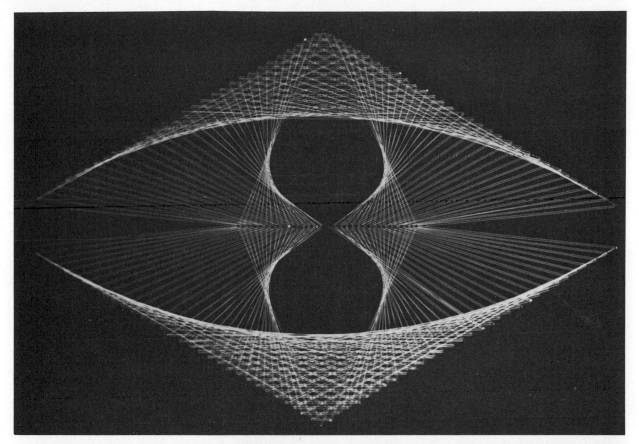

Illus. 344. Note the illusion of depth in this ultra-modern construction. It is far easier to build than it looks.

in Illus. 345. Wide angles that are nearly straight lines produce long, narrow forms. Angles that are not so wide, produce thicker forms.

To make the design shown, place an equal (and an even) number of pins along lines BH, HJ, KL, and LM. Place half that number of pins on lines GA and AI (pins L, A, and H each count in 2 lines).

Start stringing from the midpoint A and pass your wire around pins B and C, then bring it back towards pin D. Go around only the one pin in the middle row, then go back up and around E and F. Complete this twisting process when you reach G by proceeding to H and tying your wire. Repeat this pattern on lines AI and HJ. Do the same with AG and KL, AI and LM.

Once you have done the 4 twisting operations,

all you have left to do is construct arcs in the angles BHJ and KLM.

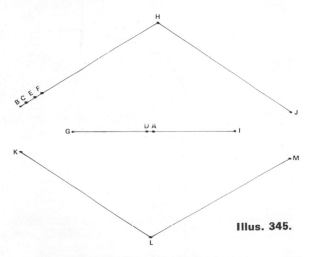

Illus. 345.

Four-Leaf Clover

To produce the design in Illus. 347, draw a circle and divide it into 4 equal segments—that is, make 4 right angles at the midpoint by constructing 2 diameters perpendicular to each other. Place pins around the outside of the circle at $\frac{3}{16}$-inch intervals, and insert pins the same distance apart along both diameters.

Following the pattern in Illus. 346, attach your wire firmly to pin A at the midpoint. Pass the wire around pin B, then bring it back just short of the midpoint to pin C. From there go to D, then E, then F, then G, and so on, until you have used all the pins along the first segment of the circle. Since the segment of the circle is longer than the radius, increase the space between the pins on the circumference so that the number equals the number of pins on the radius. Alternatively, you can keep the spacing the same and put more pins on the circumference, either turning the corner when

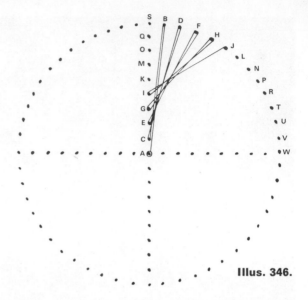

Illus. 346.

you come to the end of the radius and connecting pins along the circumference until you reach pin W-S to T, T to B, B to U, and so on— or stop short along the circumference when you have connected the last pin of the radius.

Illus. 347. The four-leaf clover looks particularly striking on a black background with silvered or steel wire.

Illus. 348. To create this double rosette, complete the inner rosette first, then the outer circle, following the pattern in Illus. 349.

Proceed clockwise to the next segment of the circle, until all 4 segments have been completed in the same manner. At this point, you will have linear structures suggesting the appearance of half leaves. To get whole leaves, repeat what you have already done but this time go counter-clockwise working the opposite side of each angle.

Double Rosette

Divide a circle into 6 equal parts. Using a protractor, mark off 6 angles of 60° each. Now, draw a smaller circle using the same midpoint. Place pins at $\frac{3}{16}$-inch intervals around the circumferences of both circles and all 3 diameters as indicated in Illus. 349.

Start from the midpoint A, then go up to pin B, back to pin C and follow through to complete the smaller rosette. For the outer rosette, begin at the pin marked R in Illus. 349 (at the intersection of the inner circle and a radius). Go to S, T, U, and so on, to complete

the design. Since there are more pins on the circumference than on the portion of the radius, stop short along the circle when the last pin of the radius is connected.

Always work in the same direction to produce even, precise work. When doing the four-leaf clover or the double rosette, for example, first do the 4 arcs to the right, then work back towards the left.

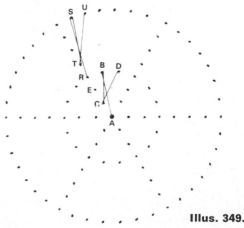

Illus. 349.

Fish

Following the outline in Illus. 351, draw 2 straight lines, AB and CD, which intersect at E. Add 2 straight lines AF and CF, meeting at F. Set pins at $\frac{3}{16}$-inch intervals on lines AE and AF. Now, it is very important to have the same

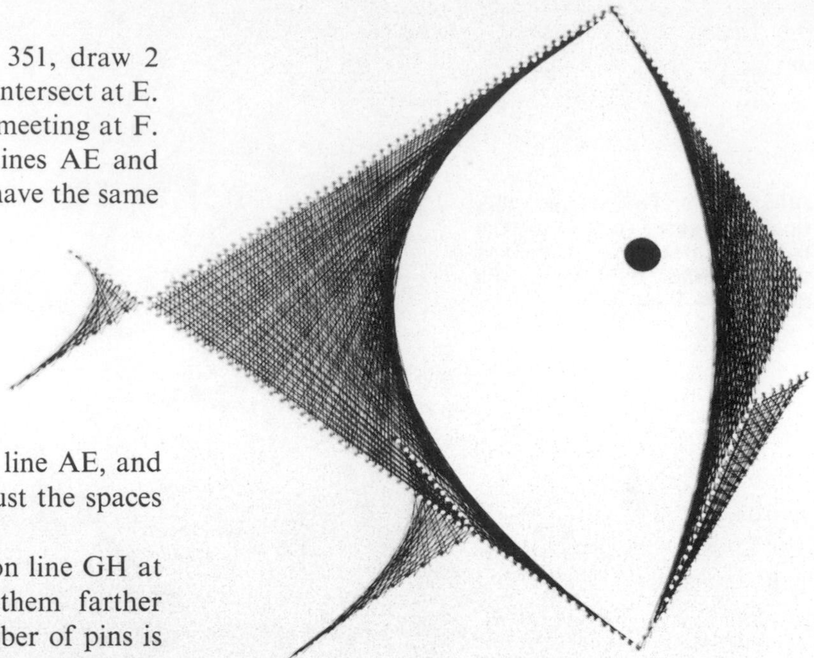

Illus. 350. Completed fish.

number of pins on line CE as on line AE, and on line CF as on line AF, so adjust the spaces on these lines accordingly.

For the lower fin, set the pins on line GH at the normal interval, but place them farther apart on line HI, so that the number of pins is the same for each line. Do the same thing for the fish's tail, making the pins on line BE farther apart than those on line DE so that, again, the number of pins on each line is the same.

The mouth of the fish must be done another way. To create the effect in Illus. 309, the light fish on the dark background, set pins on line CL equal in number to the pins from C to

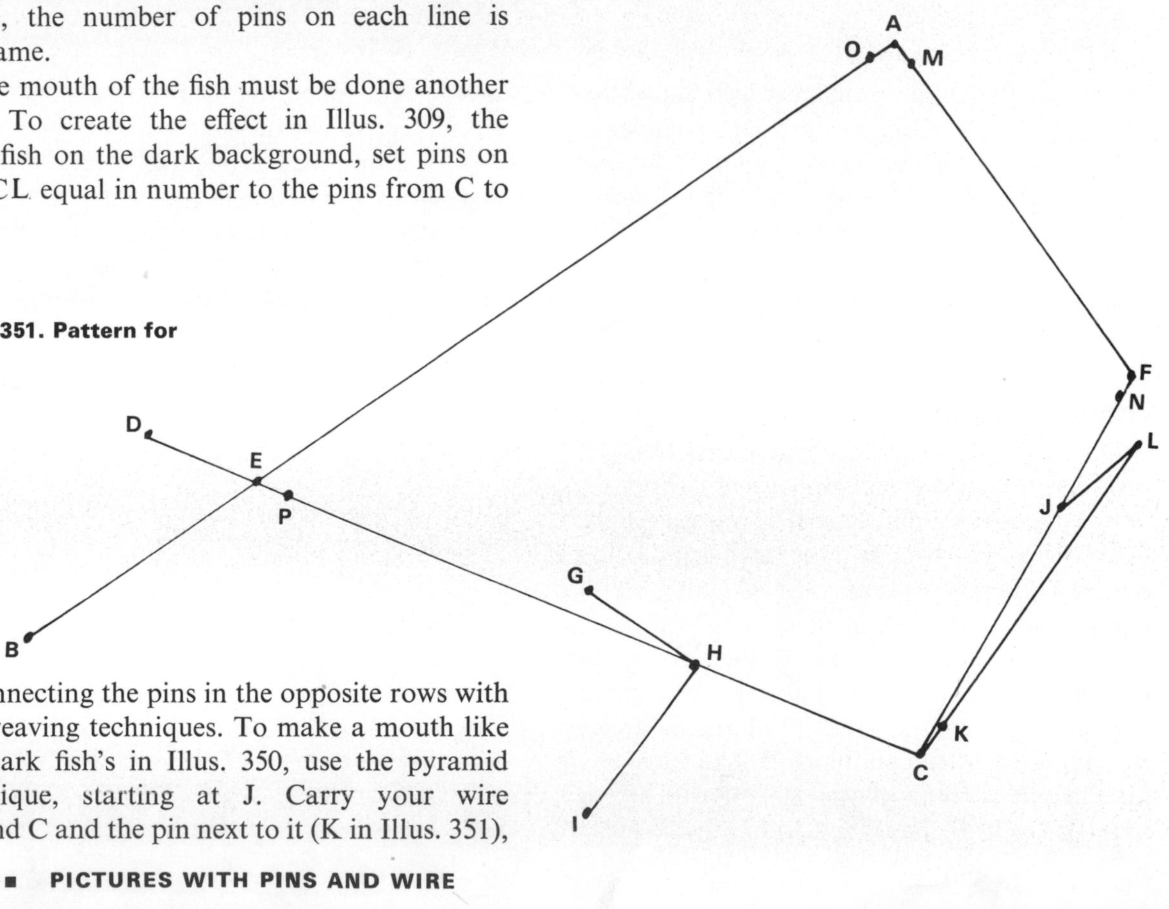

Illus. 351. Pattern for fish.

J, connecting the pins in the opposite rows with the weaving techniques. To make a mouth like the dark fish's in Illus. 350, use the pyramid technique, starting at J. Carry your wire around C and the pin next to it (K in Illus. 351), then back to J, repeating the pattern until you reach pin L.

For the body of the fish, form an arc by tying the wire to pin A, going to F, then back to M, the first pin down from A. Proceed to N, the first pin down from F, and continue this pattern until you reach C. To complete the body, start again at A, going to E, then up to O, the pin next to A. Go down to P and so on until you reach pin C.

For the tail, make an arc, beginning at B and going to E.

The fish picture is only one of many linear structures you can make by varying the basic arc design. It is just a matter of finding a subject and using your imagination in working out the different patterns.

Boat

The boat in Illus. 353 was worked on a plywood board 32 × 28 inches. Draw 3 angles as in Illus. 352, 2 acute (ABC and DEF) and 1 obtuse (GHI). Make line AB equal to line BC so they will have the same number of pins set at $\frac{3}{16}$-inch intervals. Make line DE twice as long as line EF and set twice as many pins along it. Line GH must also be longer than line HI, but keep the number of pins on each line the same by spacing those on GH farther apart.

Form arcs in each of the 3 angles. For the mast, simply run a wire from J to K, going twice around each pin. Do the mast before the hull, so that pin K is covered up when you do the lower arc.

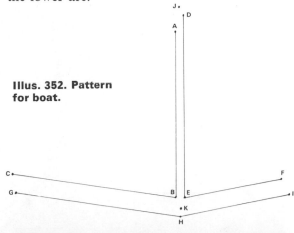

Illus. 352. Pattern for boat.

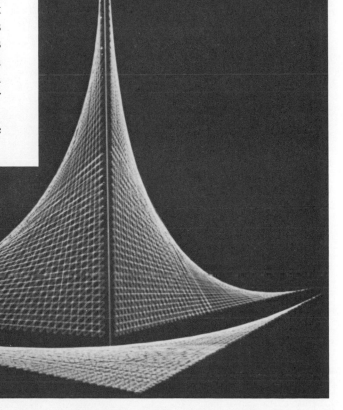

Illus. 353. Boat.

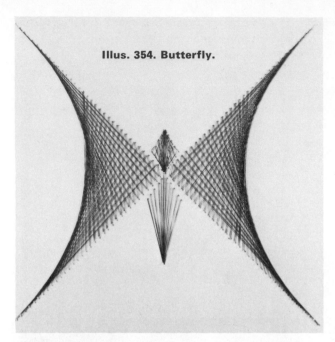
Illus. 354. Butterfly.

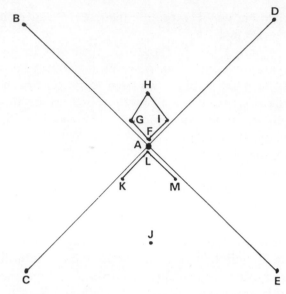
Illus. 355. Pattern for butterfly.

Butterfly

Arrange your pins as shown in Illus. 355. To make the wings, construct 2 arcs in the angles BAC and DAE. For the lower part of the body, make a pyramid, connecting pin J to one pin at a time along lines KL and LM.

Form the head of the butterfly with 2 pyramids, the first connecting pin F with one pin at a time along lines GH and HI. Make the second pyramid by starting from the opposite side at pin H and proceeding along GF and FI.

Cat

This project introduces a new technique, connecting pins along the circumference of the same circle to produce a design of the type shown in Illus. 356. As you will see, the closer together the pins that you connect, the nearer to the circumference the inner circle formed by the wires will be. The farther apart the pins you connect, the closer to the middle the inner circle will be.

Set your pins according to the pattern in Illus. 358. Start at pin A, carrying the wire to pin B, back to C, then to D and E, and so on, until you reach pin L. Refer to Illus. 357 showing the finished project to see the effect.

The fine, flourishing tail begins at pin O. From there, go to pin P, then back to Q, continuing until you reach U.

For the main part of the head, make arcs within the form of a circle, connecting pins about 45° (1/8th of the circumference) apart. Start at pin K at the base of one ear and continue until you reach pin N at the base of the other ear. Form the ears by stringing arcs in the angles MYK and MZN.

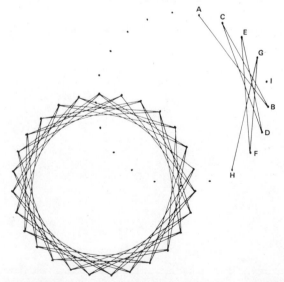
Illus. 356. Use the pattern shown here to create circles like the one at left.

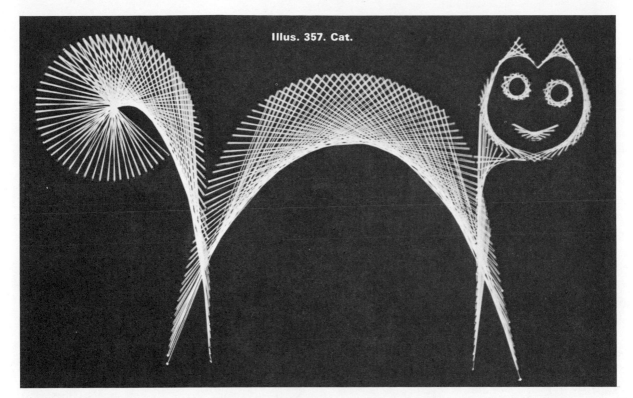

Illus. 357. Cat.

Make the cat's eyes by completing 2 small circles with the method shown in Illus. 356. Make the mouth by stringing a curved line the same way you did the outline of the head.

To give the cat its fourth leg, make a pyramid by starting at F, proceeding to G, then to H. For the neck, make a small arc from I, connecting with the pins on the circle forming the head.

Begin from I and go around V, then back to J and around W, continuing until you have formed an arc.

This cat picture is just a point of departure for the innumerable designs you can create by modifying and combining these same basic forms. It is easy to create satisfying works of your own.

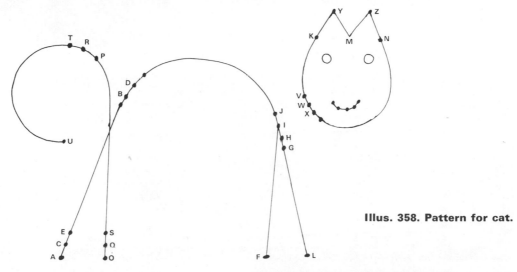

Illus. 358. Pattern for cat.

Working with Metal Foil

Thin metal, called foil, is generally used in projects that involve metal tooling or "repoussage"—the technique of raising designs on a sheet of metal so that they stand out from the flat background. Most foil is made of copper or aluminum and the thickness of the metal you use is important. Thickness is expressed in terms of gauge, and 36-gauge is right for most metal-tooling projects. This gauge is heavy enough for plaques, mobiles and free-standing sculpture, yet soft enough to be cut with a scissors and worked with simple wooden tools. The 36-gauge foil is usually sold in rolls. Aluminum is only about one third the cost of copper, but both are relatively inexpensive. Heavier metal is sold in sheets and is not only more expensive, but more difficult to work. Do not try to tool sheet metal thicker than 20-gauge.

You can try your hand at tooling without buying any metal. Just use the aluminum containers for frozen meals, pies and such that come your way. Either aluminum or copper foil can be cut with ordinary household scissors. The only other "tools" you need are blunt instruments, such as the end of a spoon handle, lollipop sticks, ice-cream sticks, or wooden stir sticks. Inexpensive boxwood

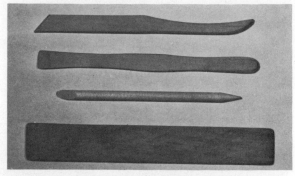

Illus. 359. Boxwood modelling tools.

modelling tools are also available at hobby shops (Illus. 359). These generally come in sets and both ends of the tools are used to achieve various textures and patterns. You can also buy steel tools for use on thicker sheets (Illus. 360).

Illus. 360. Steel modelling tools.

Illus. 361. This decorative embossed panel, modelled after an ancient Egyptian fresco, is the work of a group of teenagers.

A hard rubber mat makes an ideal support for working but you can also use a thick felt mat. Rubber, however, has both the resistance and suppleness necessary for an embossing support (a triple thickness of blotters or a pad of newspapers will serve the same purpose).

Each of the regular modelling tools has a definite purpose. The curved, flat ends are used to smooth large surfaces, the ball ends to emboss large sections, and the narrow, pointed ends to emphasize the finer details.

A soft marking pencil, such as a china marker, a grease pencil, or chalk is required to mark patterns on the metal. For glueing metal, an epoxy cement is best.

Technique

Before beginning a project using an entire sheet of metal, you should experiment on some scraps to determine the resistance of the metal to the pressure of your hand. Take some aluminum about 0.1 mm. thick—this will be especially malleable and easy to work with. First make several very simple linear outlines with the pointed end of the No. 1 modelling tool (Illus. 362). Do not press hard—a little light pressure is advisable to start.

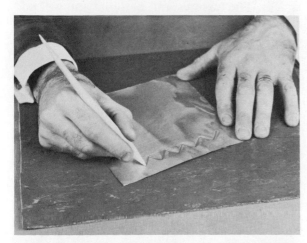
Illus. 362. Make several outlines on a piece of scrap metal to master the proper touch.

Turn the sheet over and define the outlines of your design with the pointed end of the No. 2 tool (Illus. 363).

Illus. 363. When you have a pleasing design, turn the sheet over and define the outlines.

Complete several experiments until you feel really sure of yourself. Do not hurry—the major requirement for obtaining a carefully done piece of work is patience. If you try to emboss a large area too quickly, you risk thinning out the metal beyond its resistance limit. It will become fragile and more and more difficult to work with. You also risk breaking through the sheet with the tool. If an accident of this type should happen in your first attempts, do not worry—you need to learn the limits to the amount of embossing you can obtain in relation to the resistance of the metal.

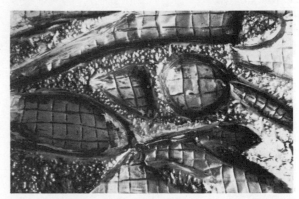
Illus. 364. The raised dots in this example come from stippling the reverse side.

Texturing

You may also want to give some of the areas of your work a textured finish. Parallel lines, checkerboard patterns, tiny star shapes, circles,

Illus. 365. The variety of textures and patterns here creates a rich, ornamental effect.

triangles, and squares are just a few of the possibilities. Try to limit the kinds of designs and textures you use for any one project, but do experiment with different kinds of tools—the edge of a spoon or even a toothpick as well as the usual modelling tools. Repetition and balance are important in creating effective tooled designs just as they are in all arts and crafts.

Save your practice pieces for inspiration when you are working on a project. Be sure to note what tool you used so you can re-create the texture again when you need it. Remember to leave some of the areas smooth and plain as shown in these examples, so that your designs don't become too "busy."

It is wise to experiment in this way on whatever metal you intend to use for a specific project. In time, it will become second nature.

Tool a Free-Form Picture

Even the youngest craftsman can make a handsome, free-form tooled picture in very little time! First, make a simple "scribble" drawing on a piece of paper (Illus. 367). Let the lines run off the paper and back on again. Keep your design free of minute details and shapes. The textures and patterns you will add later to the metal will give the composition plenty of variety and interest.

Illus. 366. This dogwood blossom design features grooved "veins" and a stippled background.

Illus. 367. Keep the lines of your design simple to leave room for texturing.

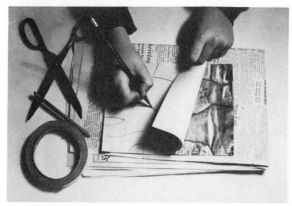

Illus. 368. Place your paper sketch over the metal and trace the lines with a pencil.

Now, cut a piece of aluminum or copper foil the exact size of your drawing and lay it on your support mat. Tape your line drawing onto the foil so it won't shift while you trace over the lines of the design with a pencil. The cushion beneath the metal allows you to create a sharp distinct line on the metal (Illus. 368).

When the transfer is complete, study your design to decide which areas you want to be raised and which to be recessed. Call these areas "ups" and "downs" to avoid confusion. You will tool the ups from the back side of the metal and the downs from the front side. Mark your ups and downs on the line drawing, so you won't lose track of what you are doing and accidentally tool an area from the wrong side.

When you decide which areas are to be ups, first work from the reverse side with the point of a tool, making a line approximately ¼ inch within each of the up shapes. Then turn back to the front side, and with the blunt end of your tool, rub carefully all the down areas just up to the original lines. The line you made inside the ups should then create a sort of "cliff" between the ups and downs. Then reverse the sheet and rub all the up areas. Alternate this procedure back and forth until

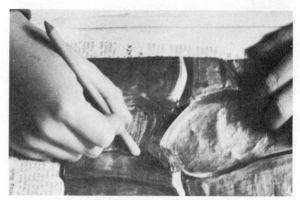

Illus. 369. Rub in the "ups" and "downs" with a blunt tool.

your ups and downs are firmly established (Illus. 369).

Now you can enhance your picture with the addition of textures and patterns. For your first try, use one or two uniform textures. In Illus. 370, the craftsman is using the point of a

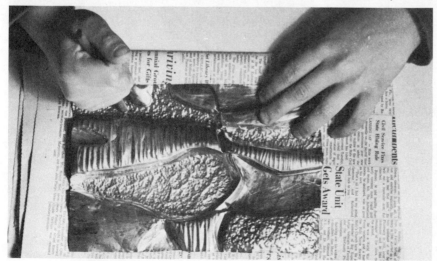

Illus. 370. Refer to Illus. 364-366 for texturing ideas, or just create your own.

wooden stick to create a stippled effect in the down areas, and a striped pattern in the up areas. When you are working with the point of any tool, be careful that you do not puncture the metal. Always practice working a texture on a piece of scrap metal first, to acquire the right touch.

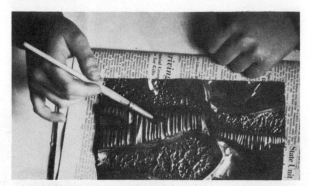

Illus. 371. Brush on diluted liver of sulphur for an antiqued effect.

Antiquing

As a final touch, you can give an antique finish to your design. For antiquing a work on copper foil, use liver of sulphur which oxidizes copper. For antiquing aluminum foil, follow the directions on page 142.

Liver of sulphur (potassium sulphide) is available at your pharmacy, as well as in craft supply shops, and is perfectly safe to handle, since it is not harmful to the skin.

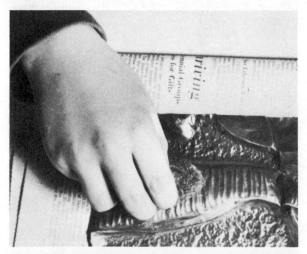

Illus. 372. Bring up the highlights of the antiqued piece with steel wool.

First dissolve a few lumps of liver of sulphur in a pint of water. Although you can use a brush to apply the solution to the copper, a sponge is more useful because you can use it to wipe off any excess fluid from the inner recesses of the design. (If it is left there, it might turn a chalky color later on.) Also, the hairs of some paint-brushes sometimes curl tightly when exposed to liver of sulphur.

After giving your picture a thorough sponging, allow it to dry. The copper should turn black. Depending upon the humidity and amount of solution you applied, the drying will take somewhere in the vicinity of 20 minutes. When you are sure it is completely dry, rub the

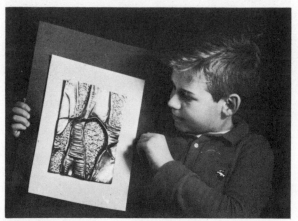

Illus. 373. As you can see, metal tooling is so easy a child can do it.

copper lightly with fine-grained steel wool to create a contrast of highlights and darker areas (Illus. 372). The low areas and the textures will remain darker and the raised shapes should begin to show their copper color.

In time, the dark areas of the copper may become light grey or chalky, since the oxidation process can continue beyond the rubbing stage. To avoid this, apply a coat of shellac, varnish, or clear lacquer as a last step. If you want a matt finish, use a spray shellac.

As you can see in Illus. 373, you can glue your copper-foil picture to tagboard, using white glue, and then glue the tagboard to a piece of black construction paper, creating a double border.

Cut Outs

For a slightly more ambitious project, you may want to try your hand at tooling and cutting out a design from the bottom of an aluminum cake or frozen lasagna container.

Illus. 374. A cut-out tooled flower.

To begin, flatten out and smooth the aluminum pan as shown in Illus. 375. If there are any lines or raised areas embossed on the pan, use the blunt end of a modelling tool to eliminate them so they will not interfere with your tooled design.

Next, make a simple flower sketch and place it on the aluminum, making sure you have a pad of newspapers beneath the metal. Using an old ballpoint pen (with no ink in it), transfer the design onto the aluminum by tracing over it

Illus. 375. First remove any embossed areas on the container with a blunt tool.

(Illus. 376). Then go over the lines on the aluminum itself with the ballpoint pen to strengthen them (Illus. 377).

Now, with the ballpoint pen, draw a line approximately $\frac{1}{8}$ inch inside the contours of all the up shapes (Illus. 378) on the *reverse* side.

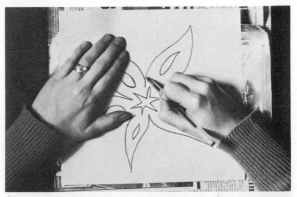

Illus. 376. Transfer your design to the metal surface.

Illus. 377. Deepen the lines with an empty ballpoint pen.

Illus. 378. On the reverse side, outline the design $\frac{1}{8}$ inch inside the ups.

Staying on the reverse side, rub the areas inside the double line with the blunt end of a tool (Illus. 379). Then turn to the front side and rub the down areas; avoid touching the parts between the double lines.

As shown in Illus. 380, add patterns and textures with the sharp point of a tool. In Illus. 381, a line pattern is being added to the reverse side of the up areas to simulate leaf textures.

Illus. 381. Then, on the reverse side, put in line patterns on the leaves with a pointed tool.

Illus. 379. Still on the reverse side, rub in the ⅛-inch area between the two lines.

Antiquing Aluminum

Now your aluminum flower is ready for antiquing. You will use India ink for this process because liver of sulphur, which you used to antique your copper piece, does not oxidize aluminum. India ink can be tricky to apply because it has a tendency to resist the smooth metal and collect into droplets and puddles. To prevent this, rub the aluminum first with a piece of steel wool (Illus. 382). This will dull the surface and remove oily fingerprints which might also cause resistance. If the ink still resists the metal, add a little kitchen cleanser to the ink.

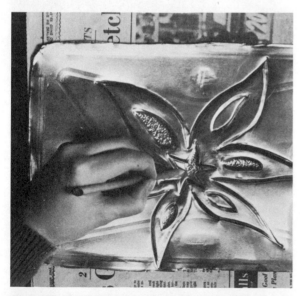

Illus. 380. On the front side, add a stippled texture to some of the down areas. The remaining areas will be cut out after antiquing.

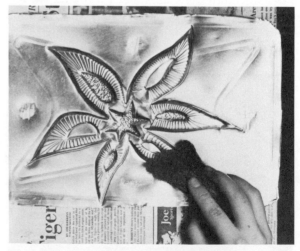

Illus. 382. Now you are ready to antique your design with India ink. Begin by rubbing the aluminum surface with steel wool.

Liberally paint the flower surface with ink (Illus. 383, left). When the ink is nearly dry, rub lightly with a paper towel and then with steel wool (Illus. 384, right).

Spread the ink all over the surface with a brush (Illus. 383). When the ink is almost completely dry, rub the surface with a paper towel and steel wool. Be careful not to rub the aluminum too hard or you will remove too much ink (Illus. 384). The downs and the little recesses in your textures should remain fairly dark in order to provide contrast with shiny ups.

Now you can cut out your flower. Use heavy scissors to cut out the large shapes and a utility knife or single-edged razor blade for the small areas (Illus. 385). Never cut out before you have inked and buffed the metal, because the steel wool will tear or bend the edges of the aluminum.

Intaglio

Besides designs in relief, you can make very effective hollowed-out decorations by a process similar to intaglio printing—a process where the metal is cut into, treated, inked and scraped. The ink remaining in the etched lines is then transferred from the plate to produce a print. Metalcrafting intaglio, however, is a simple process and combines well with repoussage.

The design in Illus. 386 was sketched on a sheet of tracing paper, attached to the metal sheet with transparent tape, and placed on a mat. After lightly retracing the outlines of the design with a ballpoint pen, lift the tracing paper and use a metal stylus to go over the light tracing left on the metal. A little drop of oil on the stylus will help it move easily. After the outline is deeply etched into the metal,

Illus. 385. Cut away the excess.

Illus. 386. Intaglio.

soak a brush in water and coat it lightly with Castile soap. Then using black gouache, cover the entire surface of the metal. When this is *thoroughly* dry, polish the sheet with fine emery paper or steel wool, taking care to always rub in the same direction and with a consistent pressure to avoid roughness. The grooves, not touched by the emery paper, will remain black, while all the other parts of the surface will return to their original color.

Illus. 387. Sunburst designs.

Metal Foil Projects

There are innumerable possibilities for creating useful and decorative objects. On the following pages are suggestions for simple projects to adorn your daily surroundings, create a particular atmosphere for a holiday, or as last-minute gift ideas—especially for all those days when you feel creative but not very energetic!

Sunbursts

Use a 4-inch-square piece of aluminum foil to work these attractive designs. Place this square on a flat, hard surface and, in order to avoid making an impression in the metal, use a grease pencil or soft chalk to draw in the diagonals of the square. Their point of intersection is the middle of the sheet. Measure about 1 inch out from this point on each diagonal

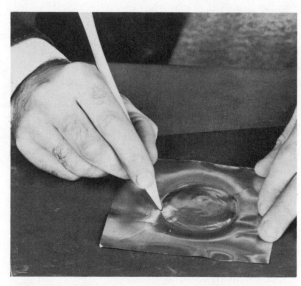

Illus. 389. Define the edge of the outline with the pointed end of the modelling tool.

and use these four points as a guide to mark a circle. Then measure 1 inch out from the circle on each diagonal—these will be the sun's rays. Draw in a number of rays to use as a guide for the embossing. Do not worry if you make a mistake because you can erase it easily by rubbing with your finger or a cloth.

Now place the square on your mat. Using the rounded edge of the No. 1 tool, move it in a circular fashion within the outline of the sun, exerting a constant and consistent pressure all

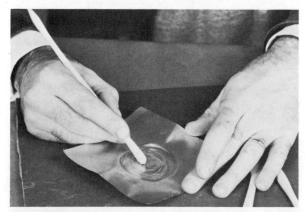

Illus. 388. Use the rounded end of the No. 1 tool with a circular motion, exerting a steady pressure, to form a depression.

the time (Illus. 388). As soon as you have formed a hollowed-out depression, turn the sheet over and define the edges of the repoussage with the sharp edge of the No. 1 modelling tool (Illus. 389). Turn the sheet back over once more and hollow it out even deeper (Illus. 390). Repeat this operation as many times as necessary until you obtain the desired amount of embossing, taking care not to overdo it, thereby weakening the metal.

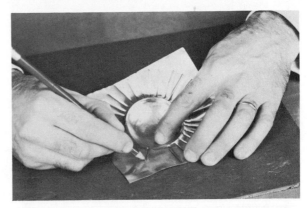

Illus. 391. Once the central area is completed, draw in the rays of the sun.

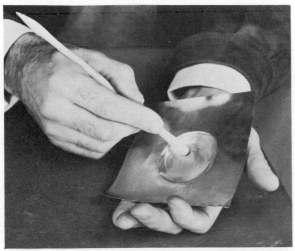

Illus. 390. Turn the sheet over again and deepen the hollow until the embossing is satisfactory.

Draw in the rays of the sun with crayon or grease pencil (Illus. 391) and work them in the same way as the circle. Turn the sheet over and sharpen the edges of the rays with the pointed end of either the No. 1 or No. 2 tool. Flatten the areas round the rays with the wide end of No. 3 modelling tool (Illus. 392). When you are satisfied with the effect, proceed to make some of the interesting sunburst designs on page 144.

Following this procedure, working alternately on both sides of the metal to define the embossing, the metal will not be extended past the limit of its resistance and the sections that are not embossed will remain flat.

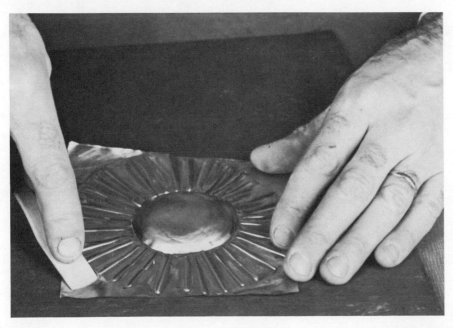

Illus. 392. After defining again the outlines of both the circle and the rays, flatten the metal between the rays with the No. 3 modelling tool.

Wall Plaques

Tooled copper and aluminum are ideal materials for making unique wall plaques and hangings. You can make plaques from flat pieces of foil and mount them on various materials, frame them, or even create intriguing cut-out designs with their own frames.

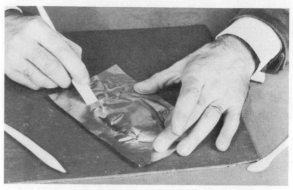

Illus. 394. After embossing the fins and the tail, work the body again to achieve a greater depth.

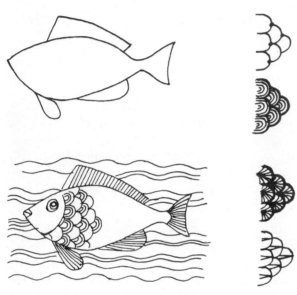

Illus. 393. You can use these patterns to make the embossed fish in Illus. 396.

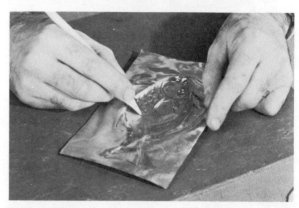

Illus. 395. Using the pointed end of the No. 1 tool, outline the lines in the fins and tail, the eye, the gills and then the scales.

Illus. 396. Just as you did for the sunburst, define the outlines of the embossing. Use the pointed end of the No. 1 tool to make wavy water lines around your fish.

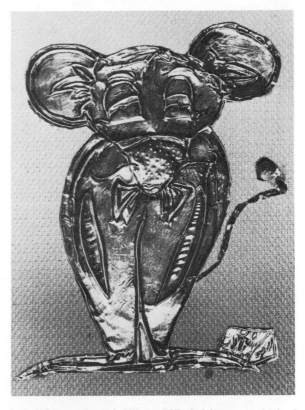

A bright-eyed owl (Illus. 397, left) or a comical mouse (Illus. 398, above) make charming embossed wall ornaments.

Illus. 399. A copper bird plaque is shown framed by burlap (hessian) and white wood.

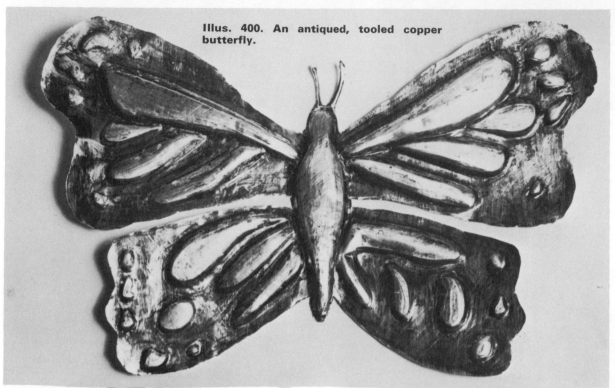

Illus. 400. An antiqued, tooled copper butterfly.

Illus. 401. This attractive floral cut-out design was made using just ordinary scissors.

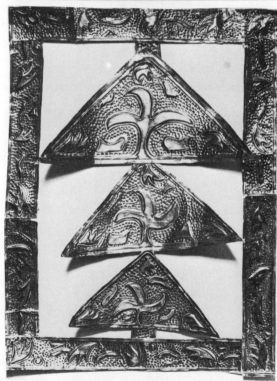

Illus. 402. The individual pieces of this design were cut from aluminum and assembled with epoxy cement.

A Medallion Plaque

To make a medallion such as the one in Illus. 405, you will probably want to use a model or reproduction as a basis for your design. You can either make a sketch or you can trace it. For this first step, draw or trace the outlines and the main lines only.

Turn the tracing *face down* on the sheet of metal. (If you don't, the embossing will be reversed.) Tape the paper securely to the metal. Now, transfer the design to the metal by going

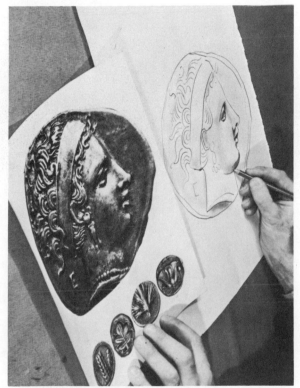

Illus. 403. Either trace or draw freehand the main outlines of the design on tracing paper.

over it with a hard pencil or a ballpoint pen, bearing down hard enough to make an impression on the metal.

Tool the whole surface until it is sufficiently hollowed out. Then emboss the specific areas such as nose, or cheek, beginning with the smallest part and working up to the largest. Then, on the tracing paper, draw the fine details—eye, mouth, ear, hair, and transfer them to the metal as you did the main lines.

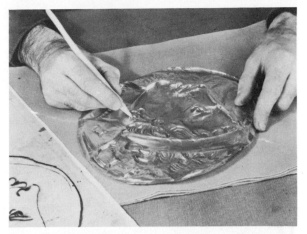

Illus. 404. Once the traced outlines are hollowed out of the metal, emboss the details, beginning with the smallest.

Emboss these details, turning the sheet over frequently and defining the relief. When you do this on small areas, place a finger on the underside of the part you are defining and press slightly against the tool. In this way, you will lessen the likelihood of breaking through the metal.

For a detailed piece of relief such as this plaque, it is wise to fill the hollows with plaster so that they do not crush. A metal-foil cement is available for this purpose from craft supply houses. You can make a satisfactory temporary "plaster" by mixing flour and water together to a very thick consistency. After applying, let it dry thoroughly.

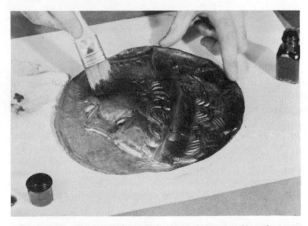

Illus. 405. When the embossing is completed, coat the surface with an artificial patina, as described on page 44.

Mobiles

Lightness, brilliance, color—these are the qualities required in the material used in making mobiles. And nothing could be better suited than the aluminum and copper foil you use for embossing—it is ideal for making eye-catching objects, and light enough to move at the slightest breeze. Also, the pieces of metal act as a wind chime as they touch against each other. The following objects can either be combined to make mobiles, or you can compose mobiles of similar elements—fish mobiles, bird mobiles, and so on. (The small stars and angels on pages 152 and 153 make an impressive Christmas mobile.) You can use string, nylon thread, or very fine wire to suspend the figures.

Be sure to make paper patterns before working with the metal—it's easier to correct a mistake on paper than on metal!

Bird of Paradise

Illus. 406. Cut the patterns shown from two sheets of metal, delicately notching the end of the long tail and the base of the wings. After embossing the two pieces of the bird, put a dab of glue in slits "a" and "b" and assemble.

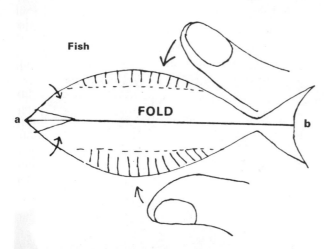

Fish

FOLD

Illus. 407. This stylized fish may be made several times for a fish mobile or combined with other aquatic creatures. Since your mobile parts will be small, keep the form and design as simple as possible. Emboss simple scales, gills and eyes. Cut the fish from a single piece of metal and fold lightly along the median line (a-b) from head to tail, creating a three-dimensional effect as shown in the rear view below.

rear view

Carousel

Illus. 408. The roof of this charming carousel mobile is made of an aluminum pie plate. Holes are poked through the plate so the braided cord which holds the figures can be inserted and knotted.

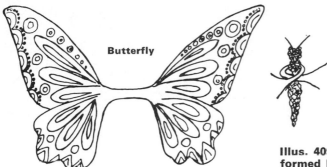

Butterfly

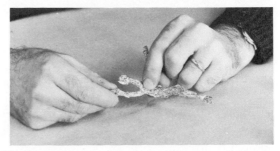

Illus. 409. The butterfly is made in two parts: the body, formed by crushing very thin metal (see photo above), and the wings, attached by coiling the band in the middle around the crushed-metal body.

Illus. 411. Tool twelve aluminum discs of the same size, glue them together in four rows of three, then glue the rows together with epoxy glue on the overlapping edges as shown. Use leather thongs to attach this construction to a thirteenth small disc and hang from the ceiling.

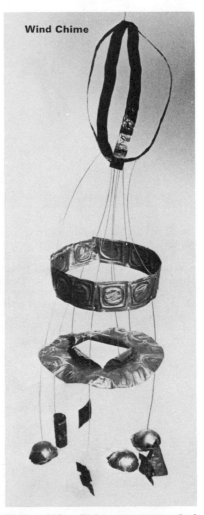

Wind Chime

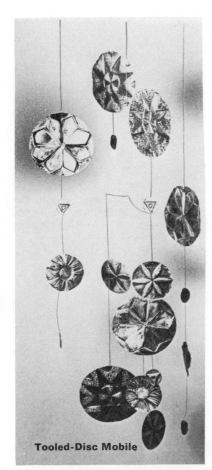

Tooled-Disc Mobile

Illus. 410. Let your imagination take over when tooling the discs which make up this mobile. Arrange them to suit your taste, then attach them with nylon thread to a wooden cross and suspend the cross from the ceiling.

Hanging Construction

Illus. 412. This copper wind chime is held together with nylon thread laced through pierced holes. The small pieces at bottom tinkle when the breeze blows.

Christmas Ornaments

One of the most effective ways to put your tooling to use is in making shiny Christmas tree ornaments. The special quality of tooled and antiqued aluminum or copper is ideal for holiday decoration.

Stars

Illus. 413. To make the six-sided star shown above, cut out a tracing-paper circle and mark off six equal parts. Cut out the resulting triangles and trace this design on a piece of aluminum. Cut out the star, trace the lines going through the middle of the star and emboss the sections as shown in Illus. 414 (below). Fold each point by pressing on each side as illustrated.

Illus. 415 (above) and 416 (below) show the special quality of handmade Christmas tree ornaments. You could make two stars like the one in Illus. 415 and glue them back-to-back.

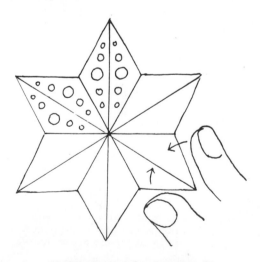

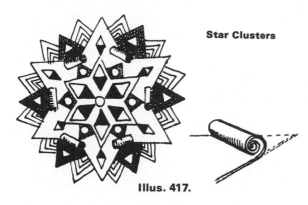

Star Clusters

Illus. 417.

Using sheets of different colored aluminum, first make paper patterns of several stars of various sizes, then cut them out of metal. Decorate with embossed designs and glue the stars, at their middles, one on top of the other, placing each in a different position. You can make special decorations by rolling back a few of the points (Illus. 417, above) or by cutting out little triangles in the points and folding them back (Illus. 418, bottom).

Angels

Illus. 420. This embossed angel can be hung as a Christmas tree ornament or serve as part of a mobile.

Illus. 418.

Illus. 419.

The angel in Illus. 420 can be hung as a Christmas tree ornament or serve as part of a mobile. It is very easy to make. Another method is to make the figures free-standing by using cones of metal for the bodies. Although you can either mount or suspend them from the Christmas tree, you might prefer to make an entire Nativity scene composed of cone figures—shepherds, animals, wise men and kings.

Illus. 421.

The angel in Illus. 419 (left) is tooled from a single sheet of metal. Illus. 421 (above) shows an angel with a cone body. Of course, you must emboss the metal before rolling it into a cone. Insert the head in the small opening at the top of the cone and glue the wings in place.

Illus. 422. Cut out a rectangle from either copper or aluminum sheet. Cut out the shapes on the upper edge as shown at "a" at right. Emboss your design (either the pattern shown here or your own creation). After completing the decoration, turn down the cut-out edge ("c") and make slits on the lower edge to form little prongs ("b"). Bend the sheet into a cylinder and attach it to a circular base of the same, but thicker, metal. To do this, cut a hole in the base slightly larger than the cylinder and insert the cylinder from underneath. Then bend

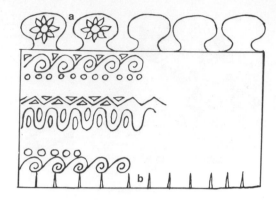

up the little prongs ("d") and glue them from underneath with epoxy cement.

Candleholders

A candleholder, tooled and antiqued, will add a lovely bright sparkle to your dinner table.

Lantern

A decorative metal lantern has the advantage over paper lanterns of not catching fire from the flame of a candle.

Tags and Labels

Practical as well as decorative, these markers are made from embossed metal. The embossed inscription, adorned with a design of your

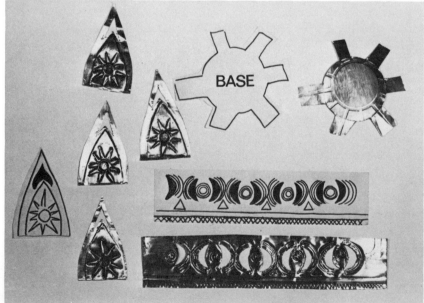

The candleholder in Illus. 423 (above) is easy yet elegant. Simply cut out and emboss the pieces as shown in Illus. 424 (left). Bend up the base tabs and glue inside the body. Glue the prong parts into place. A similar project is pictured in color Illus. D1.

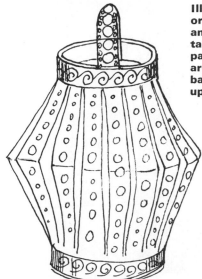

Illus. 425. Make this decorative lantern from a sheet of medium-thin copper or aluminum. The base ("a") is a metal circle with the edge notched ¼ inch and then turned up perpendicular to the surface. The body is made from a rectangular sheet, folded down the middle and cut as in "b". Make a paper pattern first to see how, when the body is rolled into a cylinder and the ends are pushed together, the lantern shape appears. Emboss the body, glue the base prongs to the inside of the body and, if you like, add a handle on the upper edge.

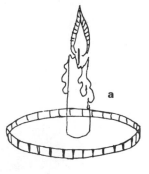

a

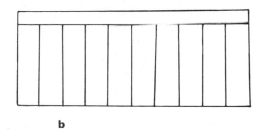

b

Illus. 426. Tags and labels.

choice, can indicate the contents of a chest or small box, a jar or bottle.

You will need small chains to hang round the neck of jars or bottles (Illus. 426). Use copper or aluminum 0.1 mm. thick for the embossed piece. Glue this on a sheet of the same size, but thicker. The form and design of this type of tag should be conceived as a function of its use—do not forget when you choose a design that the lettering must be legible and that an excess of detail will spoil the effect.

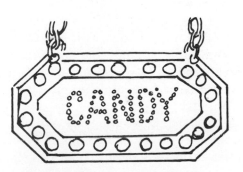

Bird Feeder

Here is a tooled aluminum creation that is sure to win you many fine-feathered friends.

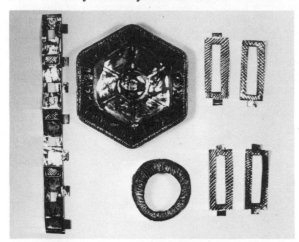

Illus. 427 (left) shows all of the pieces you'll need to construct a bird feeder for your yard. The hexagonal container serves as a base to hold the seed. The long band has tabs which are inserted into slits cut along the bottom of the base. The strips that serve as walls also have tabs, which are either inserted through cut slits or glued to other parts of the feeder. The completed feeder is shown in Illus. 428 (right) and also in color Illus. E3.

Illus. 429. Two simple wooden boxes have been transformed into decorative chests with embossed metal coverings.

Decorative Boxes

Of all the materials which you might choose to cover simple wooden boxes or chests, embossed metal is certainly one of the richest and most attractive. It transforms the most commonplace cigar box into a receptacle fit for a king's rings!

The first step in covering any box with metal is to measure all the dimensions of the box and transfer them to a sheet of paper as shown in

Illus. 430. Begin with the lid, adding $\frac{1}{2}$ inch to each end of the two long sides so that you will have an overlap to turn under later. Make the pattern for the sides of the box in the same way, adding $\frac{1}{2}$ inch on each side, top and bottom (see Illus. 431). Then draw the bottom exactly, not adding on for overlap.

Once you have made the paper patterns, cut out the metal to the exact dimensions. Decide upon the decoration—Illus. 432 through Illus.

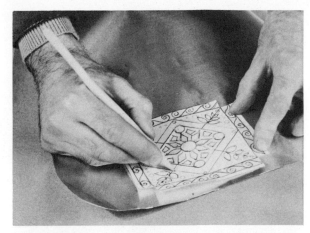

Illus. 430. Transfer your design to the metal with a modelling tool, pencil or ballpoint pen.

434 show three possible designs for your repoussage. For a regular-shaped object, such as a box, geometric or symmetrical designs are particularly suitable. If the design is symmetrical as in the illustrations, you will want to trace diagonals and medians on each of the visible sides. This will make it easier for you to lay out the corresponding elements of the design. After you have embossed the metal in the chosen design, you are ready to cover the box.

Begin by sizing both the wood and metal with a glue recommended for metals, preferably epoxy. One by one, place each sheet of metal on the corresponding wooden surface, pressing on it heavily for several minutes. Carefully turn the overlapping edges towards the inside of the box. You can temporarily staple the

Illus. 431. Test each piece before glueing to ensure a perfect fit.

metal pieces (you will pull out the staples later) to hold them in place while the glue is drying. An ordinary stapler will do the job, but you could also, in order to insure a greater bond as well as to decorate your work, fasten the pieces with round-topped copper carpet tacks as on the box at the left in Illus. 429. However, if these penetrate to the interior, be sure to cut the sharp ends off.

Your chest will be even more elegant if you provide it with four little wooden or cork legs which you can varnish. For a really finished look, cover the interior with a fabric that will hide the roughness of the folded-over metal.

Illus. 432.

Illus. 433.

Illus. 434.

Inlays

Jewelry makers of former times very often inlaid in their gold or silver work precious stones whose brilliance was admirably set off by the lustrous metal and which gave great sumptuousness to the pieces. There is no reason why you cannot emulate their work, but less expensively, by inlaying on the surface of the metal varicolored and shiny glass stones. Even small marbles will do. Much of the work shown here can be inlaid, particularly chests and boxes.

Whatever the material you choose to use as inlay—colored stones, fragments of polished glass, marbles, shiny beads—it should not simply be glued on to the metal but *set* into it

Illus. 436. This little round box with inlaid stones boasts a black velvet lining.

Illus. 435. What is underneath this richly adorned surface? A plain cigar box!

and glued. After having chosen the positions for the inlays, cut in the metal with a jeweler's scissors a hole the same size as the stone to be inlaid (Illus. 437a). Cut out as many little strips of metal as there are stones to be inlaid. The lengths of these strips will be equal to the perimeters of the stones and slightly wider than the thickness of the stones.

At the base of each strip, about one quarter of the width, cut regularly spaced notches as shown in Illus. 437b. Bend these tiny cut strips outwards and curve the entire strip round until it assumes the shape of the stone (Illus. 437c and Illus. 438). Coat the outside of the top of the

strip with glue and place the piece in the opening from the underside so that the flattened, notched part holds it in place. Press the tiny strips tightly against the bottom of the sheet to insure a firm grip. Then when these are firmly dried, glue the stone in position in the setting.

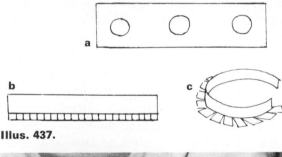

Illus. 437.

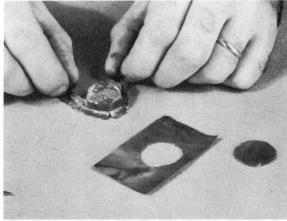

Illus. 438. The setting is placed into the hole from the underside and the stone glued into it.

Stabiles

A stabile, in contrast to a mobile, stays in place and is motionless. They should be designed to present an interesting and balanced appearance from all sides. To make stunning stabiles like those shown here, you can either use one piece of aluminum or copper and roll it into a cylinder (Illus. 439 and Illus. 440) or cut out individual pieces and put them together with epoxy (see Illus. 441 and Illus. 442). Whichever way you choose, be sure to complete your tooling and antiquing before assembling.

Illus. 439 (above) shows the stabile constructed from the pattern in Illus. 440 (below).

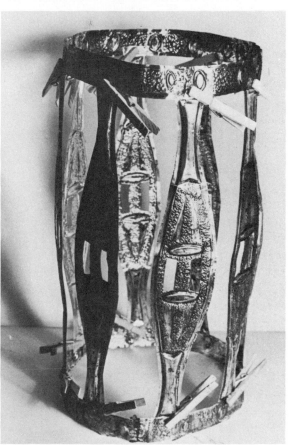

Illus. 441 (above). Clothespins are used to hold the pieces in Illus. 442 (below) for glueing.

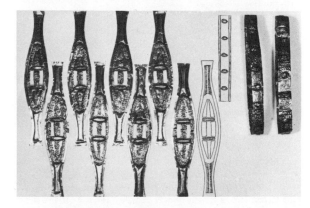

Working with Heavy Sheet Metal

The simple and elementary handling of sheet metal results in a wide range of forms and structures which can be used for many purposes. They evoke a lot of joy when given as presents: joy for the one who creates them and joy for the one who receives them.

The basic materials you need are pieces of sheet metal made of medium-hard copper or brass. The sheet metal should not be thicker than 36-to 20-gauge.

By bending, cutting, perforating, hammering and soldering the metal you can create objects of both beauty and utility.

Sheet metal can be decorated by incisions made with a chisel and hammer or with a pair of scissors. "Werindus" sheet-metal shears cuts out of the sheet metal a 3-mm.-wide strip which rolls itself up. At the end of each incision there remains a curl which sometimes has a very decorative effect.

Another possibility is provided by the use of a punch and a hammer. You can knock out small discs from the sheet metal—either wholly or, by holding the punch inclined, partly so that the

Illus. 444. The holes were made with a punch, the rolled strips with "Werindus" sheet-metal shears.

discs still remain connected at one spot to the whole piece, from which they can be bent up.

To perforate the sheet metal, place it on a wooden board; now, with the aid of a hammer and punching tool (a nail, chisel, squared iron, etc., according to the desired form and size) simply punch the holes through. The jagged edges give a decorative, scraper-like effect. The arrangement of the perforated holes and the choice of the size of the holes permits unlimited possibilities.

Solder, too, may be used for ornamentation. The soldering flame has to be handled very carefully in order to prevent the solder—as a result of excess heat—from simply flowing out flatly without forming a shape. In addition, pieces of wire to be soldered on the metal surface can be bent and arranged in order to create an ornamental effect.

Any or all of these treatments may certainly be combined.

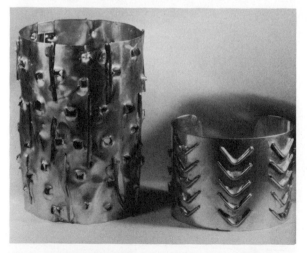

Illus. 443. The candleholder (left) was perforated; the bracelet is brass with copper wire soldered on.

A Brass Bowl

You can create a useful and attractive brass bowl by following these simple, step-by-step instructions.

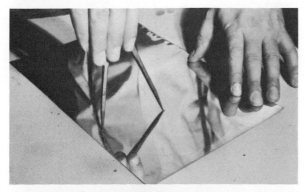
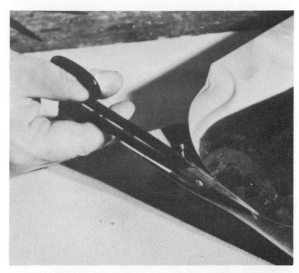

First outline a circle on the metal sheet with the compass (Illus. 445, left). Then cut it out with jeweler's scissors (Illus. 446, right).

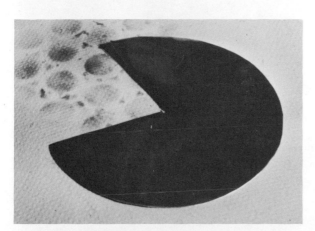

Illus. 447 shows the circle with a section about $\frac{1}{4}$ the total area cut away. Save this section for use in the base. Now bend the metal circle into a cone shape, overlapping the edges where the section was cut out (Illus. 448, right).

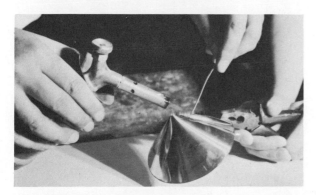

Illus. 449. Solder the edges together while a helper holds the cone with pliers.

Illus. 450. Cut two more quarter circles the same size as the first section you cut out of the metal circle. Bend each section in the middle.

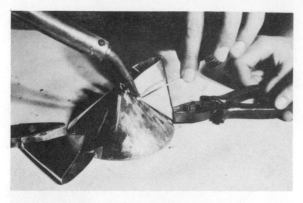

Illus. 451 (left) and Illus. 452 (right). Solder each bent section to the bottom of the cone. Use a soldering iron so that the soldered seam of the cone is not weakened.

Illus. 453 (left). The completed bowl will be useful as an ashtray or candy dish. You can use the same basic cone shape and solder on wire legs if you prefer (Illus. 454, right).

Sheet Metal and Stones

On excursions and walking tours, you can often discover the "preciousness" of very ordinary stones. Streaks of iron and minerals, etc., give many stones color and brightness. These stones can be used for wall decorations by mounting them on brass or copper sheet metal.

The form of the sheet-metal base must be shaped in a way that leads the eye towards the stone. The stone should not appear as a mere decoration on the sheet metal; it should be the focal point.

The stone is held either by unobtrusive pieces of sheet metal soldered onto the base or by sheet-metal parts which are soldered on consciously as part of the design.

Illus. 455. This abstract setting for a stone uses simple metal strips.

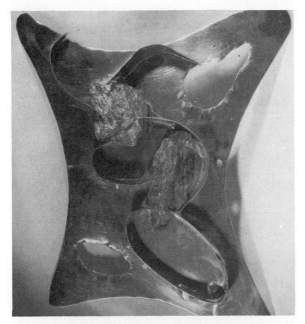

Illus. 456. This abstract rock setting is decorated with abstract holes cut with hammer and chisel.

Illus. 457. You can use solder for decorating your work, as shown in the patterned use of bits of solder in this stone setting.

3-Dimensional Abstract Sculpture

The simple soldering together of similarly shaped rectangular pieces of sheet metal at right angles to one another can result in an attractive 3-dimensional abstract sculpture.

Illus. 458. Pieces of metal soldered in an abstract design reflect light off the many angled surfaces.

Illus. 459. For this imaginative fruit, the different parts were cut out in segments and soldered into their round shape.

Figures of Sheet Metal

Full, imaginative figures can be created by piecing together various parts of sheet metal and soldering together the cut edges. The resulting figure, like a cartoon character, will be extremely simplified, but can convey great meaning. Use your imagination, and keep it simple.

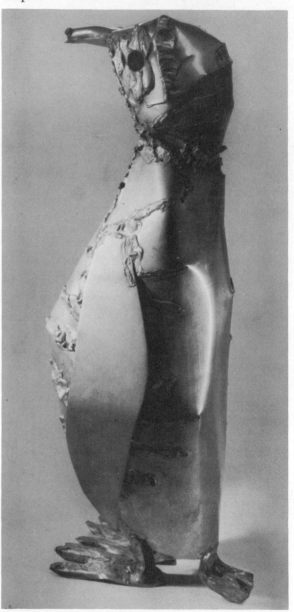

Illus. 461. With this penguin, and the rooster in color Illus. F2, the various techniques of working with sheet metal are used to produce a complete sculpture.

Illus. 460. The figure on the right was made from three pieces of shaped metal. The figure on the left uses more pieces, but the same process.

Crafting with Silver Wire and Sheet Silver

Silver, besides being one of the most attractive of Nature's metals, is also one of the most malleable, or softest, of all metals, natural or man-made. In addition, it is far less expensive than, say, gold. Besides the satisfaction you will find in your completed silver jewelry, you will discover the joy of working with this lovely metal. It has a texture and other qualities that are far different from ordinary metals.

You are going to be amazed at the ease with which you can produce stunning, individual jewelry—*without any difficult techniques*, such as sawing, drilling, or soldering. With your own two hands and a minimum of materials and tools, you can turn out the most intricate, finely wrought silver jewelry imaginable.

Do not be deceived by the elaborate appearance of some of the projects in this section. Every piece is as simple as the few techniques you will learn right in the beginning!

The first thing you will need, of course, is silver wire and sheet silver. You will use *wire* in almost all of the projects in this section. There are many different sizes and shapes available which you can purchase from a metal supply house, as well as through specialized hobby shops. You will find round, flat, rectangular, square, beaded, half-round, etc. However, for your beginning work, you will use only round and flat.

Round wire is difficult to work with in the heavier gauges, so keep to the 16- to 24-gauge area. Silver flat wire comes in various widths, but you will find the ⅛-inch width suitable for your jewelry. A piece of 18-gauge flat wire can be hammered out to make it wider if so desired.

You will generally want to use the higher gauge (lightweight) wires which, incidentally, are the least expensive. Silver is sold by weight and therefore the lower gauge, or thicker, wires, are heavier and cost more. Also, the thinner the silver, the more malleable it is.

The same holds true for *sheet silver*. This you will find available in a variety of sizes and shapes—strips, circles, squares, and so on, in gauges from 10 to 28. You will, of course, as with the wire, want to use the lighter-weight pieces, say, from 18-gauge up. It is advisable to use none heavier than 24-gauge, and preferably 28-gauge.

You need not use silver findings unless you wish to—you can purchase very inexpensive metal findings. However, in much of your silverwork you are going to make your own clasps and such, but for earrings, you will probably want ready-made findings.

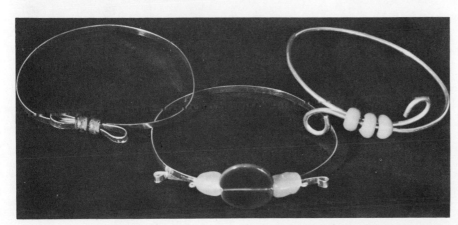

Illus. 462. You have your choice of wire and beads for these charming, easy-to-make bracelets.

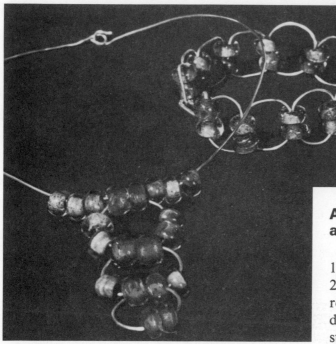

Illus. 463. All you need is one piece of wire and some beads for a stunning necklace or bracelet. The necklace is described below, the bracelet on page 167.

A Looped-Wire and Bead Necklace

You will need:
18- or 20-gauge silver round wire
20 beads, 12 light and 8 dark
round-nose pliers
diagonal cutting pliers
string
tape measure or yardstick

Tools used for all metalwork will be needed here. Special tools might be *diagonal cutting pliers*, also called diagonal wire cutters, which have a cutting jaw at an angle up to the point. Use them for cutting off both round and flat wire. There is a type that has a cutter on one jaw in combination with a round or flat jaw. These are less suitable for getting into tight places where it is necessary to snip off wire ends.

Metal-cutting shears, called plate shears, are necessary only for cutting thicker metals such as earring findings. A simple, very sharp scissors is sufficient for your sheet-silver cutting.

A rawhide or rubber mallet and a small anvil are handy for hammering and flattening. These are inexpensive and worth the small investment.

The necklace in Illus. 463 is so easy to make from just one piece of silver wire, you might end up making dozens of them for friends and relatives.

Take a very long piece of string and place it around your neck. Decide what length you wish the large neckloop to be, remove the string and measure the length. An average size is 15 inches.

Now using the string again, follow Illus. 464 through Illus. 468 until you have formed three

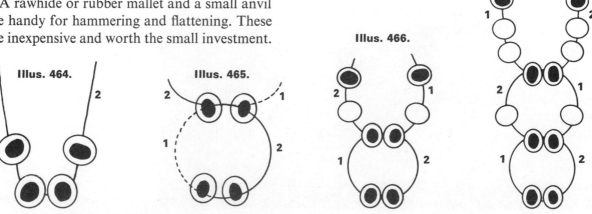

Illus. 464.

Illus. 465.

Illus. 466.

Illus. 467.

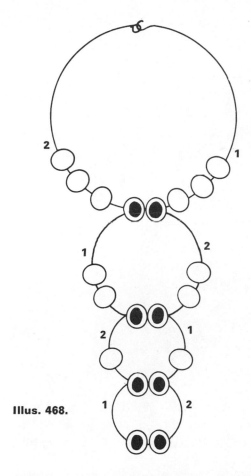

Illus. 468.

same way to the point where you want loop #2 (Illus. 466). Thread two more dark beads on, cross the strands over again, and thread four light-colored beads on, two on each side, and complete loop #3 by threading on two more dark beads (Illus. 467).

Add the six light beads shown, three on each side, and bend your two strands into the neck-loop shape. Make a simple clasp at the end as shown in Illus. 468, using the round-nose pliers for this bending procedure. Snip off any excess wire with your diagonal cutting pliers.

A Looped-Wire and Bead Bracelet

You will need:
20-gauge silver round wire
14 beads
round-nose pliers
diagonal cutting pliers
rolling pin
string
transparent tape
tape measure or yardstick

Although the bracelet in Illus. 463 has 24 beads and 12 loops, be a little less ambitious for your first wire and bead bracelet, or you will have to make loops that are too small to handle at this point. Be satisfied with 8 loops and 14 beads. Do not use more than two beads per "twist" unless they are very small.

Take your string and form 8 overlapping loops all stretched out in a line. Use tape to hold the loops together. Pick it up carefully and place it around your wrist. Adjust the loops as necessary—smaller or larger in order to fit. Take note of the two ends, undo the string and measure. An average length is 24 inches. Again, as you did with your necklace, allow a little extra for clasping.

You can now thread your beads onto the wire in the same way as with the necklace, crossing and threading two beads at a time. For this project, you will find your round-nose pliers or a simple home-made device which

small loops and the neckloop, allowing at least 1½ inches for clasping purposes. Undo your "string necklace" and measure the total length. It will probably be about 40 inches long.

Now you are ready to work with your silver wire and beads. Cut a piece of wire at least 6 inches longer than you need to allow for adjustments. You are not wasting wire—you will use many small pieces in your work.

With your hands, bend the wire in the middle into the shape shown in Illus. 464. Slide two dark-colored beads on as shown. Then bend wire strand 1 and strand 2 together and thread two more dark beads on both wires. Now bend strand 1 over strand 2 and work the beads gradually downwards to the point where you want your first loop (Illus. 465).

Thread two light-colored beads onto the two strands just as you did before by pressing the upper ends together. Work these down in the you may already have (see Illus. 469) most help-ful to aid you with the bending.

The spool stanchion is easy to make. Take two wooden spools of the desired size and nail them down with small nails onto a hard surface. Then bend the wire around the spools as shown, being sure each set of beads in this case is in place as you work each loop.

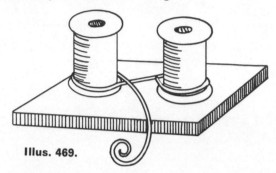

Illus. 469.

Now, since your bracelet is still flat, in order to form it into wrist shape, use a wooden or plastic rolling pin to form it on. Work carefully, using your pliers and hands, until the desired shape is attained. For your bracelet, it is best to use the clasp shown in Illus. 50. Shape as shown.

Neckloop with Pendant and Matching Earrings

You will need:
silver round wire, 12-gauge most desirable, 16-gauge satisfactory
silver flat wire
beads
sheet silver, 26-gauge
silver round wire, 24-gauge
strong needle
sharp scissors
round-nose pliers
paper
knitting needle
spring-type earring findings
epoxy cement

Using the string method, measure off a piece of 12- or 16-gauge round wire the desired length for the large neckloop. Bend the ends into a hook catch as shown in Illus. 470.

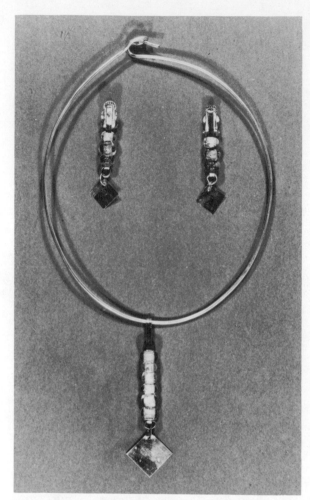

Illus. 470. This beautiful silver round-wire set will look like you bought it at a jewelry store.

To make the pendant, take a piece of flat wire long enough to accommodate 5 or 6 beads, plus allowance for bending the end around the neckloop at the top, and at the bottom for hooking on the square. (Remember, it is always wise to use string for your preliminary measurements.)

Do not cut out your sheet-silver square until you have made a paper pattern. This way you can change its size at will—once you cut the sheet-silver square, you can do nothing but make it smaller! Place the pattern on the corner of a silver sheet so you will have two straight edges already cut for you. With a grease pencil, sketch in the other two sides and

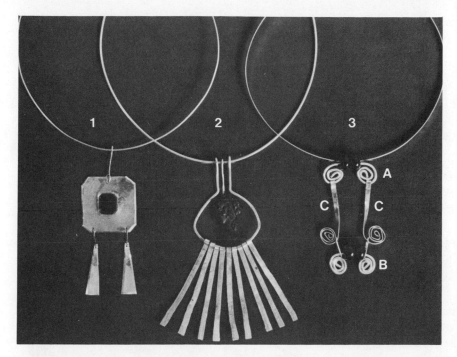

Illus. 471. For these three elegant necklaces, see directions for (1) below; (2) on page 170; and (3) on page 171.

cut, using sharp scissors. Then with a strong needle, pierce one corner so you have a hole that will accommodate 24-gauge wire.

Now make tiny 24-gauge loops (jump rings) by winding a length of wire around a knitting needle. You will need 6 for this project, but you can make a number of them at this time for use later. Remove the "spiral" from the needle and cut across one side as shown in Illus. 472, using the diagonal cutting pliers. Attach two rings to the square, closing both tightly. This you can do by squeezing with your fingers.

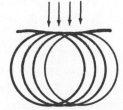

Illus. 472. Cut the spiral as indicated for wire jump rings.

Now bend the flat-wire strip around the neckloop using round-nose pliers. String your beads on. Bend the bottom end of the flat wire up and hook the second ring onto it. Bend shut with the pliers.

Make the matching earrings in the same way as you did the pendant. You will undoubtedly use fewer beads and smaller squares, however. With epoxy cement, attach ready-made ear clips to the top end of the flat wire. If they overlap on the side, use your metal-cutting shears to trim them down *before you glue*, or else glue strips of sheet silver the equivalent width of the findings over the flat wire. (If you ever do make a mistake in glueing or decide you want to make a change, there is an epoxy cement remover available.)

A Wire Neckloop and Jewelled Silver Pendant

You will need:
18-gauge silver round wire or lighter
24-gauge silver round wire
sheet silver, 26-gauge or lighter
a square bead, not too small
string
strong needle
embossing tools
epoxy cement

This is neckloop (1) in Illus. 471.

You will want to use a lightweight wire for this project because the necklace should have a very delicate appearance. If you wish, use a lighter wire than 18-gauge.

Since this type of necklace looks best as a choker, measure off your neck length with your string and cut a corresponding piece of silver round wire. An average length is 15 inches or 16 inches. The loop should be as close to a circle as possible, so shape your wire very carefully, holding one end with the flat-nose pliers and the other with the round-nose pliers. To achieve the best results, you might shape it around a half-gallon or gallon bottle, such as is used for mineral water or wine. Be sure you fill the bottle with liquid so it won't tip during the bending process, or enlist the aid of a friend to hold it steady. Make a simple clasp as in Illus. 468.

Next, make paper patterns for the square silver pendant and long triangular pieces attached to it. Make these fairly good-sized, say a 2-inch square and 2-inch-long triangles. When you are satisfied with the proportions, outline the patterns on the sheet silver and cut. Pierce the square with a strong needle in three places as shown in Illus. 471. Pierce the triangles at the narrow ends.

Illus. 473. A: wrong. B: right.

This square can be embossed. You will find directions for this in the section on embossing.

When you have finished the embossing, cut 1-inch-long pieces of the 24-gauge silver round wire and make the attachment pieces for the square and triangles. Bend these in the fashion shown in Illus. 473 which shows the right way and the wrong way to make this type of attachment loop. Before closing them over completely, insert the ends in the holes you pierced, as well as around the neckloop.

You are now ready to attach the decorative bead in the middle by simply glueing it on with epoxy cement, and you are finished!

A Neckloop with a Flat-Wire and Cameo Pendant

You will need:
18-gauge silver round wire
18-gauge silver flat wire, ⅛ inch wide
large decorative bead, or cameo as shown
rawhide or rubber mallet (in a pinch you can wrap felt around an ordinary hammer)
anvil
epoxy cement

This is neckloop (2) in Illus. 471.

Make a choker-type neckloop as you did on page 168.

To decide on the size of the wire which will enclose the cameo, use the string method as

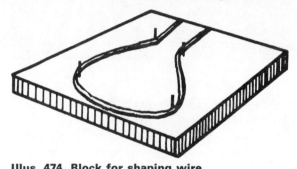

Illus. 474. Block for shaping wire.

before—it should require approximately 10 inches allowing for the two lengths attached to the neckloop. Use the silver round wire for this part and lay it on the anvil. With the mallet, tap *lightly* along its length until it has two flattened surfaces. Do not flatten it out completely. You will find it has stretched out somewhat. (A tip on hammering: excessive hammering will toughen the metal, so keep this in mind when you work.)

In order to bend this wire into the shape shown, you can use any form you might have handy that is similar or you can make a form yourself very easily. Take a block of wood, and hammer nails into your desired pattern as shown in Illus. 474. Then bend the wire around the nails until it has the shape you want. Be sure to snip the heads off the nails so that you can lift the wire off easily.

Before attaching this to the neckloop, make your flat-wire strands. Prior to cutting the individual pieces, decide how long they are to be. Since they will be attached to a curved surface, make them all the same length, and they will appear to form a similar curve (see Illus. 471). Suppose you choose 2 inches for the length and 9 strands altogether. Simply multiply, and cut an 18-inch length of flat wire. Hammer this out as much as you please on your anvil. Then measure off each 2-inch length and cut. Attach them by bending the ends over the finished part of the pendant and squeezing. Then attach the entire piece to the neckloop with simple bends as shown.

The large bead or cameo is hooked onto the neckloop with a piece of flattened round wire which, in turn, is glued onto the back of the cameo.

A Flat-Wire Neckloop with Spiral and Bead Pendant

You will need:
18-gauge silver flat wire
18-gauge silver round wire
24-gauge silver round wire
4 large-eyed beads
very narrow string
round-nose pliers
flat-nose pliers

This is neckloop (3) in Illus. 471.

Form a choker-type neckloop as before, this time using the 18-gauge flat wire. Do not fashion a clasp immediately—leave the ends free until later on.

The three spiralled parts A, B and C will be made separately and put together. A and B are made of round wire and C of flat wire.

Take your narrow string and make a form with spiralled ends as shown at A in Illus. 471 in proportion to the neckloop. Unravel and measure. Piece B will be similar but somewhat smaller; however, allow the same length for each. You can make tighter spirals for Part B,

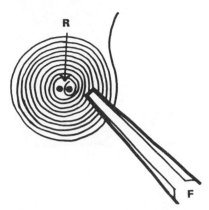

Illus. 475. Spiralling requires both round-nose (R) and flat-nose (F) pliers.

if you wish. Jot down the measurement, so you won't forget.

Two identical pieces of flat wire comprise Part C. Use a piece of string again to determine how long you want these pieces and make a note of it. They should be the same length, of course, or Part B will hang lopsided.

Cut your first piece of round wire. Then, with your round-nose pliers, grip one end, and with the aid of the flat-nose pliers, wrap a spiral around at least two times (Illus. 475). Now slip two beads on from the other end and proceed to wrap another, similar spiral at that end. Don't worry if they are not exactly alike —the distinction of hand-made jewelry is that it is rarely precision-wrought!

Make Part C in exactly the same way, forming somewhat tighter spirals and also adding two beads as shown.

Now cut your two pieces for Part C from the flat wire. Make your spirals as before and then, as in Illus. 476, using the round-nose pliers (R), twist the flat wire around the flat-nose pliers (F) a *quarter-turn* (90°) as shown.

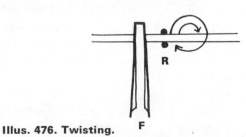

Illus. 476. Twisting.

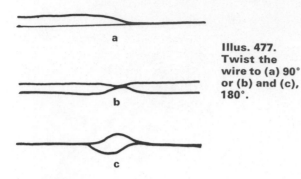

Illus. 477. Twist the wire to (a) 90° or (b) and (c), 180°.

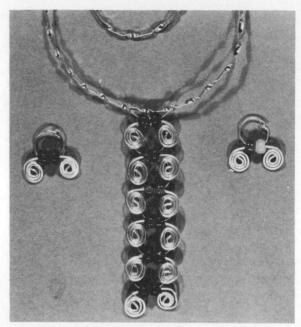

Illus. 478. Twisted-wire neckloop with spiral and bead pendant.

You are now ready to attach the various pieces together. Take Part A and thread it onto the neckloop through the eyes of the beads until it is in the exact middle. Join Part C to Part A by inserting the two ends into the lower spirals and bending them over on the reverse side into hooks. Part B and Part C are joined together with the same 24-gauge wire loops which you used on page 170.

Make a clasp on the neckloop and wear your new creation with pride.

Twisted-Wire Neckloop with Spiral and Bead Pendant

You will need:
18-gauge silver flat wire
20-gauge silver round wire
24-gauge silver round wire
12 beads with large eyes
round-nose pliers
flat-nose pliers

This elaborate-looking necklace is simpler than you think—it merely combines techniques you have already learned—threading, twisting and spiralling. Each part is made separately and then joined together.

Since you will lose some length in your neckloop because of the twists, allow at least 3 inches more when you take your string measurement. You can always snip off any leftover wire, but you cannot add any!

Now, with your round-nose pliers, twist the flat wire around the flat-nose pliers a *half-turn* (180°) as shown in Illus. 477. Continue this process until your neckloop is complete. A simple way to measure off each section between twists is to use the width of the flat-nose pliers as a guide. As we said before, don't be worried if it doesn't come out looking absolutely perfect. That would be impossible even for the most skilled silverworker without the aid of machines which, after all, have no place in hand-wrought work.

Since all of the spiralled parts are made separately and are all the same size, measure once only with your string as you did before. You will make six of these parts, but cut just one piece first from your 18-gauge round wire to make sure it is correct. Then proceed to spiral one end, slip on two beads and spiral the other end, exactly as you did for Parts A and B in Illus. 471. Continue until you have made all six pieces.

Take your 24-gauge wire, and proceed to "thread" it through each pair of beads as you did for your first necklace on page 166. Attach the two strands to your neckloop with a few twists. Snip off any loose ends, and make a necklace clasp as shown in Illus. 468.

Illus. 479. Wire and bead belt.

A Linked Wire and Bead Belt

You will need:

24-gauge silver round wire

quantity of glass or plastic beads with small eyes

round-nose pliers

flat-nose pliers

The individual links of this delicate-looking belt (Illus. 479) are made in two different lengths. Make a string measurement of your waist. The number of beads and links will depend upon how long your belt will be. This belt is based upon a 28-inch or 30-inch waist. Fourteen 1-inch links and fourteen ½-inch links which add up to 21 inches have been used.

Then about 6 inches of round wire on each end was used to string two rows of beads. However, this belt has spirals on the ends which not only serve to hold the beads, but can be used as a clasp by simply hooking them one over the other.

Make your links in the same way as you made the connecting links in Illus. 473. Every other link will be a short one on which you will thread one bead before closing the ends. Be sure to hook each link onto the next one before

closing tightly. Actually, it is wise not to squeeze them tight until you have completed all the links in case you want to make an adjustment.

For the two end pieces which are hooked onto the last links, use about 16 inches of round wire for each. Make your spirals using the pliers. String the beads on. Snip the leftovers, if any, leaving ¾ inch for a hook.

You can make all kinds of variations of this belt, or you might wish to make a matching bracelet or earrings.

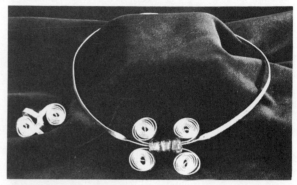

Illus. 480.

Spiralled Flat-Wire and Bead Choker

You will need:

18-gauge silver flat wire, ⅛ inch wide

24-gauge silver flat wire

3 beads with extra large eyes

round-nose and flat-nose pliers

Make your choker from the 18-gauge flat wire, allowing a little for two twists. Do not make the clasp until later.

Cut two 16-inch pieces of 24-gauge flat wire. Form spirals with your pliers on *one* end of each. Pass the free ends of both through the three beads so they are in the relative positions shown in Illus. 480. Then spiral the other two ends.

Slip the choker through the beads and *between* the other two pieces of wire. Then, with the pliers, twist the flat wire a quarter-turn (90°). Make a clasp with the ends and you're finished.

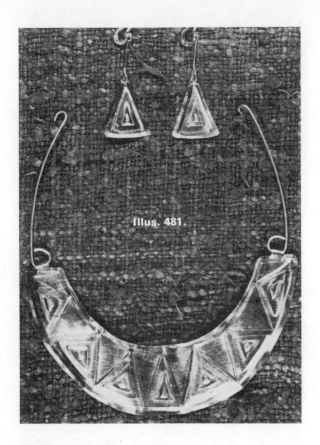

Illus. 481.

used in Illus. 482. You need not use this design, however, but keep it simple since this is a fairly large piece of silver and you won't want to spoil it.

Transfer your outline in grease pencil to the silver, as well as the design. Cut, not forgetting the tabs. Work lightly and carefully on your embossing with the bone folder, being sure to use the mat.

Form the wire pieces from the heavy round wire after measuring with string and the paper pattern. The two tabs will form the attachment, so do not tightly close the bottom wire loops yet.

Roll the tabs toward the back using a knitting needle until you have formed cylinders

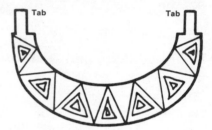

Illus. 482. Don't forget tabs for attaching the wire.

of a size that will accommodate the wire. Slip the wires through and squeeze tight.

Make matching earrings as shown in Illus. 481 (also using paper patterns) and hook onto ready-made findings of either the ear-clip or screwback type in the style called "pierced look." These have tiny hooks at the base for attaching dangles.

Silver Gorget and Matching Earrings

You will need:
26-gauge sheet silver
16-gauge, or heavier, round wire
24-gauge, or lighter, round wire
earring findings
scissors
paper and grease pencil
pliers and knitting needle
bone folder and embossing mat

Here you can achieve a medieval look by fashioning a silver gorget, originally a crescent-shaped piece of armor worn to protect the throat in the 15th century.

Make a paper pattern of the sheet-silver crescent alone and measure it (using string for the wire pieces) around your neck. Allow for two tabs on each end.

Sketch your design now on the paper. Notice the variance in shape and size of the triangles

A Personalized Silver and Bead Barrette

You will need:
18- or 20-gauge sheet silver
26-gauge round wire
large, bulbous bead
barrette finding, ready-made
plate shears
round-nose pliers
tweezers
heavy needle
epoxy cement
bone folder and embossing mat

Illus. 483. A personalized barrette.

this around the bead as many times as you can, but don't bury the bead! Do this by holding about ½ inch of wire at the back with the pliers and use a tweezer for wrapping. (A good idea to prevent marring is to cover the tweezer ends with adhesive tape.) Make a few twists at the back to secure it and snip off the excess.

Cement the finished barrette to a ready-made finding.

Spiralled Flat-Wire Belt and Armband

You will need:
18-gauge silver flat wire
round-nose and flat-nose pliers
string
tape measure

Both the belt and the armband in Illus. 484 are made from just two pieces of flat wire.

The length of the belt will depend upon how you are going to wear it—around your waist or on your hips. Use the string method for measuring, and allow at least 5 inches on each end for spiralling. After spiralling, twist the wire just in back of the spirals 90° (Illus. 477) upward. In Illus. 484, these are the small spirals on top.

The two large spirals which seem to disappear

Make a paper pattern of your chosen monogram as in Illus. 483. Since a barrette receives a certain amount of bending and pressure, do not use very thin sheet silver. Although 18-gauge is most often used for such things as money clips and tie clips, you can use, if necessary, 22-gauge. Use plate shears for cutting out your transferred pattern.

Keep your embossing as simple as possible since you will find you must work heavier silver more times on each side.

Cement the bead on and create an "artificial bezel" by piercing a hole alongside it and drawing a length of 26-gauge wire through. Wrap

Illus. 484. The spiralled belt and armband set are elegant examples of what you can create with simple tools and materials.

into the small spirals are actually made from one piece and looped *over* the small spirals on the end of the belt, serving as a clasp. After cutting approximately a 10-inch length of flat wire, make the two spirals and then cross them over each other using the pliers. You will find that to make them lie flat in relationship to each other you must make a 45° twist in each.

The armband, or slip-on bracelet, does not have a clasp, so allow for being able to get it over your hand. (Use string to measure.)

First make the back part of the bracelet, bending into a large semicircle a length of wire with a small spiral on either end. Again, allow 5 inches for these spirals.

Then take a longer piece of flat wire which should be equal to the remaining semicircle, plus about 10 inches. Thread this through each spiral and bring the long ends toward you. Wind larger spirals on each end. Then bend the whole thing back toward the other part till the two spirals meet. Give each a 90° twist upward, so they are in the position illustrated.

Wire-and-Bead-Decorated Belt

You will need:
22-gauge round wire
beads
heavy velvet ribbon
flat-nose pliers

Here is an elegant belt to wear on special occasions. The design easily can be adapted to matching accessories—bracelet, necklace, earrings. You are going to make a different kind of spiral now.

Wrap a length of wire around a dowel or any solid cylindrical object as shown in Illus. 58, at least ten times, leaving 2½ inches of straight wire on both ends. Remove, and with the flat-nose pliers, squeeze the coil until it assumes an elongated shape. Then pull the loops apart so that they fan out as shown. The silver is soft and malleable. Press the two straight ends together, thread on a bead, and then form the ends into two "belt loops."

Make at least a dozen of these ornaments and

Illus. 485. The decorative wire flourishes on this wire-and-bead-decorated belt have a floral look.

slip on the velvet band. A simple bow or knot serves as an appropriate clasp.

A Flat-Wire Key Ring

You will need:
narrow silver flat wire
flat-nose pliers
round-nose pliers
scissors

Here is a key ring (Illus. 486) you will never find in any shop in the world! Make an oval loop about 3 inches in length with the flat wire. Give each end a 90° twist and form loops that will hook onto each other as a clasp. These twists will prevent keys from slipping off easily.

With one piece of flat wire about 12 inches long, form a loose spiral on each end. Then bend carefully into the four elongated loops as shown. Cut four 1-inch lengths of wire and wrap around each loop as shown to form secure clips.

Make a third spiralled piece and suspend it from the middle of the main part. Attach the assembly onto the large loop with two flat-wire round rings.

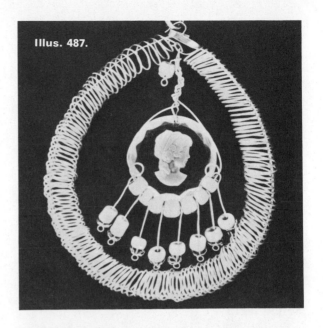

Illus. 487.

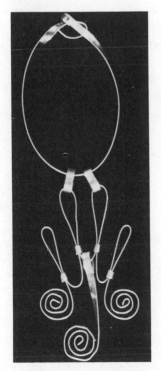

Illus. 486. Flat-wire
key ring.

A Round-Wire Wall Decoration

You will need:
20-gauge silver round wire
18-gauge silver flat wire
beads
brooch
bead cups
epoxy cement

You can make this lovely ornament (Illus. 487) any size you wish. Using the same method for the belt you made on page 176, wind the round wire round a cylinder. Slip a length of flat wire through the resulting spiral and form into a long oval. Make a 90° twist on each flat-wire end.

Form the middle piece by shaping a circle the appropriate size to accommodate the brooch. Then form a twisted end, slip a bead and cup on, and attach where the spiralled ends meet. Glue the brooch onto the circular portion.

Make the pendant parts from equal-length pieces of wire with a single bead and cup strung on and attached to the main section with tiny loops.

This piece can be used in many ways—on a Christmas tree, a mirror, in a window, or even in a car window!

Working with Solid Silver

Working with solid silver is not difficult. The techniques are easily mastered and the possibilities for expression of your own originality make it a fascinating hobby. The assumption is that the users of this book are untutored in silver-working, but have always longed to "do something with silver." The directions are simply stated and the photographs, taken during actual teaching sessions, are aimed at illustrating the text.

The projects in this section require the most simple materials and designs. The articles for which detailed directions are given are merely stepping stones to an endless variety of jewelry and related items. For example, you can also apply the techniques you use to make the most simple ring to the most complex pendant or belt buckle.

Realizing that any hobby can become quite expensive, the designs selected require a minimum of materials. The list of essential tools has been compiled so as to include only those most necessary for the beginning hobbyist. With proper use and care, these implements will last many years.

You can purchase any tools and materials you need (including the silver) from metal supply houses or craft or hobby suppliers who carry silversmithing equipment. Also, lapidary shops sometimes carry silversmithing equipment.

Silver, like other metals, is sized by gauges—the higher the gauge number, the finer or thinner the silver.

The designs in this section are only suggestions. The thrill of using your own ideas and creating new patterns is what makes any artistic effort worthwhile. Do not be afraid to experiment—let yourself go!

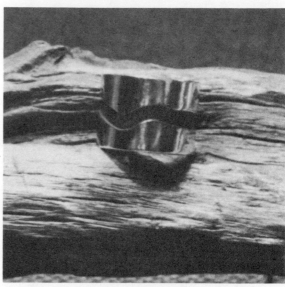

Illus. 488. The completed basic overlay ring.

Basic Overlay Ring

You will need:
scissors
notebook with unlined paper
white liquid glue (Elmer's)
transparent tape
construction paper (light and dark)
felt pen (black, fine-tip)
soft drawing pencil
metal ruler

To begin your first silver ring, divide a sheet of unlined paper into ring widths. This is your design sheet. Beginning at the top of the sheet, start to fill in all of the ring widths (Illus. 489). Doodle, make crosses, circles, squares, rectangles, straight lines, squiggly lines, and so on. Vary the size of the designs. Try to arrange them so they are attractive and pleasing to your

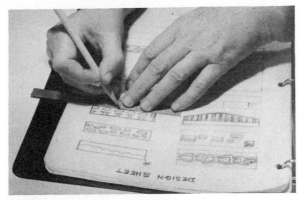

Illus. 489. Fill in the design sheet with various patterns.

eye. Find a little pattern that satisfies you and repeat it several times in one ring width.

When you have filled all of the spaces on the design sheet, go back over them. Blacken some parts out with a pencil, shade others. Think of some of the patterns as being holes or absence of material, others as being raised.

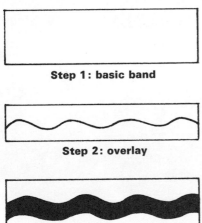

Step 1: basic band

Step 2: overlay

Step 3: completed pattern

Illus. 490. Pattern for basic overlay ring.

The first project is shown in Illus. 490, which has been divided into the three steps necessary for pattern construction.

STEP 1: Cut a strip of dark construction paper 1 inch wide. Wrap it around the desired ring finger and transparent tape it in place. Bend your finger. If the paper feels sharp and as

though it would cut, the band is too wide. Keep trimming it to narrower widths until it feels comfortable.

To find the proper ring size, place the pattern for the basic band over the knuckle of the ring finger. It should be snug but should slide on and off without forcing. Mark the size and cut off the excess, leaving about $\frac{1}{4}$ inch beyond the mark to allow a strip for glueing. Now that you have determined the proper length and width for the band, trace and cut out a duplicate of it (minus the glue strip) for the final pattern.

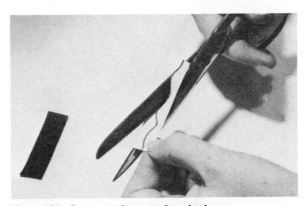

Illus. 491. Cut out the overlay design.

STEP 2: The overlay design for this particular ring, although as long, is not as wide as the basic band (Step 1). Draw the design on white construction paper. Cut it out as shown in Illus. 491. Copy the overlay design for the final pattern. *Do not cut the copy in half yet.*

STEP 3: The reason for the narrow overlay band becomes clear at this point. Glue the two pieces of the white overlay band to the outside edges of the basic band. See Illus. 492. Observe

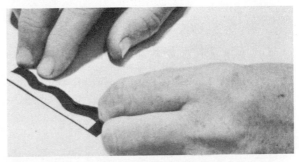

Illus. 492. Glue the overlay pieces to the band.

that the narrow overlay band, when cut in two and spread apart, makes a wide, dark middle strip. If you want a narrower center strip, increase the width of the overlay.

Make the mock-up round and glue it. This gives you a visual example of the completed ring. Think of the dark strip down the center as being an oxidized area—that is, treated with liver of sulphur, or its commercial equivalent, to turn it black. The white strips represent the areas which will be highly polished. Try on the mock-up ring (see Illus. 493), look at it, analyze it. Does it look well on your hand? Is it too wide? Too narrow? Adjust the ring to fit your needs, and you are ready to proceed with its production.

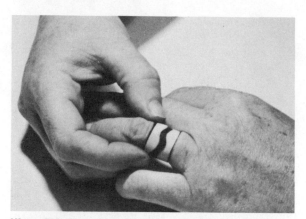

Illus. 493. Try on the finished mock-up ring.

Transferring the Design to Silver

You will need:
metal ruler
duplicate paper pattern
two 1 × 6 sheets of sterling silver, one 18-gauge, one 22 gauge
scribe

To transfer your final design to silver, lay the basic band pattern flush with *one corner* and *the edge* of the 18-gauge silver. Using the scribe, lightly trace the pattern outline. Hold the scribe firmly; an unnecessary slip could cause a deep scratch that would be very difficult to remove.

Remove the pattern. Now, "true up" the outline using metal ruler and scribe.

Illus. 494. Scribe the outline of the overlay onto 22-gauge silver.

Follow the same procedure to scribe the outline of the overlay pattern in the 22-gauge silver (see Illus. 494). When you have finished the outline, cut the paper pattern down the wavy center line. Then, place half of the overlay pattern flush with the corner and outside edge of the silver. Scribe the center line as shown in Illus. 495.

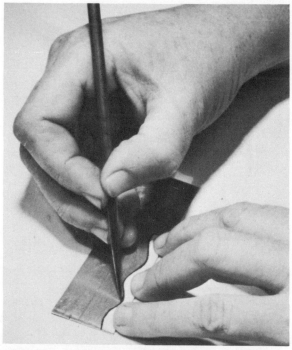

Illus. 495. Scribe the center line of the overlay.

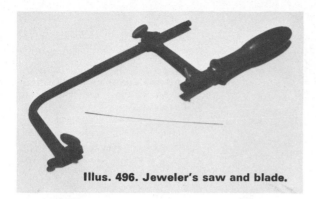

Illus. 496. Jeweler's saw and blade.

Sawing the Design

You will need:
one C-clamp
saw blades, size 2/0
one jeweler's saw, 3-inch (see Illus. 496)
bench vice
one sheet fine emery paper
fine, half-round, 6-inch file
flat 6-inch file
half-round needle file
home-made bench pin (see Illus. 497)

The jeweler's saw has a rather fragile appearance that is misleading. It is a powerful and sturdy tool, which, if used properly, is capable of cutting the hardest of metals. Since this saw cuts only on the downward stroke, you must always set the blade so the teeth face *out* from the frame, and *down* towards the handle.

Loosen the wing nuts at each end of the jeweler's saw frame. Fasten the blade in the top holder first. Place the tip of the frame against the edge of the table, while holding it by the handle with your left hand. Push firmly against the table until the frame bends slightly and fasten the blade in the bottom holder. Fastened properly, the blade should make a musical ping when you strum it with your thumb.

Now, fasten the bench pin to the work bench with the C-clamp. To judge the correct position accurately, let your right arm hang loosely at your side. Bend your arm at the elbow and raise your hand until it touches the edge of the table. You should center the V in the bench pin here. Mount the vice on the right of the

bench pin. (Reverse this procedure if you are left-handed.) See Illus. 497.

Illus. 497. Proper position of the bench pin and vice.

Hold the jeweler's saw in a vertical position (see Illus. 498). As mentioned earlier, this saw cuts only on the downward stroke, so its motion is up and down and not forward as with a hand saw. You pull it downwards, gently slide it up,

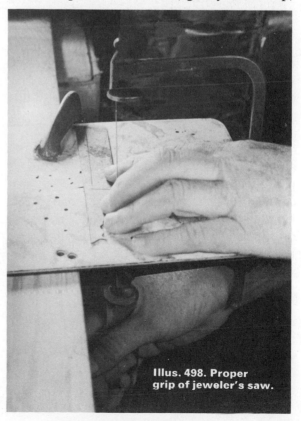

Illus. 498. Proper grip of jeweler's saw.

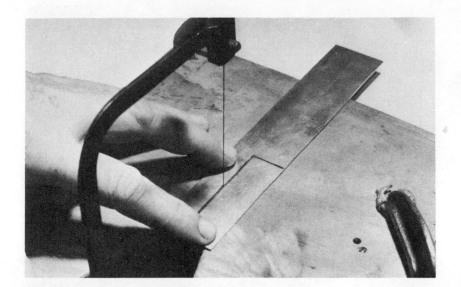

Illus. 499. Hold your fingers and the silver as shown here when sawing out the basic band.

and pull it downwards again. Frequent breakage of saw blades usually means you have tilted the saw forward or that you have forced or rushed the sawing. Take your time—try to make the motions as smooth as possible.

Place the 18-gauge silver on the bench pin, scribed side up. Put the saw blade up against the beginning of the scribe mark. Place the first and second fingers of your left hand, one on each side of the blade, on the silver (see Illus. 499). Hold the silver down firmly and tightly against the bench pin. If at any time while sawing, the silver slaps against the board, you are holding it too loosely.

On the first try, do not saw on the mark but alongside it. Stay as close as possible, but do not permit the saw to cross over the line. You can control the direction of the cut by one of two methods: either move your hand to change the direction of the saw or move the silver right or left. The choice is up to you.

Saw past the corner of the outline by about $\frac{1}{16}$ inch. When you reach this point, relax— let the saw coast with the up-and-down movement. Very gently, a little at a time, turn the near end of the silver towards your right hand until the saw blade is parallel to the scribe mark at the end of the band (see Illus. 500). Finish the cut, keeping the saw parallel to the line.

Cut out the overlay scribed on the piece of

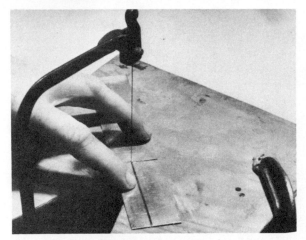

Illus. 500. To turn the corner, gently turn the silver towards your right hand.

22-gauge silver in the same manner, with one exception: saw the wavy center line first (see Illus. 501). This time you must saw *exactly* on the line. When you reach $\frac{1}{16}$ inch beyond the

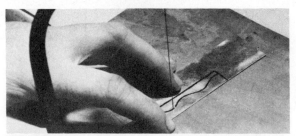

Illus. 501. Saw the wavy center line of the overlay first.

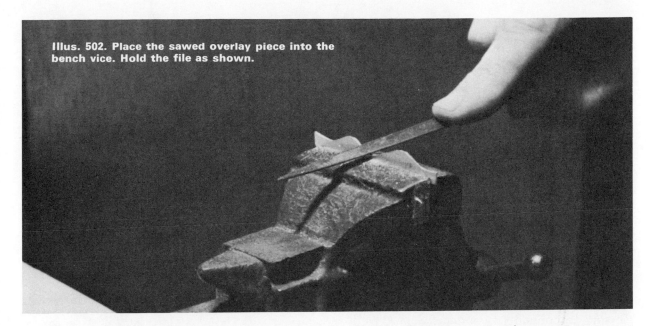

Illus. 502. Place the sawed overlay piece into the bench vice. Hold the file as shown.

scribed end of the band, back the saw out of the cut by pulling gently and moving the saw up and down. Be sure to hold the silver down firmly so that you do not break the saw blade.

Saw the long outline mark next. Turn the corner as described earlier. Cut the end of the band about $\frac{1}{16}$ inch longer than the mark.

Filing

With all your pieces cut out, you are now ready to file. Place the overlay design, one piece at a time, in the vice as shown in Illus. 502. Hold the file in your right hand on a level plane (Illus. 503). It is important that you do not allow the file to dip at the tip or the handle end. Turn the round side of the file down towards the silver. Use the whole cutting surface of the file and follow the wavy surface of the design. File with a movement which is both forward and to the side, until you have removed all of the saw marks. Repeat this on both pieces of the overlay design.

Keep a small box handy in your work area so that you may sweep up filings and save them for later use.

Next, use a small piece of medium emery paper rolled into a tube in the manner pictured in Illus. 503. Remove all the file marks on both overlay pieces.

It is important that all of the surfaces that you plan to solder are clean—that is, free of dirt, oxides, and oil from fingers. You may clean the pieces by rubbing the surfaces shiny with fine emery paper. Once cleaned, do not touch the surfaces to be soldered with your fingers; use tweezers whenever possible.

Illus. 503. Use medium emery paper to remove file marks from overlay pieces.

Soldering

Soldering silver is like soldering other metals except that you need a propane torch and a lighter for the torch. A soldering iron does not give us enough heat.

Besides the torch you need:

self-pickling flux

hard, medium and easy solder with box for storage

pickling pan (copper or oven-proof glass)

jeweler's shears

copper tongs

tweezers (soldering tweezers or an old pair of household tweezers)

binding or stove wire (fine and heavy)

asbestos pad

3-inch square charcoal block

pickling compound (a commercial product is recommended as it is safer than sulphuric acid)

POINTS IN SOLDERING:

Sterling silver melts at 1,640°F. (893°C.)
Hard solder melts at 1,475°F. (802°C.)
Medium solder melts at 1,390°F. (756°C.)
Easy solder melts at 1,325°F. (718°C.)

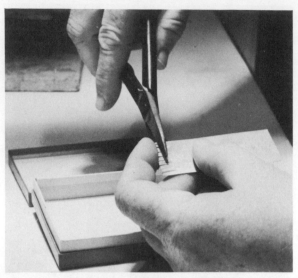

Illus. 504. Cut solder into little squares for use.

Before proceeding further, take the time to bind the edge of the charcoal block with some binding wire. This little trick prolongs the block's usefulness considerably and prevents it from splitting apart through repeated use.

The strips of hard, medium and easy solder all look the same to anyone who is not an expert. So, take no chances. Mark each piece

Illus. 505. Flux the band and apply solder squares with tweezers or the flux brush, as shown here.

with a scribe as you take it from the envelope. For example, scratch the letter "H" all the way up the center of the hard solder strip. Then, no matter how small the last scrap, it will still be easy to identify. A small lozenge or cigarette box is ideal for solder storage.

Clean the piece of hard solder on both sides of one end with emery paper. Make a number of narrow cuts with the jeweler's shears (about $\frac{1}{2}$ inch long) up the length of the solder. The strips will curl as you cut. Straighten them out by rubbing on the side opposite the curl with the jeweler's shears. To prevent the solder squares from flying as you cut them, hold the solder in your left hand. Place the index finger of that hand across the end of the solder where you have made the $\frac{1}{2}$-inch cuts. Hold the solder over the lid of the solder box and, with the shears, cut across the width of the strips so you form little squares about $\frac{1}{16}$ inch (see Illus. 504).

You must first thoroughly flux all surfaces (solder and silver) that you plan to join together. Flux is a borax mixture which helps prevent oxides and permits the smooth flow of

Illus. 506. Pin the ring to the charcoal block with L-shaped pieces of wire.

the solder as it melts and becomes liquid. You may apply flux with a brush or hold the pieces of silver or solder with tweezers and dip them in the flux bottle.

After you have fluxed the basic band, place it on the charcoal block with the cleaned, fluxed side *up*. Now apply solder squares in one of two ways: with tweezers or with a flux brush. If using tweezers, dip each square in the flux as you place it on the band. If using the flux brush, you must moisten it for the application of each piece. (See Illus. 505.) Place solder under the overlay so it conforms to the wavy design, one piece at the crest of the wave and one at the ebb (where the design narrows). Repeat this to the end of the band. Make sure there is one piece of solder directly in the center of each overlay piece at each end of the band. With the tweezers, place the overlay pieces, cleaned and fluxed side *down*, in position. There should be no solder pieces showing. If you discover any, push them underneath the edge of the overlay with tweezers.

It is only permissible to touch, with your fingers, any surface that you are not going to solder.

NOTE: *Oxide prevention.* Oxides are the result of heating the metal during the soldering or the annealing process which follows. On prolonged soldering projects, it is possible to hold oxidation to a minimum by fluxing the entire object. Parts that are in direct contact with the charcoal block need not be fluxed as it offers its own protection against oxidation. If you heat the object to be soldered quickly and efficiently, the oxides will not have time to burn deeply into the silver.

From the coil of binding wire, cut six lengths, each $\frac{1}{2}$ inch long. Bend each piece at about $\frac{1}{3}$ its length into an L shape. Pin the ring to the charcoal block with these wires. Use three on each side to be soldered (one on each end, one in the middle) as in Illus. 506. When this is finished, take a quick survey to make sure the ring parts are in proper alignment and make any adjustments necessary.

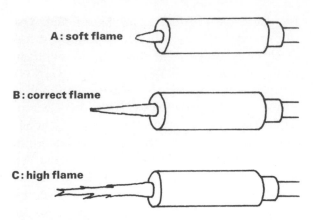

A: soft flame

B: correct flame

C: high flame

Illus. 507. Various flames on the soldering torch.

Torches

There are several kinds of torches available that you may use for soldering silver.

The propane torch in the illustrations here has a disposable cylinder, is economical, and is available in hardware departments or from mail-order suppliers. It has a clean, easily controlled flame.

You can also use a gas-air torch which utilizes a combination of gas and compressed air. The gas can be either manufactured illuminating gas, natural gas or propane. Air pressure is supplied by a foot bellows or by a motor-driven compressor.

Acetylene torches are portable, and although they are initially expensive to buy, the refill tanks are low in cost and readily available.

Another recommended torch unit uses a tank of oxygen and the natural gas that is normally supplied in homes. Many artists are using this set-up.

Following are some important facts to remember when deciding which flame you should use to solder (see Illus. 507): The flame shown in Illus. 507A is called a soft flame. You use this occasionally to dry flux on complicated soldering projects. Drying the flux this slowly (for a second or two) prevents it from bubbling and causing the solder to jump out of place. You can also use this flame, sometimes, to solder delicate parts together, such as two fine wires.

The flame shown in Illus. 507B is the correct flame for most soldering projects. Notice the sharp point in the middle of the flame. The tip of this point indicates the hottest area of the entire flame. The tip should always be near, but not touching, the surface of the object being soldered.

In Illus. 507C, the torch has been turned higher for illustration. When the hot tip disappears, the heat dissipates. You should not use this flame, as it will not heat as effectively and will cause unnecessary fire scale and oxides.

Using the Torch

Follow a pattern with the tip of the flame when soldering—a figure eight or, as will be done on this ring, the letter "N." To make the N, for example, solder up one side, down the middle and up the other side. This technique helps to assure that you heat all parts of the item to be soldered uniformly.

When the solder reaches its liquid state and begins to flow, it is a thin, bright, silvery line, and will probably appear first in the middle of the overlay. During this period (two or three

Illus. 508. Draw solder, by the heat of the flame, to specific areas of the ring.

Illus. 509. Place the pickle pan on a stove or hot plate, and, with copper tongs, place the ring in the simmering solution.

seconds), you may draw solder by the heat of the flame to specific areas of the work (see Illus. 508). To ensure that the solder has completely melted under the overlay, run the torch up and down both outside edges of the ring. The correct approach to soldering is to heat quickly and uniformly at all times, thus avoiding excess fire scale and oxides.

Now, using tweezers, remove the ring from the charcoal block and quench it in water. Then, pickle it.

Pickling

Pickling is a cleansing, conditioning process. To mix a pickling solution, carefully follow the directions on the container of solution which you have bought. Sparex #2 is one commercial pickling solution. It is granular and easy to measure. You mix it with water to use it.

You can make your own pickling solution by adding one part sulphuric acid to 10 parts water. *You must add the acid to the water*, or the mixture will explode. Sulphuric acid, however, is dangerous—if spilled, it eats holes in clothes, floors, and so on. To neutralize it on your skin, rinse the area with cold water and apply a paste of baking soda to the area.

You may stir pickle with anything made of oven-proof glass, stainless steel or copper. Note that the smallest bit of iron in the solution causes any silver placed in it to discolor.

Place the pickle pan on the stove or a hot plate. Turn it on *low*. The solution should simmer, but not boil. Using copper tongs, place the ring in the pickle. When all signs of oxidation have disappeared and the silver is frosty white, remove the ring and rinse it thoroughly in cold water.

Rinse the pickle pan in cold water and dust it with baking soda before storing it away. This will neutralize any acid remaining in it after use.

If you plan to store pickle between projects, keep it in a well labelled glass jar. Be sure it is out of the reach of children, but never above your own eye level.

CAUTION: Always do pickling in a well ventilated room. Because you should always consider the solution *acid*, *never* stand directly over the pan while it is steaming, as the fumes can be potent. If pickle should spatter on your skin, you may neutralize it by running cold water over the area. If irritation persists, apply a paste of baking soda mixed with water to the area.

Illus. 510. After pickling, trim the ends of the ring length so they are square.

find these in the scrap pile of a new building site or a lumber yard. Drill a hole through the middle of each piece, then saw the blocks in half (see Illus. 511). Smooth each half with sand-paper. Cover two halves with moleskin across the top and down into the groove. With a felt-tip marking pen, label the end of one block TRIPOLI and the other ROUGE (these terms will be discussed further). Set these aside. You will use them later in polishing. Use another half, as is, as the forming block.

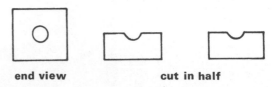

end view   cut in half

Illus. 511. How to make polishing blocks.

Trim, with the saw and file, the ends of the ring length so they are square (Illus. 510). Solder will not fill in gaps caused by imperfect workmanship.

Annealing

In annealing you heat the silver until it begins to turn a dull red, then immediately quench it in cold water or pickle. When silver is pounded or stretched, it hardens. You may return it to its softer, more workable state by annealing.

Anneal the ring length now.

Forming

You will need some more tools for forming, namely a ring mandrel and a hammer with one metal end and one plastic end, and a hand drill. Also, purchase a box of a commercial product used in the care of feet called "moleskin," a felt-like material with an adhesive back, easily cut to size.

To make polishing blocks, use two 5-inch lengths of 4 × 4 wood. Sometimes, you may

Place one end of the ring length across the groove in the forming block. Hold the dowel in position as shown in Illus. 512, and strike it (not the silver) with the hammer. Move to the other end of the silver and repeat. Frequently, switch the ring length end for end. Continue this procedure, gradually working towards the middle until the length is rounded.

Try the ring on for size. If it is too large, you may trim *small* sections off each end in the following manner: Place the ring in the bench

Illus. 512. Bend the ring length in the forming block using a dowel and hammer.

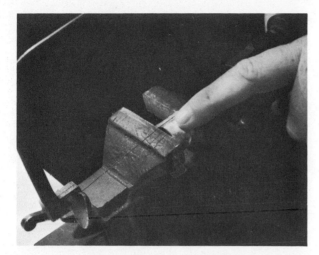

Illus. 513. Trim the ring if it is too big.

vice with the joint on top as in Illus. 513. Lay the saw blade on top of the mark scribed for the cut. Guide the blade with your index finger to prevent it from slipping. Gently move the saw back and forth until the cut is complete. Repeat on the opposite side. File the ends to ensure a smooth, close-fitting joint. Round the ring again and try it on. It should be snug, for polishing enlarges it slightly.

Anneal and pickle the ring again, using the method previously described. In a heavy-gauge ring such as this, it may be difficult to bend the ring ends together using only your fingers or the forming block. If such is the case, you may insert the ring in the bench vice, as shown in Illus. 514, and bend one side at a time until

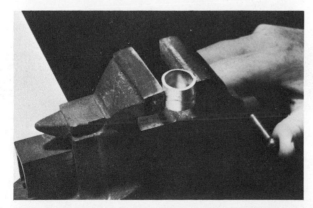

Illus. 514. Bend the ring ends together in the bench vice if you have trouble in the forming block.

both ends are flush. (It would be wise to line the jaws of the bench vice with two small pieces of moleskin to avoid marring the silver.) This will flatten the ring, but it is not essential that it be perfectly round at this time. Run the tip of one finger across the joint. If you feel any ridges, the ends are not flush. Keep bending until the ridges disappear.

Clean the ring joint inside and out with emery. Do the same to both sides of one end of the *medium* solder. Cut a thin strip of solder long enough to cover the ring joint from one edge to the other. Flux the solder.

With tweezers, place the ring on the charcoal block, joint side *down*. Flux the joint and place the strip of fluxed solder inside, directly on top of the joint (see Illus. 515).

Heat the ring in a pattern as described earlier (see page 186). Move the heat across the top, down the right edge, inside the bottom and up the left edge. Repeat this pattern until the solder begins to melt. Only then concentrate the heat on the solder.

Illus. 515. Place fluxed solder directly on top of the fluxed joint. To solder the ring joint, move the heat in a pattern until the solder begins to melt. Then, concentrate the heat on the joint.

Pickle and rinse the ring. Inspect the ring closely to see if the joint is properly soldered. Re-solder where necessary.

If the soldering turned out well, very little filing is necessary. If, however, there are rough, uneven spots, you may smooth them out with the 6-inch file. Let the file follow the contour of the ring. Hold the file level and do not allow it to dip on one side or the other. When you have finished, go over the area with a fine, half-round, 6-inch file using the same method.

Use the rounded side of your needle file to clean the solder bits from the inside of the ring joint (see Illus. 516). Use the whole length of the cutting edge in a movement that is both forward and to the side. Do not allow the file to dip at either end.

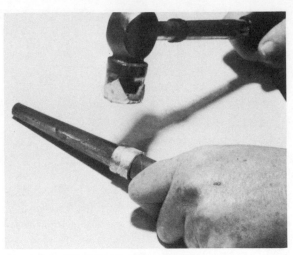

Illus. 517. Round the ring on the mandrel.

of the hammer to avoid marring the ring. Push the ring as far up on the mandrel as possible. Strike the ring on the high side, completely around its circumference. Reverse the ring and repeat this operation on the other edge. Keep forcing the ring as high on the mandrel as it will go. Follow this procedure until the ring is perfectly round.

To file the outside edges of the ring evenly, lay the ring on your flat 6-inch file and move it back and forth across the file's entire cutting surface (see Illus. 518). Turn the ring several times during the process. When both edges of the ring are smooth, repeat the same steps using the 6-inch half-round fine file.

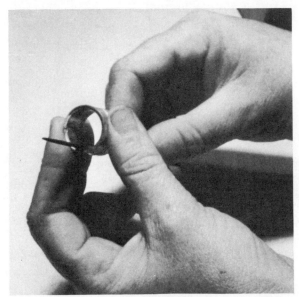

Illus. 516. Clean bits of solder from the inside of the ring joint with the needle file.

Now, you may round the ring on the mandrel as shown in Illus. 517. Notice that a small square of moleskin has been applied to the plastic end

Illus. 518. File the outside edges of the ring on the flat 6-inch file.

Hand Polishing

Now you are ready to polish your ring. The purpose of polishing is to wear away the surface of the metal to the depth of the deepest blemish —that is, fire scales and scratches. Fire scales, as well as fire flakes and fire coat, are common names for cupric or cuprous oxides—discolorations which appear on the surface of silver after it has been heated. Because pure silver, or fine silver, is too soft to work with, alloys are added to harden the silver (such silver is called sterling silver). Fire scale results when the base metal of the alloy added separates on the surface of the silver.

You can remove such blemishes by rubbing the surface of the metal first with emery sticks and then with felt buffs that have been charged with polishing compounds.

You will need:

dowels of various sizes

tripoli, a coarse polishing compound which you use in the primary polishing steps; it actually cuts away the surface of the silver and re-

Illus. 519. Clean the inside of the ring with an emery dowel.

moves scratches and fire scale; take care not to destroy the sharpness of the design when using this polishing agent; keep the tripoli cake and the tripoli-charged buffs apart from the other polishing materials; a plastic bag is ideal for storage

tripoli felt buffs: one dowel and one paddle covered with moleskin and charged with tripoli; write TRIPOLI on the handle of each to distinguish them from ROUGE

emery paper: glue various grades to paddles and dowels with white liquid glue

emery dowel and paddle

jeweler's rouge, a fine polishing agent composed of red iron oxide with a wax base; used to obtain a final high polish on silver

rouge felt buffs, one dowel and one paddle covered with moleskin and charged with rouge; each should have ROUGE written on the handle; keep buffs in a separate plastic bag

liver of sulphur (or commercial equivalent) which you paint in diluted form on silver in selected areas to cause it to oxidize (turn dark); you may use a commercial equivalent as it comes from the bottle

paint paddle, obtainable in a paint store free of charge

coping saw, to cut paint paddles into polishing sticks of desired lengths and widths

polishing blocks, with the top surface of each block covered with moleskin; mark one block TRIPOLI and the other ROUGE

watercolor brush, small, to apply oxidizer to desired areas of project

ammonia, mixed with detergent and warm water; use to clean tripoli or rouge from projects

scrub bowl to use for ammonia, detergent and warm water solution when scrubbing tripoli and rouge from projects

toothbrush, a soft one, also for the above process

STEP 1: Using the forming block for support, clean all the surfaces of the ring with the medium emery stick and dowel (Illus. 519). You can remove most deep scratches and surface blemishes with this step. Repeat the above, using the fine emery stick until you achieve a fine matt surface.

STEP 2: Using the tripoli polishing block for support, buff the inside and outside surfaces of

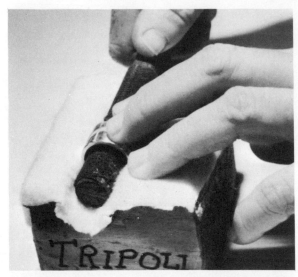

Illus. 520. Polish the inside of the ring with the tripoli dowel.

the ring with the tripoli dowel (Illus. 520). Use as much pressure as possible. This process actually moves the surface of the silver, filling in fine scratches and producing a soft lustrous finish.

STEP 3: Mix one capful of ammonia and one capful of detergent in warm water. Scrub the ring with a soft brush, as in Illus. 521, until you have removed all traces of tripoli compound. At this point, fire flake—small shadows on the surface of the metal—begins to appear. If not completely removed, these little areas will tarnish quickly and spoil the appearance of the ring. To remove fire flake, repeat the polishing steps from the fine emery stick to the tripoli buffs. Pressure with the tripoli buffs shortens the process. Always scrub the silver object with the ammonia solution before proceeding to the next step.

Place a lump of liver of sulphur, the size of a small coin, in a small bottle (a spice or vitamin bottle will do). Fill the bottle 4/5ths full with cold water. Put the cap on and shake until the liver of sulphur is dissolved. (You may use the commercial equivalent of liver of sulphur as it comes from the bottle.)

Paint the middle strip of the ring with this solution using a watercolor brush (see Illus.

522). Let it stand for a few minutes. When the area is dark enough, dry the ring thoroughly with a paper towel.

NOTE: Some craftsmen prefer to heat these solutions to obtain a darker oxide. However, if you do this, be prepared for the smell, which is very pungent.

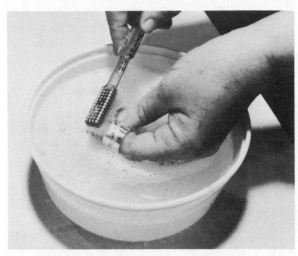

Illus. 521. Scrub the ring in a solution of ammonia and detergent.

With STEP 4, the ring gains dimension and depth. Rouge is a very fine polishing agent that gives silver its highest shine. Follow the directions previously described in the use of tripoli. Lightly brush the ring in the solution used in Illus. 521 and dry it with a paper towel.

Your finished project should look like Illus. 488. The same procedure, more or less, is used in making all silver rings.

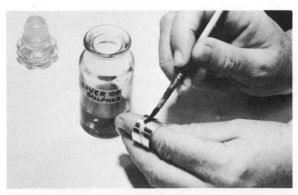

Illus. 522. Paint the area you want oxidized with liver of sulphur.

Illus. 523 (left) and Illus. 524 (right). Two textured variations of the overlay ring.

Texturing

Texturing is used in silversmithing to break up the flat surfaces of a project in order to reflect light and bring out the design.

The two rings in Illus. 523 and 524 require much more patience and skill in soldering, but they are actually simple variations of the ring in Illus. 488. Use the overlay pattern (Step 2) shown in Illus. 491 for the wavy strips used on these rings.

Take care in soldering these little strips. Be very sure that you firmly fasten the work to the charcoal block and that you securely solder all parts of the strips to the basic band before you round the ring. If you do not do this, the strips will distort when bent.

Drilling

Groupings of drill and burr holes of assorted sizes can create some interesting effects. Place the ring part to be drilled on a hardwood or steel block and make a "starter" mark with a punch and hammer. This mark keeps the drill from skidding and leaving unwanted scars on the surface of the silver. Then fasten the ring part to the bench pin with a C-clamp and drill.

You may place a burr in an already-drilled hole to enlarge it (see Illus. 525).

Illus. 525. Examples of drill and burr texturing.

Illus. 526. This handsome ring combines nail-set texturing and oval cutouts.

Nail-Set Texturing

This is a simple and inexpensive way of texturing. You must remember, however, that when you hammer silver, you stretch and harden it. Therefore, you should do most texturing *before* you assemble the parts for soldering. You must then anneal the textured piece.

The ring in Illus. 526, a very simple one, consists of two parts: the basic band and the overlay (see Illus. 527). The pattern illustrated shows some textured areas as well as dark ovals which you will cut out.

Cut out and fit the pattern and construct a mock-up ring, as shown in Illus. 528. When you are sure of a good fit, scribe the outline of the basic band on a piece of 18-gauge silver and saw it out. Scribe the ovals next.

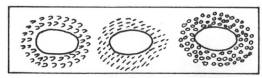

basic band with texturing

overlay

Illus. 527. Pattern for the textured ring in Illus. 526.

You should place all projects you plan to texture on a hardwood or steel block. Then hold the nail set firmly against the silver and strike with a hammer, one blow per mark.

For this ring, place the basic band, scribed side up, on the polished steel block. Using a punch and hammer, strike a mark in the middle of each oval. Fasten the band to the bench pin, using a C-clamp. Place the tip of the drill in the punch mark and drill a hole.

When you have completed drilling, remove the band from the C-clamp. Loosen the top clamp of the saw frame and pull the loose end of the saw blade through the drilled hole. Fasten the saw blade again and saw in an arc towards the scribe mark. Take care to stay as close to the line as possible without allowing the saw to cross over it.

Illus. 528. Paper mock-up of the textured ring in Illus. 526.

When you have cut out all of the ovals, place the basic band in the bench vice so the scribed marks are visible. Use the half-round needle file and file the oval until the cut is even with the scribe mark. Roll a small piece of emery paper into a tube and remove the file marks from the inside of the ovals.

Scribe and saw out the overlay employing the techniques just used. Place the overlay on top of the basic band and lightly scribe the outline of the larger ovals. Then place the basic band on the steel block, scribed side up.

You may actually do texturing with any instrument which leaves an interesting mark.

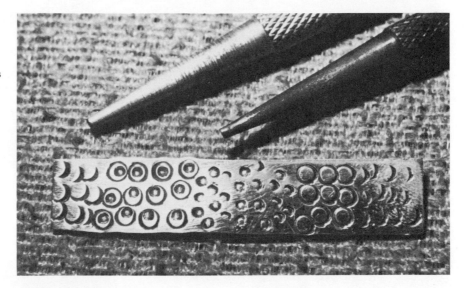

Illus. 529. Various examples of nail-set texturing.

For this design a small screwdriver, a nail set and a small dapping punch were used. You may hold the nail set straight up and down or tilt it slightly. You may also vary the force of the blows from the hammer (see Illus. 529).

Texturing should cross slightly over the lightly scribed line. When you have completed this step, you are ready to solder the two parts together. Use the techniques for soldering you learned while making the first ring.

When you have rounded the ring and soldered the ring joint, file the edges. Taper the outside edges slightly to remove any uncomfortable sharpness.

Turn the half-round, 6-inch file, round side

Illus. 530. This textured ring has seven oval insets on the overlay band.

down, and file the holes in the basic band to remove any sharp edges. Finish the ring following the procedures outlined for the basic overlay ring.

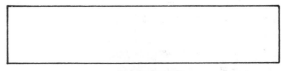

basic band

overlay with seven insets

Illus. 531. Pattern for the textured ring in Illus. 530.

The ring in Illus. 530, similar to the one in Illus. 526, is smart and easily executed. It consists of nine parts: the basic band, the overlay, and seven oval insets (see the pattern in Illus. 531). Follow the procedures and techniques you used on the previous ring, with the following differences: use 22-gauge silver for the basic band and 18-gauge silver, which is heavier, for the overlay and insets.

Illus. 532. The texture on this ring was produced by filing.

Filed Surfaces

The pattern for the ring in Illus. 532 has two parts: the basic band and the overlay (see Illus. 533). You should file this ring before soldering the overlay to the basic band.

Firmly fasten the item you want to file to the bench pin with a C-clamp or hold it in the bench vice. Any line you decide to file should go all the way across the ring surface. Be careful not to allow the file to dip at either end (see Illus. 534).

After filing, complete the ring as you did the previous overlay rings.

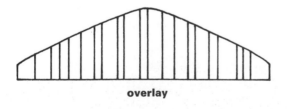

overlay

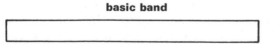

basic band

Illus. 533. Pattern for the filed textured ring in Illus. 532.

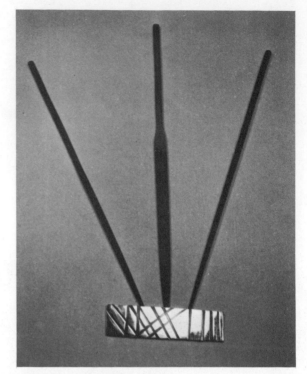

Illus. 534. Examples of filings.

Shot

Shot is the name given to little balls of silver which you can solder to a surface for texture. You can make shot from scrap silver or from uniform lengths cut from silver wire. Then heat the scraps on the charcoal block until they melt and form balls. Pickle the shot balls, and they are ready to use.

Illus. 535. Ring textured with shot.

Table Ring

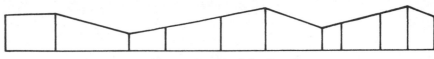

inside band marked for bending

A table ring has a table or base to which you attach a ring band. The pattern in this case consists of four parts: the outside band, the inside design, the table to which they are fastened, and the ring band (see Illus. 536).

Cut out the outside band from paper. Bend where indicated and glue. It is not necessary to have a perfect rectangle or absolute "squared" corners. When the glue is dry, use this as a pattern for the table. To do this, place the outside band on a piece of dark construction paper and trace round it with a pencil. Cut out the tracing on the outside of the pencil mark. Glue the two pieces together.

Then, cut out the inside design and bend where the pattern is marked. Fit this into the already constructed part. When you are sure of the fit, lift this piece out, put a small amount of the glue on the bottom of the table and refit

outside band marked for bending

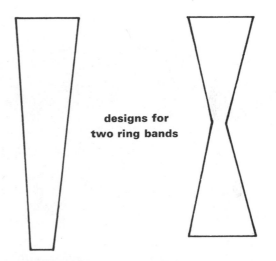

designs for
two ring bands

Illus. 536. Pattern for the table ring.

the piece. You may hold the parts together with a little piece of transparent tape across the top until they dry.

Two possible patterns for ring bands are shown in Illus. 536. Both bands are very adaptable and you may use them over and over on different rings. When fitting the mock-up ring band, leave a gap of about ⅛ inch between the ends of the band. Glue them to the table top this way.

When you are sure the mock-up is comfortable and of the right proportions, scribe round the outside band pattern on a piece of 18-gauge silver, and cut it out. When you have sawed the part out, file the two ends of the band carefully to ensure a square, snug-fitting joint for soldering. Use the paper pattern as a guide and bend the outside band.

Illus. 537. Paper mock-up of the table ring in Illus. 544.

Using a small piece of emery paper, clean both sides of the joint to be soldered. Take care not to touch these areas with your fingers after cleaning. Then, bind the band, as shown in Illus. 538, with a piece of wire. This prevents the ends from spreading apart when heated.

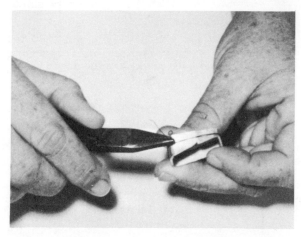

Illus. 538. Bind the outside band before soldering.

Flux the entire piece and place it, joint *down*, on the charcoal block. Cut a thin strip of *hard* solder, just long enough to cover the width of the joint. Flux it and place it in position. Solder. Remember to follow a pattern with the torch while soldering so all parts of the band will be equally hot. If you do not do this

properly, the solder will run to one side of the joint only.

Quench the band in water. Remove the binding wire. The band should require little or no filing if soldered properly. Be very sure there are no little pieces of the binding wire left on the band, as iron discolors silver if the two are pickled together. Rinse in cold water and dry. Place the band, bottom *down*, on the flat 6-inch file and file until smooth and uniform.

Illus. 540. Flux all ring parts, fit them together, and place the ring on the charcoal block.

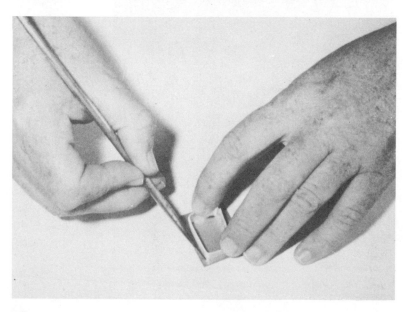

Illus. 539. Scribe the outline of the soldered band on a piece of 22-gauge silver for the table.

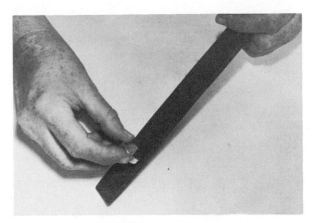

Illus. 541. File the two ends of the band until they are very thin on the inside edges.

Use the soldered band as a guide and scribe its outline on a piece of 22-gauge silver (see Illus. 539). Be sure to saw on the outside edge of scribe mark. Do not file at this time, but clean the side of the table to be soldered with emery paper.

Use four L-shaped wires to pin the two pieces to the charcoal block. Flux. Place snippets of *hard* solder against the side of the band all around.

Use a piece of 26-gauge silver for the inside design and follow the same procedures you used in sawing the outside band. File the ends and finish with emery paper. Use as a guide the paper pattern and bend the design, starting at the inside. Some small adjustments may be necessary to ensure a proper fit. File the bottom of the design as you did the outside band.

Flux all parts to be soldered, fit them together and place them on the charcoal block. Pin the work down with L-shaped wires as shown in Illus. 540.

Use *medium* solder, being sure that the pieces touch the design as well as the bottom of the table. Solder, pickle and rinse. Trim in bench vice.

Some filing should be needed where you joined the table and outside band. When you have completed that, lay a piece of emery paper face *up* on the table and rub the sides of the ring on it until all of the file marks have disappeared.

NOTE: *Do not file the ring on top yet.* It is much easier to handle after you have attached the ring band.

Saw out the ring band next from 18-gauge silver. File the ends carefully and finish with emery paper. Bend the band using the method you learned with the first ring. Leave a gap at the ends of the band about $\frac{1}{8}$ inch wide.

To file the sides of the ring band, hold the band firmly in your left hand. File both sides at once with the flat 6-inch file. Start at the bottom of the band and make one sweep with the file all the way to the top. After you have filed the band evenly, run the file a few times round both edges to remove the sharpness and make the band more comfortable to wear. Remove all file marks with emery paper. Next, file the two ends of the band flat until they are very thin on the inside edges (see Illus. 541). When this is finished, the band is ready for soldering.

Place the table design face *down*, on the charcoal block after fluxing. Flux the band, including the flattened ends, and stand it on the bottom of the table in the proper position. Cut two thin strips of *easy* solder just long enough to cover the ends of the band. Flux and place in position (see Illus. 542). Solder, pickle and rinse.

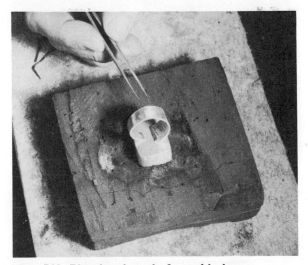

Illus. 542. Ring band ready for soldering.

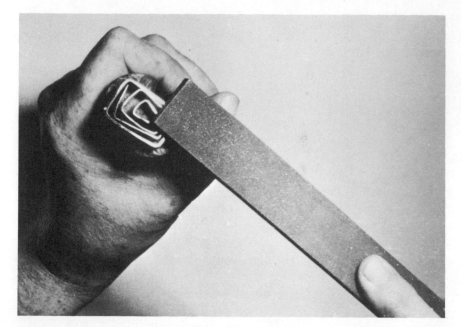

It is now time to file the ring top. Place the ring in the ring clamp. Again, use the flat 6-inch file and follow the contour of the design. Keep filing until the top is completely level (see Illus. 543).

Polish as described before. See Illus. 544 for the finished ring.

Now that you know the basic techniques for making a table ring, you can attempt to construct others which require much more patience and skill.

Illus. 544. The finished table ring.

Illus. 545. Another possible table ring which you can construct.

outside band marked for bending

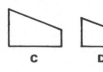

A   B

Illus. 546. Pattern for the table ring in Illus. 545.

C   D

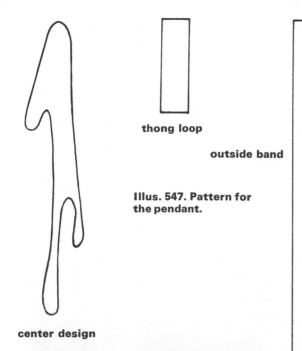

thong loop

outside band

Illus. 547. Pattern for the pendant.

center design

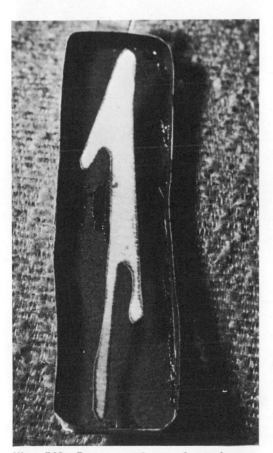

Illus. 548. Paper mock-up of pendant.

Pendants

The construction of pendants, such as the one here, is much the same as the construction of a table ring. The first step is, as always, the mock-up (see Illus. 547 and 548).

Note that the middle of the design in this pendant is elevated from the floor of the pendant with two silver blocks. The outside band is made of 18-gauge silver. Because of the length, it is necessary to piece this band on the side and away from where it will be bent. The design and floor of the pendant are made of 22-gauge silver.

Illus. 549. The pendant parts are ready to be soldered, pinned to the charcoal block.

Saw out the parts as usual. Bend the outside band using the paper pattern as a guide. Solder, pickle and rinse. Use the soldered outside band as a guide for scribing the floor of the pendant.

Ready the parts for soldering and then use four L-shaped pins to fasten them to the charcoal block as in Illus. 549. NOTE: Use *hard* solder on this step. Lean the snippets against the side so they touch the bottom of the pendant. Solder, pickle and rinse.

Prepare the middle design for soldering. Take special care in finishing this part as it is the focal point of the pendant. Cut four pieces of 18-gauge silver $\frac{1}{2}$ inch long and $\frac{1}{16}$ inch wide. You do not have to finish these pieces as they block up the middle design. Prepare them for soldering and join them together, using *hard* solder, to form two silver blocks. Pickle and rinse.

Use the middle design as a guide and position the silver blocks in a spot that gives the most support to them. Mark the spot with the scribe and remove the block. Flux everything thoroughly. Place two pieces of *medium* solder on each end of the marked spot. Place the block on top of this. Dry the flux slowly with a soft flame so the block does not jump out of place. Solder, pickle and rinse

Cut a strip of 18-gauge silver, one inch long and $\frac{1}{4}$ inch wide, for the thong loop. File the ends so they are smooth. Using round-nose pliers, bend it into a circle. Place this in the bench vice and file the two ends flat. File both sides of the circle. Remove all file marks with emery paper. Prepare the thong for soldering.

Use *easy* solder for the middle design. Flux all parts thoroughly. Place three fluxed snippets of solder on each block that will support the middle design. Dry the flux with a soft flame. Position the design and pin it to the charcoal block.

Dig a small hole in the charcoal block at the end where you will solder the thong loop to help support and center it. The loop should fit snugly against the outside band. Cut a piece of solder as wide as the loop and place it on

top of the loop where it will join. Dry the flux with a soft flame. Solder, pickle and rinse. Then follow the procedures for polishing to finish your first pendant.

The pendant shown in Illus. 552 is an exercise in effect. To make this pendant, cut lengths of silver tubing and then solder them to the floor of the pendant. Upon completion of this step, file the design smooth.

For the pendant in Illus. 553, cut silver tubing in varying lengths and solder it to the floor of the pendant. When you have completed this, solder a silver ball to each piece of tubing.

Illus. 550. The thong loop is ready for soldering.

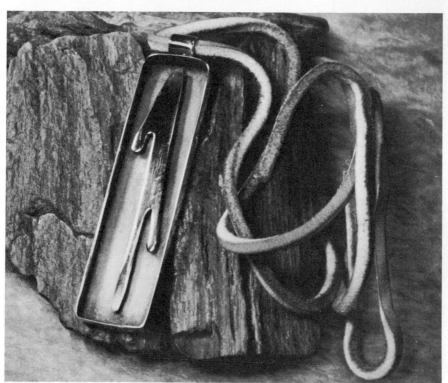

Illus. 551. Attach a leather thong or other hanging device to complete your pendant.

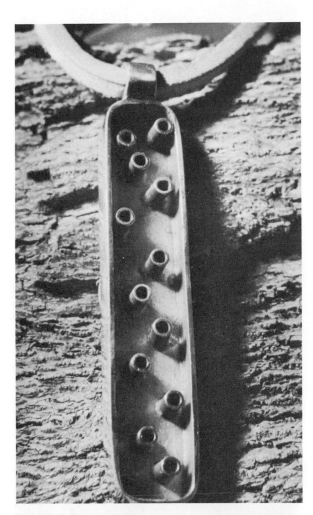

Illus. 552. Simply solder lengths of 8-gauge heavy-wall sterling silver tubing to the floor of a pendant to create this effect.

Illus. 553. Silver tubing, soldered to the floor of a pendant and topped with shot balls, created this unique pendant.

Silver and Wood Inlay

The combination of silver and wood is pleasant and attractive. Teak is used for the examples here, but any kind of hardwood is adaptable to this type of inlay. Cut the wood you plan to use into a slab $\frac{1}{4}$ inch thick. Place the design for the pendant shape (see Illus. 554 for one idea) on the slab and trace the outline with a pencil. Use the jeweler's saw to cut it out.

Mark, with a pencil, the area you plan to cut out for the insertion of the thong loop. Fasten the pendant to the bench pin with a small C-clamp and drill a hole in the middle of the marked area. Unfasten the top of the saw blade, slip it through the hole and fasten it once more. Saw out the area. Remove the saw blade.

Scribe the outline of the center design on a piece of 22-gauge silver and cut it out. File the

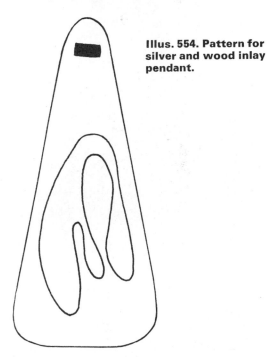

Illus. 554. Pattern for silver and wood inlay pendant.

design carefully and when it is finished to your liking, trace its outline on the wood with a pencil.

Fasten the pendant to the bench pin with the C-clamp. Using a sharp carving tool, follow the outline of the design until you have made a cut all the way round it. With a flat-bladed carving tool, carve a bed for the silver design. Try to achieve a uniform depth of $\frac{1}{16}$ inch. Fit the design often and whittle away unwanted wood a little at a time. Your aim is to achieve the closest fit possible.

When you have completed the fitting, place a layer of wood putty in the cavity and force the silver design down into the bed. A good tool for this is a pencil with an eraser.

Next, sand the pendant, using medium sandpaper first, going with the grain of the wood. When your sanding has almost reached the level of the silver inlay, switch to fine emery paper. Sand with the emery until the silver and

Illus. 556. The silver glows brightly in its wooden setting in the finished pendant.

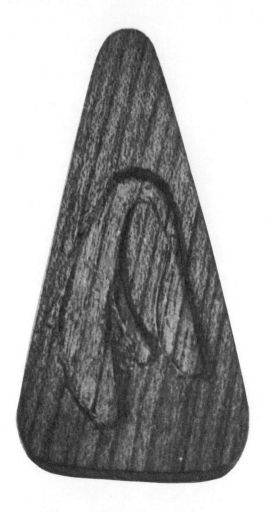

Illus. 555. Inlay design for pendant after carving.

wood are all at the same level and you have achieved a fine matt finish on all parts of the silver.

You may finish the wood in any of several ways. Two of the easiest methods are to rub it with linseed oil or to leave it natural. Or, you may use neutral shoe wax and then buff it to a high gloss.

Saw out the thong loop, using 18-gauge silver. File the edges and rub to a matt finish with emery. With a flat-nose pliers, make the first bend in the thong loop. Insert the silver in the hole and finish bending.

Index

Suppliers

For general metalcrafting supplies, try your local craft or hobby shop, of the following:

Allcraft Tool and Supply Co.
215 Park Avenue
Hicksville, NY 11801

Australian Silver Craft Centre
104 Bathurst Street
Sydney 2000

California Crafts Supply
1419 N. Central Park Ave.
Anaheim, CA 92802

Camden Art Centre (S.A.) Pty. Ltd.
210 Rundale Street
Adelaide, Australia 5000

C.C.M. Arts and Crafts, Inc.
9520 Baltimore Avenue
College Park, MD 20740

Craftsmen's Distributors Ltd.
1597 London Road
London, S.W.16
England

Kraft Korner
5864 Mayfield Road
Cleveland, OH 44124

X-Acto Inc.
48–41 Van Dam Street
Long Island City, NY 11101

For supplies of horseshoe nails, you can contact the following companies:

Griffith Saddlery & Leather Ltd.
P.O. Box 633
240 Norfolk Street, Area Code 519
Stratford, Ontario
Canada

H. W. Mangelsen and Sons, Inc.
8200 J Street
Omaha, Nebraska 68127

Mustadfors Bruks AB
P.O. Box 10
S-660 10 DALS LÅNGED
Sweden

Mustad Manufacturing Co.
Old Mill Road
Porteshead near Bristol
England